## PENGUIN BOOKS

### THE COLLECTING BOOK

ELLEN LIMAN

*has written extensively in the design field*

*and is the author of*

The Spacemaker Book

Decorating Your Room:
A Do-It-Yourself Guide for Children

Decorating Your Country Place

The Money Saver's Guide to Decorating

*Mrs. Liman lives in New York City with her husband,*
*Arthur, and her children, Lewis, Emily and Douglas.*

LEWIS LIMAN,

*an undergraduate at Harvard College, has been an*
*avid collector of political memorabilia since kindergarten.*

Toys

Tobacco Humidor

Hat Box Band

Vending Machine

Period Clothing

Spark Plugs

*Advertising Mirror*

# The Collecting Book

by Ellen Liman with Lewis Liman

## PENGUIN BOOKS

*Photographs*

*Dolls*

Book Design by *Jos. Trautwein*

Penguin Books Ltd, Harmondsworth,
Middlesex, England
Penguin Books, 625 Madison Avenue,
New York, New York 10022, U.S.A.
Penguin Books Australia Ltd, Ringwood,
Victoria, Australia
Penguin Books Canada Limited, 2801 John Street,
Markham, Ontario, Canada L3R 1B4
Penguin Books (N.Z.) Ltd, 182–190 Wairau Road,
Auckland 10, New Zealand

First published 1980

**Library of Congress Cataloging
in Publication Data**

Liman, Ellen.
   The collecting book.
   1. Collectors and collecting.   I. Liman,
Lewis, joint author. II.  Title.
AM231.L55      790.13′2      79-25165
ISBN 0 14 00.5268 2

Typesetting by Printworks, Inc.

CREDITS: *FRONT COVER, Buckles (Cooper-Hewitt Museum, The Smithsonian Institution National Museum of Design),* Dog *(Cooper-Hewitt Museum, The Smithsonian Institution National Museum of Design),* Dolls *(Museum of the City of New York),* Comic Books *(Collection Douglas Propp),* Picture Puzzle *(Museum of the City of New York),* Coach Toy *(Museum of the City of New York). BACK COVER,* Advertising Signs *(Collection of Leonard Schechter),* Eyeglasses *(Cooper-Hewitt Museum, The Smithsonian Institution National Museum of Design),* Trade Card, Carter's Pills *(The Museum of the City of New York),* Paper Doll *(Collection of Anne Tolstoi Wallach),* Political Buttons *(Collection of Lewis Liman),* Vases *(Cooper-Hewitt Museum, The Smithsonian Institution National Museum of Design),* Doll House *(Museum of the City of New York).*

CREDITS: p.3, Wooden Toy Bicycle and Man *(Shelburne Museum),* p.4, Humidor *(The U.S. Tobacco Museum),* Hat Box Band *(Bella L. Landauer Collection of American Ephemera, Metropolitan Museum of Art),* p.5, Advertising Mirror *(Collection Burt Purmell, Photograph Collection Keith DeLillis)* Doll *(The New York Historical Society, New York City),* p.7, Wall Clocks *(Ellen K. Blauer),* p.8 *(Collection Philip Snyder),* p.9, Hat Box *(Cooper-Hewitt Museum),* p.11, Earthenware Platter *(Museum of The City of New York),* p.12, Comic Art, *(United Features Syndicate, Collection Jerome Muller),* p.16, Advertising Signs *(Collection Leonard Schechter),* p.18, Theatre Poster *(Museum of the City of New York),* p. 19, Lindbergh Menu *(Museum of the City of New York),* p.19, Matchholders *(Collection Sarah Lee Singer),* Ambrotype by Mathew Brady c. 1854 *(Janet Lehr, Inc.),* p.21, World's Fair Toy, *(Collection Larry Zim, The New York Historical Society, New York City),* Cigarbands *(Collection Arthur Liman)* Political Buttons *(Collection Lewis Liman),* p.22 Sheet Music *(Museum of the City of New York),* p.23, Dolls *(Shelburne Museum).*

# CONTENTS

*Minatures*

Christmas Ornaments

*Hat Box*

## THE COLLECTOR

*Those who pick, dig and erect;*
*also select store and collect.*
*Don't throw it away,*
*collectors are here to stay.*
*What you collect today,*
*tomorrow someone will pay.*
*The old takes the place of new,*
*becomes likeable as an old shoe.*
*The collection for you*
*makes for something to do;*
*and as your collection grows,*
*you then have something to show.*
*If it's money you need,*
*use your collection for seed.*
*In no time at all,*
*collectors will call.*
*Which now gives you a chance,*
*to have something in advance.*
*To build your collection,*
*to one of great perfection.*

*by "ROBBIE" ROBERTSON*

# INTRODUCTION

Collections, like a book about them, can go on forever. The subject is overwhelming, ever-changing and never-ending. So in this book, which is both a survey of the collecting field and a how-to guide, we have tried to present a cross section of what is happening, told in large part by the collectors themselves.

The people we interviewed were as diverse as their collections: as young as nine and as old as 90; well-known and little-known; rich and poor; casual and compulsive. They collect for a variety of different reasons, many of which are unknown even to them. Some collect purely for pleasure, others for prestige or for profit. Some are hoarders and some are historians and some just like the challenge of the hunt. Many have become authorities in their fields, authors of books, presidents of organizations. They enjoy the sharing and social life of clubs and conventions and proudly display—and often use—their collections. Many others prefer privacy; they do not discuss their collections—they store them in closets or in vaults, hidden from public scrutiny. But, however different their motives and personalities, collectors have a lot in common. Their experiences, activities and, in fact, their advice seem almost

*"A passion which transcends the barriers of age, sex, and society, which can entirely occupy the minds of the most profound as of the most superficial . . . which excites emulation and allows people to singularize themselves while remaining within the framework of morality and social organization, is collecting."*

—PHILLIPE JULIAN,
*The Collectors* (Charles E. Tuttle Co.)

Earthenware

interchangeable. For example, the trading tactics of a bank collector are useful for the collector of comic art and vice versa; the cleaning tips of the tool collector are equally applicable to typewriters or toys; and information about advertising and appraisals, about fakes or forming a club, are relevant to bottle, book and barbed-wire collectors alike.

Given the infinite amount of information in a constantly fluctuating field, this book cannot begin to be all-inclusive. It is designed, rather, to be a catalyst—a jumping-off point —that suggests some of the options available to the collector today. The rest of the job, the follow-through, is up to you!

In each section we have included one or more sources of further information: a collector, a publication or an organization. Many have generously agreed to send a free sample of their newsletter or magazine or to answer questions as long as the requested handling costs are covered and a legal-size SASE (self-addressed stamped envelope with adequate postage) enclosed. There are special listings in the book for mail-order companies, including book distributors who sell books on collecting; for reference books that give names of museums, more organizations and publications; and, most importantly, for free sample copies of general collecting papers and magazines (reading their articles and advertisements will surely lead you to whatever you want, no matter how obscure). One caveat: Addresses and prices were current at the time of writing but may have changed by the time you read this. We apologize. We also apologize for the collections, clubs and publications that were unintentionally omitted and hope to include them in a future edition.

We would still like to hear from you if you have an unusual collection or bit of information to pass on. Write Box 213, West Hampton, NY 11977.

*Comic Art*

**Letter to the Editor,
American Collector, April 1978**

**Garbage Cans?**

Your April editorial suggested some items not being collected. Good try, but we are beginning to think there is no such thing. Trash cans were exhibited at a show of plastic "antiques" in England a few years ago and are part of a collection in the Plastics Industry Museum. The Buten Museum of Wedgwood owns some worn Wedgwood heels, do they qualify as "used heels of shoes?" The ancient Chinese saved all fingernail and toenail clippings to be buried with them. There are many blanket collectors; old hand loomed American blankets and Indian blankets. We can't find a collector of "drumsticks of well known drummers" although we do know of several collections of violin bows. We have seen a set of drumsticks from a known drummer saved by a fan.

Years ago we tried to write an April Fool's article about a collection so silly it would be an obvious joke. The best idea was sawdust from different types of wood and we found there really is a collection like that.

Ralph and Terry Kovel are well-known writers on antiques, publish a monthly newsletter; Kovels on Antiques and Collectibles. To get a sample copy send $.50 to 22000 Shaker Blvd., Shaker Heights, OH 44122.

# QUOTES FROM COLLECTORS

*"I think discovery is one of the great joys of collecting and I wouldn't delegate that pleasure to anyone else, even if he were to offer me a free Picasso with every third purchase."*

–Dorothy Rogers, writing about
collections that are made for people by experts,
in *My Favorite Things* (Atheneum)

*"Looking back, what most collectors regret most is not the things they bought but the things they passed up. Beginners tend to start with less expensive items, but such items often appreciate more slowly than solid major items. The key to a great collection is quality, not quantity. I no longer count the number of pieces in my collection but I am continually upgrading it."*

–Jerome Muller, comic art collector

*"Any collecting hobby can become a virtual obsession, owing to the very human penchant for believing that as one object is valuable, a dozen or a hundred like objects can be a hundred or a thousand times more valuable. Hence, each like object becomes irresistible."*

–Jo Brewer, lepidopterist

*"To collect should never be a forced job that must be completed, but rather a constantly exhilirating surprise of discovery, a new treasure to add to one's others."*

–Eleanor Brenner, fashion designer

*"I don't understand . . . I just like everything. Everything looks so terrific."*

–Andy Warhol (Folk and Funk Catalogue, Museum of American Folk Art)

*"When children get old enough not to listen, their parents' collectibles become their 'children.' The collections are cared for the same way and when they are given away to a museum the parents want them to associate with the right other collections, to live on the 'right street.'"*

–Teddy Kolleck, collector of antiquities,
Mayor of Jerusalem and Chairman of the Board of The Israel Museum

*"Only if you turn artworks back to the market will they stay alive."*

–attributed to Robert von Hirsch of Basel, Switzerland, whose art collection was sold for $34 million at Sotheby Parke Bernet, London

*"Always bargain with the person with whom you are dealing, especially if it is another collector or individual who is not in the antique business. The first price quoted is usually inflated, many times because the person honestly believes he has something rare or particularly desirable but is not aware of prevailing prices. Further, seek out the person's particular interests—he may be willing to swap for items you have that are of no use or interest to you. I have swapped toy trains, military insignia, political campaign buttons, etc., for fire-fighting memorabilia.*

*"If buying a collection or pieces of a collection, one might consider 'dollar averaging,' i.e, the person may have a high price on one item and a low price on another. The worth of the low-priced item may more than compensate for the cost of the higher-priced piece and one can come out ahead. Example: I paid $425 more for a cast-iron fire toy than I felt it was worth but picked up two rare fire prints from the same person at about $150 less than actual value.*

*"Be persistent in advertising your wants. In one case I advertised over a period of five years in order to complete a set of 10 models.*

*"As your hobby grows, bring it to the attention of your local press or magazine(s) covering your field. A good story can lead people to contact you regarding swaps, buy, sell, etc. Even more important, it can lead to an exchange of information that could alert you to items or areas of your hobby that you never realized existed."*

–Gilbert Stanley, collector of fire apparatus

**ADVERTISING AGE,**
November 1977

CHICAGO—The nostalgia craze and a host of other factors appear to be sweeping a large segment of Americans into a vast market for collectibles, ranging from "manufactured" items like commemorative medallions to antique cars and toothpick holders.

A new study conducted by Leo J. Shapiro & Associates shows that one adult American out of five is a collector of something that somone could add to with a gift.

The most popular objects were coins, antiques and books, each of these categories being named by 3% of respondents. Figurines and stamps were next, each named by 2%.

But the wide diversity of collections was indicated by the catchall "other" category, which included 8% of respondents, who named 28 different items, such as music boxes, fine records, gold, H.O. railroad layout, salt and pepper shakers, sea shells, pre-Columbian artifacts, figurine bears and hores, old plates and pitchers, hand tools, milk glass, vases, toothpick holders, bottles, musical instruments, miniature furniture, beer mugs, old coal stoves, driftwood, matches and fine handkerchiefs.

A further new study by the Shapiro company delves into the collecting habits of young people, by age groups and by sex. The survey of boys and girls, ages six to seven, showed that 50% of them "collect things that are interesting or unusual." Boys were somewhat more avid collectors than girls—54% of boys said they collected things, compared with 46% for girls. The collecting urge held steady in the later teen years.

The most popular items were rocks and shells, collected by 23% of those with collections, trailed by coins and stamps, each collected by 16% of the young collectors, and baseball cards, collected by 12%.

"There are many things we don't know about collectors," Mr. Shapiro said. "But we do know that, among young people, the collecting urge relates to an early desire to go to college, to become a professional person. Collecting is one way to start entering the adult world." –*Leo J. Shapiro,* President of the marketing research company

*Political Campaign Buttons*

# COLLECTING CLUES

## Determining Value

A final price is the lowest figure at which a dealer will sell and the highest price a buyer is willing to offer. This may be based on condition, quality, beauty, workmanship, color, size, decorative utility, scarcity (but sometimes a rare item does not command as high a price as a more common item because the common item is better known), source (marks and attribution), fashion and fad, historical interest (potential to have future value), subject (dogs sell well) and collectibility (too fragile, specialized or costly; too hard to identify, find, store or dispose of; or too easy to reproduce).

## Appraisals

A free or informal appraisal might be obtained from an auction house, pawn shop, a dealer in your specialty, e.g., coin shop for coins (telephone those that advertise in "Item Wanted") or a museum curator (who generally will identify objects but will not appraise their value). If you cannot bring the

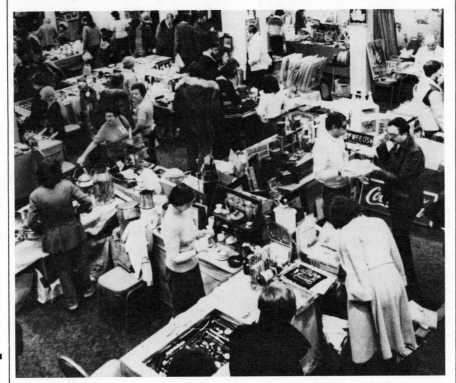

actual object send good photographs with a detailed description—and get more than one opinion if necessary.

To find a professional appraiser, call the appraisal society in your area, consult organizations for their membership listings or an antique dealer; ask an attorney or bank trust officer for their recommendation.

### Appraisers

*American Society of Appraisers*, Box 17265, Dulles Airport, Washington, DC 20041 (703-620-3838). *Membership Directory* gives listings by geography and category (free).

*Appraisers Association of America*, 541 Lexington Avenue, New York, NY 10022 (212-753-5039). *Membership Directory* gives listings by geography and category ($3 postpaid).

**PRICE GUIDES**   These guides should be used with some caution as they may be based on the author's educated opinion or "guess," on an average price or on what a dealer would like to have received but has not; or they may be privately printed to inflate prices.

**THE SELF-EDUCATED EXPERT**   In the final analysis, the smart collector is the knowledgeable collector, with a good memory for figures. There is no substitute for reading, talking to dealers and fellow collectors, comparison shopping by reading advertisements in collecting publications, and attending fairs, shows and auctions (refer to auction prices realized listings).

# Buying Right

**SHOPPING TOOLS** *Tape Measure;* *Magnifying Glass* to find any identifying marks, notations, dates, labels or trademarks (a rubbing can be made of some marks by placing thin paper over them and rubbing with a soft pencil, shown to an expert or compared with those in books); *Pocket Knife* (for scratching through paint); *Magnet* (to test for solid brass, bronze or copper—these will not attract a magnet, but plated-over iron will); *Shopping Bags; Soft Packing Material; Ropes, Blankets, Luggage Rack* for large collectibles and *CASH*.

### Shopping tips

- Collectibles can be bought at specialist dealers, at antique shows and flea markets, at auctions, at garage and tag sales, and privately through mail-order and merchandise offerings.
- It is usually easier to buy than to sell (although some collectors claim the reverse is true) and what you buy at retail you may often have to sell at wholesale.
- When buying from a dealer, get a receipted bill on his letterhead with date, price, description and terms such as guarantees. When buying from a private party, be aware of these pitfalls: lack of recourse, poor repair work, questionable documentation.
- A dealer may inflate the price if he thinks you are an anxious collector; on the other hand, a good or steady customer has more bargaining power.

**TRADING** The barter system is used at all levels of collecting and is sometimes highly organized within each specialty. An important point to remember is not to undervalue what you are disposing of just because you are anxious to make the trade. However, value should not be the sole reason for a transaction. Obtaining the missing link or long sought-after item may be just as important.

# SWAP TABLE

Trading notices for this department accepted at no charge Notices limited to trades only — nothing for sale accepted. Limit 20 words, including name and address. Notices will appear in one issue only renewable by sending in again. No dealer notices aceptted. We reserve the right to refuse or edit any notices.

Type or write very plainly. Give material you have first, then material you want. Give full address including zip number.

Trade notices are published in good faith but GEMS & MINERALS cannot assume responsibility for actions of traders. Write advertiser before you send material and arrange complete details of trade. Notices published in the order received subject to space available. If notice cannot appear in one issue, it will be held for the next.

ADDRESS: Swap Table, Gems & Minerals, P.O. Box 687, Mentone, California 92359.

**PREHNITE, PYROPHYLLITE AND** limonite crystals, for your crystals. Send list to Wall, 803 Cumvilk Dr., Kernersville, NC 27284.

**LOCAL FOSSILS, ROCK,** for sphere chunks of Red Trees onyx (CA), Wakefield Marble (MD), Melon plush (AZ). Arnold Richter, Fairmount, IL 61841.

**EXCELLENT MICROS AND** broadheads, for same. Write first. Marge Farkas, 1904 S. 5th St., Allentown, PA 18103.

**GENUINE HORSE COLLAR** mirror with hames, for cutting material. Prefer agate, geodes, jasper. Stan Bradley, Grass Range MT 59032.

**DEEP WATER ATLANTIC** coral heads, black tree coral, for what have you? Collect specimens. Mrs. H. Brookstone, 17401 NW 19th Ave., Opa Locka, FL 33056.

**WESTERN CRYSTAL MINERALS** specimens, for any choice crystals. Request list, indicating your trade minerals. McBroom, 6091 S. Detroit, Littleton, CO 80121.

**U.S. COMMEMORATIVE STAMPS,** for T/N crystal specimens, fluorescents or fossils. Milton S. Hershhorn, 263 N. Country Rd., Smithtown, NY 11787.

*Advertising Signs*

## Collecting By Mail

Enclose an SASE so the seller can easily respond and money can be returned, if necessary.

Don't send cash in the mail. Include a return address and use sufficient postage.

Read advertisements carefully to determine true condition (if an item arrives defective or misrepresented and it was not so advertised, return it and notify the publication); extra costs (postage and insurance may be additional if ad does not say postpaid); the right to return, etc.

## Mail-Order Auctions

Many smaller collectibles, such as stamps, autographs, political buttons and campaign collectibles are auctioned through the mail by specialized companies. The bidder sends in his bid and at a predetermined deadline date the bids are opened and the winner notified.

## Buying at Auction

Examine everything fully before bidding. Many auction houses state that they are not responsible for accurate descriptions, authenticity and condition.

Establish with yourself the maximum price you will pay and try to stick to it.

Read the conditions of sale (must you pay in cash, by certified check; how fast must merchandise be removed; is there a buyer's premium added to the purchase price).

Keep calm.

## Terminology

*Advance*—the increment by which the bid continues.

*As is*—the article as it is, including imperfections.

*Bid*—price offered.

*Book-bid*—bid left with auctioneer in advance of sale.

*Consigner*—the person or organization owning or controlling the merchandise being sold.

*Consignment*—auction merchandise not owned by the house.

*Estimate*—the price the auction house tells either the consigner to expect to receive on an item, or the buyer to expect to pay for it.

*Knocked-down*—sold.

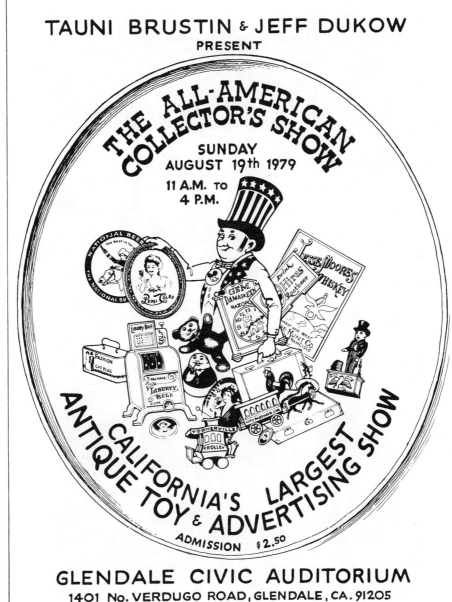

*Lot*—the unit offered for sale; may be one article or several.

*Pass*—decision made by auctioneer to skip a lot.

*Provenance*—the ownership and exhibition history of an item.

*Reserve*—the minimum price the consigner will accept for an article; sometimes silent, sometimes stated by the auctioneer.

*Unrestricted sale*—an auction in which there are no minimums or reserves, and all merchandise is to be sold to the highest bidder.

# Selling Your Collection

Sooner or later you are going to sell, if only to trade up or dispose of duplicates or less desirable items. Here's how to do it:

Friends—and word of mouth among collectors.

*Shows, Conventions and Flea Markets*—A table can cost as little as $10; price clearly, be prepared to give a discount and watch out for thieves.

*Direct Mail*—Photocopy or mimeograph list of items for sale; include pictures, a personal note, state condition, price, etc.; advertise list in collector's publications (ask for SASE).

*Dealers*—They will generally give you only half of the fair market value on items bought outright; if left on consignment they will give a prearranged percentage of the selling price.

*Auctions*—Find out what the commission rate is (generally 20 to 25 percent, either a flat rate on the whole lot or a sliding rate based on the value of each piece); how soon the sale can be scheduled and how much after it you will be paid; and if there are extra charges such as packing, delivery, storage, photography, advertising and insurance.

*Classified For-Sale Ads* (and "Wanted" Ads)—Write a precise, detailed and clear ad. Begin with a strong statement about the type of collectible, then give a full description (including condition, i.e., poor to excellent; size; marks; pattern; name; etc.) and a realistic price (or request bids). Figure in shipping and insurance costs (some customers ask for an item on approval and will pay these costs both ways); ask for an SASE (so money can be returned if item is sold, or to send list of other offerings).

*Bulletin Boards, Garage Sales*—and, if all else fails, donations to charitable organizations, thrift shops, etc. Get a receipt for tax purposes.

# Hidden Costs

**THE COST OF BUYING** These hidden costs include: price paid; taxes; appraisal; commission and insurance fees; the cost of travel, packing, shipping and research.

**THE COST OF OWNING** This includes money for: cleaning, repair and restoration; hobby publications, courses, club memberships and other educational activities (travel, conventions, etc.); interest lost on the money invested in the collection; insurance safety devices (including a vault box); display or storage equipment.

**THE COST OF SELLING** You must pay for: advertisements, telephone, postage, repair costs, photographs, packing

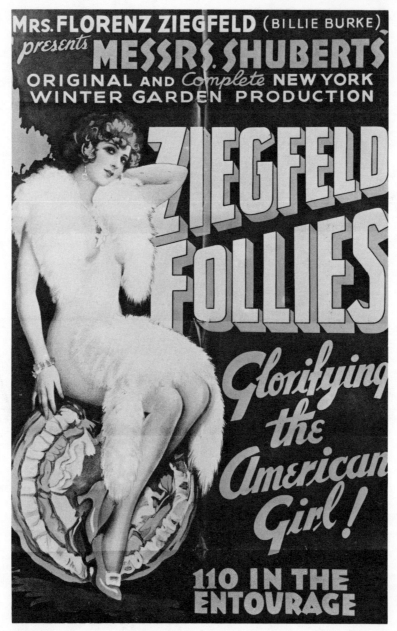

*Theatre Posters*

material, price guides and auction catalogues (to help establish the current price), stationery, photocopies, dealer or auction commission, tables or booths at conventions and shows (including cost of getting and staying there—gas, hotel, etc.).

# Care of Collections

Although the collections in this book are quite varied, there do seem to be some universal truths that apply to all of them; and a tip or bit of advice given by a collector in one area will undoubtedly hold true for others. "Mostly common sense," they say, and "proceed with caution" (and in proportion to the value of an item—obviously you can experiment with steel wool and rust remover on a cheap tin without great loss); "under- rather than overclean or restore"; "keep collectibles (especially those made from organic materials, paper, cloth, ivory, etc.) away from extremes in temperature and bright sun."

**PAPER PRODUCTS** Keep away from dampness (paper mildews) and excessive heat and dust (use plastic bags, plastic envelopes sold for this purpose, acetate sheets, manila folders or boxes for protection). Don't trim margins, cut in other ways; fold, or mend with plastic tape; store flat; and use acid-free paper when mounting.

**CHINA, POTTERY AND GLASS**
Don't use strong bleach or harsh abrasives, and dust very fragile objects with a fine, soft artist's paintbrush. Add a little ammonia to a mixture of mild detergent and water to make glass sparkle, then dry it with a lintless cloth. (See specific chapters for more information on care of collections).

**INSURANCE**    Collectors have been known to pack up their collectibles and transfer them to a vault each time they go away. One collector of fine porcelain would even take the best pieces along with her in the special velvet-lined cases she had made for traveling. When her collection was sold, she commented that as sad as she was to see it go, she was relieved to be rid of this burdensome routine. It is too bad collectors have to worry about protecting their collections; but fire, theft and breakage are facts of life that cannot be ignored, so some precautions should be considered. If you are thinking about insuring your collection, check with your collecting club to see if they sponsor an insurance plan (many do); check with your insurance agent to see exactly what your homeowners comprehensive policy covers (usually only part of the value of your home and collection) and to determine whether a special fine arts policy or addition is advisable (this insures specific items for specific amounts based on a professional appraisal or recent bill).

Then remember to have collectibles that are appreciating in value reappraised every few years and the insurance policy changed accordingly.

*Menus*

*Matchholders*

# Record Keeping

**HOW TO INVENTORY YOUR COLLECTION**  A written record is indispensable for tax and insurance purposes as well as to just keep track of what is in the collection. Any ordinary notebook can be used, but a loose-leaf that allows for changes, additions and deletions is best. The following information could be included, with one or more items to the page:

*Name of Item and Description*—condition, historical notes, purchase price and date, and from whom purchased; date sold, for how much, etc.

*Insurance and Appraisal value*—and inheritance information if relevant.

*Picture*—a photograph or photocopy of a flat object in black and white or color (objects can be numbered to correspond to numbers in the book). Two books already assembled for this purpose are:

*Personal Inventory Antiques and Collectibles,* E.G. Warman Publishing Co., Union Town, PA 15401 ($8.95)

*The Kovel's Organizer for Collectors* by Ralph and Terry Koval ($8.95, at bookstores)

# How to Photograph Your Collection

Photographing the objects in a collection is not very different from photographing the family, yet it is surprising how few collectors have done it. Assuming you know how to work the camera, just keep in mind the following simple suggestions and your margin of success and the clarity of your pictures should improve:

**ARRANGEMENT OF OBJECTS** Each one should be photographed alone (probably not where it is displayed) or in a group of a few pieces spaced so that they do not hide one another (an effective way is to place objects on steps or on boxes set up to simulate steps).

**BACKGROUND** Any other activity in the picture will be distracting, so it is best to photograph the object(s) on an area that has been covered with a cloth (or piece of cardboard) of a contrasting color (i.e., if the object is light, use a black cloth). The cloth should be both under and behind the object.

**LIGHT** It may be easiest to set up outside in open shade (not bright sunlight, which can create confusing shadows). If you are taking pictures inside, first see if there is already enough light by opening windows and putting on all the lights. Use

*Photographs*

fast Tri-X film, a camera with a good lens and a tripod or other support if necessary. If you must use additional lights (a lamp with the shade removed can sometimes be pressed into service) or a flash, watch out for reflections (in mirrors, off pictures and shiny surfaces) and "hot spots." Don't take pictures of metal, glass or glass-covered objects (and some china) head-on with a flash—tilt the flash 45 degrees or more (it can be pointed upward and the light bounced off the ceiling).

**FOCUS AND ANGLE** Don't shoot only frontally; take the picture from several angles, including from above. And don't stand too close. The picture may be out of focus if you are nearer than two to three feet, and a picture can always be enlarged for greater detail. If the camera is set so there is very little depth of field, try and place all objects in the same picture plane.

If you are using 35mm film, which is cheap, take a lot of pictures, at several exposures and from several angles. Then you'll be sure to have at least one good one.

# Collecting and the Law

**THE HOBBY PROTECTION ACT** Signed into law in 1973, this act is designed to protect hobbyists against reproduction or manufacture of imitation hobby items, and provides additional protections for American hobbyists. The law is enforced by the FTC.

The law requires that any imitation or replica items manufactured in the United States or imported into the United States must be plainly and permanently marked "COPY." (New reproductions can be so true to their historical antecedents that they can easily be mistaken for the "real thing.")

**OBJECTS WHETHER ANTIQUE OR NEW**   The law makes no distinction between the two. If they are made in whole or in part from whalebone, tortoise shell, ivory from the Asian (not African) elephant, or materials from other endangered species, they cannot be transported across state lines for the purpose of sale or brought into the country. It is a federal offense.

**IF COLLECTIBLES ARE TO BE SOLD**   It might be a good idea to check government regulations on small businesses. For example, in many states and under varying conditions, collectors who sell at flea markets or yard sales should have a resale license and should collect tax to be passed on to the state (this comes under the heading of casual or occasional sales).

**SPEAKING OF TAXES**   Capital gains or earnings from the sale of collectibles are supposed to be reported. Since many transactions are in cash or trade or in combinations of both, this is often overlooked.

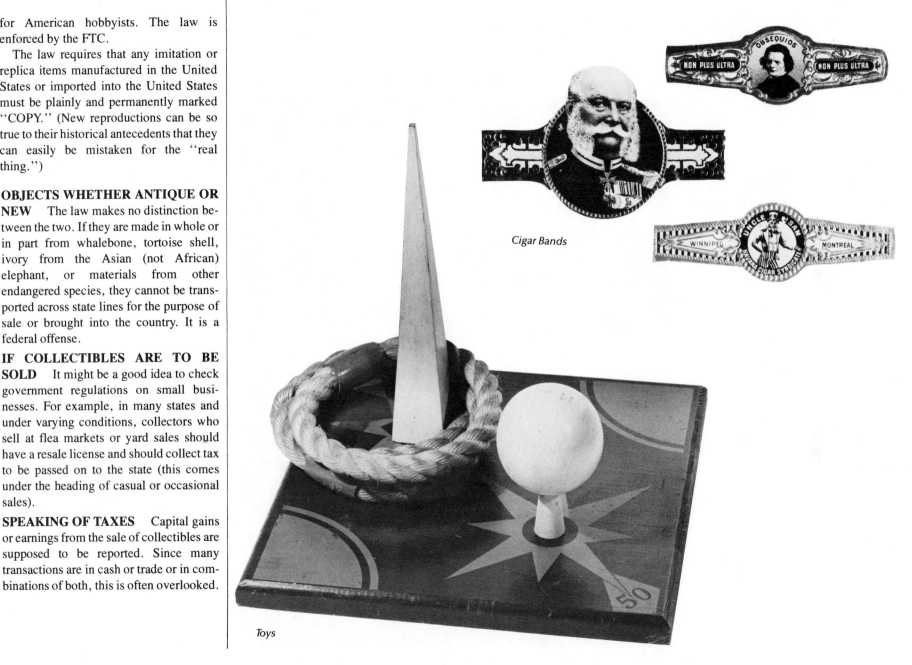

Cigar Bands

Toys

# INDEX OF INFORMATION

## Free Sample Issues of General Antiques and Collecting Publications

In some cases there is a small handling charge, as indicated in parentheses.

*American Antiques,* New Hope, Bucks County, PA 18938 (50¢)

*American Collector,* 13920 Mt. McClellan Avenue, Reno NV 89506

*The American Collectors Journal,* American Publishing Co., Box 1431, Porterville, CA 93257 (50¢)

*Antique and Collectors Mart,* Box 17063, Wichita, KS 67217

*Antique Collector,* Box 327, Ephrata, PA 17522 ($1)

*Antique Monthly,* Box 2274, Birmingham, AL 35201

*The Antique Price Report,* Box 974, Kermit, TX 79745 (25¢)

*The Antiques' Journal,* Box 1046, Dubuque, IA 52001

*The Antique Trader Weekly,* Box 1050, Dubuque, IA 52001 (50¢)

*Art and Auction,* 250 West 57th St., New York, NY 10019

*Sheet Music*

*Collectibles Monthly,* Box 2023, York, PA 17405 ($1)

*The Collector,* Drawer C, Kermit, TX 79745 (25¢)

*Collectors News,* Box 156, Grundy Center, IA 50638

*Country Americana,* Castle Press Publications, Inc., Rt. 1, Washington, NJ 07882 ($4.50 bimonthly)

*Hobbies,* Lightner Publishing Corp., 1006 S. Michigan Avenue, Chicago, IL 60605 (25¢)

*Joel Saters Antiques and Auction News,* Box 13, Marietta, PA 17547 ($1 for two issues)

*Maine Antique Digest,* Box 358, Waldoboro, ME 04572

*The New York Antique Almanac,* Box 335, Lawrence, NY 11559

*The Newtown Bee* (Antiques and the Arts Weekly), Newtown, CT 06470

*Relics,* Western Publications, Inc., Box 3338, 1012 Edgecliff Terrace, Austin, TX 78764 (35¢)

*Spinning Wheel,* American Antiques & Crafts Society, Fame Avenue, Hanover, PA 17331 ($1)

*Sotheby Parke Bernet Newsletter,* c/o Newsletter Editor (CB), 980 Madison Avenue, New York, NY 10021

*Tri-State Trader,* 27 N. Jefferson Street, Knightstown, IN 46148 (25¢)

## OTHER COLLECTING MAGAZINES

*Acquire,* 170 Fifth Avenue, New York, NY 10010

*American Art and Antiques,* 1515 Broadway, New York, NY 10036

*Americana,* 10 Rockefeller Plaza, New York, NY 10020

*The Antique Dealer Collectors Guide,* 1–3 Wine Office Court, Fleet St., London, England

*Antiques World,* Box 990, Farmingdale, NY 11737

*Apollo,* 75 Rockefeller Plaza, New York, NY 10019

*The Connoisseur,* 250 W. 55th Street, New York, NY 10019

*The Magazine Antiques,* 551 Fifth Avenue, New York, NY 10019

# Collecting by Mail

*Book Publishers and/or Distributors That Specialize in Books on Collecting—*

*Most have catalogues of collecting books that will be sent on request.*

*The Alamo Company,* 13920 Mt. McClellan Avenue, Reno, NV 89506

*Collector Books,* Box 3009, Paducah, KY 42001

*R.J. Beck Co.,* 2109 Hunter Street, Huntertown, IN 46748

*Shepard's Emporium,* 2120 Second Avenue, Seattle, WA 98121

*Nostalgia Book Club,* 165 Huguenot Street, New Rochelle, NY 10801

*American Antiques & Crafts Society,* Fame Avenue, Hanover, PA 17331

*The Collectors Shelf of Books,* 23 Crandall Street, Box 6, Westfield, NY 14787

*Hotchkiss House,* 18 Hearthstone Road, Pittsford, NY 14534

*Wallace Homestead Book Co.,* Box B1-1912, Grand Avenue, Des Moines, IA 50305

*E.G. Warman Publishing Co.,* 540 Morgan Town Road, Uniontown, PA 15401

*Dover Publications,* 11 E. Second Avenue, Mineola, NY 11501

*Publishers Central Bureau,* Dept. 526, 1 Champion Avenue, Avenel, NJ 07131

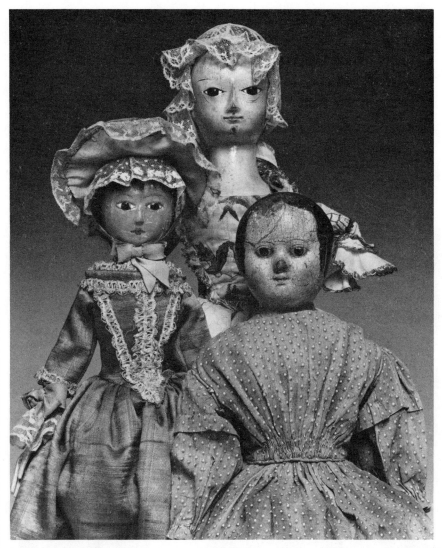

*Dolls*

# Useful Publications

Information for collectors on clubs, prices, publications, museums, dealers, shopping sources, etc. Most can be found in large libraries.

*Encyclopedia of Associations* (annual), Gale Research Co., Book Tower, Detroit, MI 48226. See Chapter 13, "Hobby and Avocational Organizations."

*The International Directory of Arts* (Frankfurt am Main). Societies, dealers, private collectors, auctioneers, appraisers, restorers; also museums, galleries, libraries, archives, universities and colleges, art associations, publishers, critics and experts.

*The Art Index,* Wilson. Index to art-related articles and museum bulletins (international).

*The Official Museum Directory.* Directory of the American Association of Museums—refers to specialized museums of the United States and Canada, such as Crime and Circus, Theatre and Transportation Museums.

*Readers' Guide to Periodicals.* Listing of articles that have appeared in major general publications.

*The Standard Periodical Directory Annual,* Oxbridge Communications, Inc. Available at Antiques and Art Goods, 1345 Sixth Avenue, New York, NY 10019. See chapter on hobbies and crafts.

*N.W. Ayers* periodicals. Not too much art and antiques, coins and stamps, but lists circulation, which is helpful for those wishing to advertise.

*Ulrich's International Periodicals Directory* (annual), Bowker. Classified guide to current periodicals, foreign and domestic.

*Writers Digest* (Annual), Cincinnati, OH. Lists major periodicals; see hobbies and crafts chapter.

*Books in Print.* Listings of trade books by author or title; look under collecting, antiques, hobbies, etc.

## Shopping Aids

*Price Indexes.* These publications are available from some of the larger auction houses, dealers and libraries, and from bookstores and book distributors listed on page 27. Auction catalogues with prices realized; dealer's catalogues with prices of merchandise offered for sale; art price annuals; classified "For Sale" advertisements; general price "guides," "Guides" (not price "gospels") by Ralph and Terry Kovel and Edwin G. Warman, and hundreds of specialized price guides

*Whitlaw's Art Directory,* 180 Madison Avenue, New York, NY 10016. A monthly publication for buying and selling collectibles (subscription $8.50).

*Have a Number: A Guide for Dating Collectible Items Through Patent Numbers* by Gary and Candy Floria, Box 6633, St. Paul, MN 55106 ($6 postpaid)

(Note: Old catalogues are also helpful in dating and describing many collectibles.)

*Flea Market USA,* Rt. 1, 470 Cantonment, FL 32533. A directory of flea markets and swap meets in 40 states ($5).

*The Yellow Pages.* For dealers, listed by specialty under "Antiques" or "General Headings."

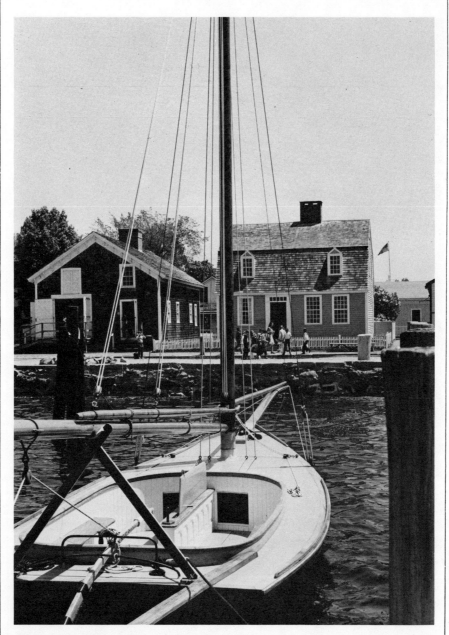

*Mystic Seaport, Mystic, Connecticut*

## Historic Restorations— Houses and Villages

This is just a partial list; to find those in your area consult local historical societies, the Chamber of Commerce, tourist bureaus, magazine and newspaper listings and *The Official Museum Directory.*

Bellingrath, *Theodore, Alabama*

La Casa Grande, *San Simeon, California*

Mystic Seaport Village, *Mystic, Connecticut*

Corbit-Sharpe House, *Wilmington, Delaware*

Henry Francis du Pont Winterthur Museum, *Wilmington, Delaware*

Whitehall, *Palm Beach, Florida*

Vizcaya, *Miami, Florida*

The Shadows-on-the-Teche, *New Iberia, Louisiana*

Hampton, *Towson, Maryland*

Old Deerfield Village, *Deerfield, Massachusetts*

Jeremiah Lee Mansion, *Marblehead, Massachusetts*

Hancock Shaker Village, *Pittsfield, Massachusetts*

Essex Institute and House of Seven Gables Settlement Association, *Salem, Massachusetts*

Mission House, *Stockbridge, Massachusetts*

Old Sturbridge Village, *Sturbridge, Massachusetts*

Old Salem, Winston Salem, North Carolina

Henry Ford Museum and Greenfield Village, *Dearborn, Michigan*

New York State Historical Association Village and Museum, *Cooperstown, New York*

Boscobel, *Garrison, New York*

Home of Franklin D. Roosevelt National Historic Site, *Hyde Park, New York*

Vanderbilt Mansion, *Hyde Park, New York*

Campbell Whittlessey House, *Rochester, New York*

Lyndhurst, *Tarrytown, New York*

Sleepy Hollow, *Tarrytown, New York*

Biltmore, *Asheville, North Carolina*

Tryon Palace, *New Bern, North Carolina*

Adena State Memorial, *Chillicothe, Ohio*

Strawberry Mansion, *Philadelphia, Pennsylvania*

The Breakers, *Newport, Rhode Island*

The Elms, *Newport, Rhode Island*

Shelburne Museum, *Shelburne, Vermont*

The Beehive House, *Salt Lake City, Utah*

Monticello, *Charlottesville, Virginia*

Mount Vernon, *Virginia*

Stratford Hall, *Stratford, Virginia*

Colonial Williamsburg and Carter's Grove Plantation, *Williamsburg, Virginia*

The White House, *Washington, D.C.*

Woodrow Wilson House, *Washington, D.C.*

## Research Institutions for Collectibles

*Special Collection of 20th Century Memorabilia,* Boston University Exhibition Hall (a research library, not a museum)

*The Popular Culture Library and Audio Center,* Bowling Green State University, Bowling Green, OH 43403

*Early American Shop (Henry Ford Museum) Dearborn, Michigan*

*Noah Webster House (Henry Ford Museum) Dearborn, Michigan*

# OFF THE BEATEN TRACK: Unique and Unusual Collections

## Onomastics: (Names)

*"You don't have to polish it, dust it or wash it and no one is going to steal it from you, so you don't have to insure it. It's the easiest kind of collection and the most charming. It doesn't cost anything and it doesn't require labor."* – GEORGE HUBBARD, *New York Post,* Jan. 9, 1975

What is it? Why, name collecting, or onomastics. To qualify for Hubbard's collection, names must be odd and authentic (no stage names, pen names, aliases), and come from a reliable source: obituary column, society page, news article, tombstone, telephone directory and so forth. He has acquired names on his travels and through the mail from collectors who swap with him. Some favorites are: *Oscar Asparagus, Three Persons Appleyard, Aphrodite Chackess, Free Love Outhouse and Sistine Madonna McClung.* While others may specialize in surnames, given names or names with a point of association with the person's occupation, Hubbard collects only full names and will be happy to receive names from readers to add to the more than 10,000 he already has. Write him at 210 East 68th Street, New York, NY 10021.

A Collection of Articles About Unusual Collections. (*Collection of Glen Wiswell*)

## Calling Cards of Celebrities

Frederick Schang, with some of his visiting cards that date back to the 18th century. The collection includes the cards of Jefferson, Twain, Pasteur, Proust, Baudelaire, Freud, Tchaikowsky and Chopin—his rarest and most valuable (written to a music student in French, it is inscribed, "I cannot give you a lesson today. I send you a thousand excuses accompanied by a warm hand clasp."). A retired concert manager, Schang is the author of *Visiting Cards of Celebrities* and he is currently writing a book about his collection of visiting cards that were used by musicians.

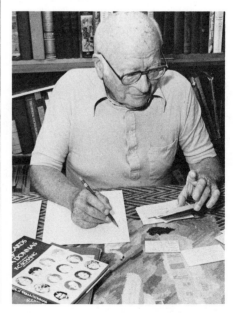

# Free Book Club

Jerry Cammarata never has to ask Information for a telephone number because he has a collection of 3,747 telephone directories from all over the country. Not only does this save money, but Jerry (known as Super Pop) uses the books to teach his two little girls skills like reading, math and spelling, and also geography, sociology, psychology and earth science. In addition, the children have the privilege of making a three-minute telephone call to anyone, anyplace in the United States. Jerry feels they learn from the conversation—telephone manners, and facts about the people, the community and the climate of the area they have reached. *(Rosey-Garrard Lou Reda Productions, Inc.)*

*Credit Cards*—John Black and Frances Hensler with their collection. *(WorldWide Photos)*

## COLLECTOR IS REAL SHARP

Berlin (UPI)—Paul Richter, an 80 year old pensioner in Leipzig, collects razor blades, just as other people collect stamps or beer steins.

The East German news agency ADN reported yesterday that Richter's collection is made up of 15,735 blades from 77 countries—"the largest collection of razor blades in the world!"

The blades are stacked according to country, in alphabetical order in his albums.

Richter who has been collecting for 32 years says a Gillette blade manufactured in Boston in 1904 is one of his rarest finds.

*Wishbones*—David Lazarus, Jr., of Cincinnati, has 166.

# The Lure of Plugs

Computer consultant Seth Rosenbaum's professional life is future-oriented but his avocational interests are involved with the past: collecting antique artificial lures. He has roughly 10,000 that date back to the 1860s. When he is not fishing with them, the lures are hung on a net strung along the walls of a closet. Rosenbaum, who has been fishing since he was seven, started collecting in the fifties when it was easy to pick up old plugs that were forgotten and left lying around on the shelves of local tackle stores. Modern merchandising methods have all but eliminated this source, so he must now rely on swapping and advertising.

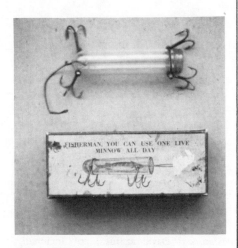

*Detroit Glass Minnow 1910.*

*Collection in a Closet*—Seth Rosenbaum with his lures.

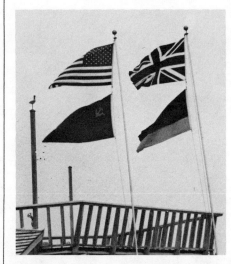

*Flags of All Countries* are stored on shelves in file folders, and flown from the beach house according to the nationality of the visitors. *(Collection of James Warren)*

*Paper Shopping Bags (Collection Cooper-Hewitt Museum, The Smithsonian Institution's National Museum of Design)*

## What Other Collectors Collect

- *Telephones; Cash Registers; Looms; Toasters*
- *Passports; Almanacs*
- *Licenses:* dog; chauffeur; police
- *Shoe Taps; Ice Skates; Hula Hoops*
- *Scientific and Drafting Instruments; Yard Calendars*
- *Shopping Bags; Mousetraps; Cattle Brands* and *Firecracker Wrappers* before 1920

*Shopping Bag c. 1966. Andy Warhol.*

# FROM LARGE-SCALE TO LILLIPUTIAN

## Oversized Americana

One of the first and certainly one of the most passionate and prolific collectors of Americana, Electra Havemeyer Webb, also had a weakness for early architecture. She "collected," rescued and preserved, among others: a light-house, a covered bridge, a jail, a school house, a country store and the Stage Coach Inn (filling them with furnishings and accessories from her other collections), and old vehicles—trains, carriages, and a boat, the S.S. Ticonderoga, a 1,220-foot, 892-ton steamship and the last sidewheeler to operate on Lake Champlain. "Some collectors have the place and look for the piece. Not I. I buy the piece and then I find the place." —E. H. Webb, as quoted in *The Proud Possessors* by Aline Saarinen (Random House)

The place in this case became the Shelburne Museum, which she founded in 1947. *(Collection of Shelburne Museum, Shelburne, Vermont)*

## The Carriage Trade

Ken Sowles' collection of over 300 buggies, or horse-drawn carriages, required more of an investment in storage space (six barns) and time (for authentic restoration) than money—the most he has paid for a carriage is $500 and he has paid as little as $5 for some. Since a carriage needs a horse to be in full working order, he also has a few of them, trained for the job. He hopes eventually to establish a museum financed by a private foundation he has set up.

## The Melville Collection at The Carriage Museum

Shoe magnate and philanthropist John Ward Melville left a legacy that included a large collection of horse-drawn vehicles and the restoration of the village—Stony Brook—they might have once paraded through.

*3 Wagons (Melville Collection, The Museum at Stony Brook)*

*Conestoga Wagon* c. 1820.

*Wells Fargo Stage Coach* c. 1868.

*Farm Cart and Hay Wagon*, early 1900.

*Long Island Railroad Caboose* 1915. Like other large-scale collectibles, it was almost free for the taking but costs a lot to move and restore.

**THE CARRIAGE ASSOCIATION** Box 3788, Portland ME 04104. "The purpose of the Association is to foster the knowledge, collecting, restoring, driving and research of horse-drawn vehicles. We publish a quarterly magazine, *The Carriage Journal*, which is available only to members upon payment of annual dues. Membership is for the calendar year and members who join late in the year receive all issues of *The Carriage Journal* for that year. This publication, which has become an authority in its field, gives restoration tips, sources for materials, historical data, driving information and other pertinent news to zealots.

We try to move our annual conferences about the country so that the greatest number of members may participate. St. Louis; Woodstock, Vermont; Dearborn and Mackinac Island in Michigan; Devon, Pennsylvania; Colorado Springs; and Monterey, California, have been some sites.

"We continue to seek out books of interest to our members and have reprinted several carriage catalogues and have arranged for the reprinting of important early books on carriages and driving. We are developing a film library of carriage events and educational films on training and driving. The Auction, held during the Annual Conference, makes available rare and hard-to-get items from members who may have some duplicates."

*Chippendale Dining Room* and *Colonial Bedroom* in the 42-room miniature castle, containing over 8,000 individual pieces. (*Collection of John and Ellen Blauer, photographs by Ellen Blauer*)

# Miniature Mania

Collecting small things for today's small spaces does seem to make sense. But the appeal is more than one of practicality. True miniatures, or tiny versions of larger objects, are big business. (A dollhouse, Titiana's Palace, begun by Sir Nevill Wilkinson in 1907, sold in 1978 for $256,500). Or as John and Ellen Blauner put it, "We think small, principally because we really do appreciate the little things in life." John has a large collection of small, perfectly scaled, authentically accurate one-inch-to-the-foot miniatures. To support his collecting habit, which dates back to early childhood, and in response to publicity, John started a miniature mail-order business called The Miniature Mart. (You might say Ellen was a mail-order bride; she was one of his suppliers, making woven accessories.)

**MAGNIFICENT MOTT MINIATURES**   As a child, Allegra Mott started collecting tiny things like the prizes from Cracker Jacks. First her collection was contained in a candy box, then a dresser drawer. Eventually, to protect and display the growing collection, she and her husband built small model structures. These now contain over 150,000 miniatures and chronicle both the lifestyle of the United States and her own. They range from a 17th-century Pilgrim cabin to a turn-of-the-century toy shop, from the Victorian home of Mr. Mott's grandparents to Allegra's childhood dwelling c. 1900 to their own 1932 ranch house. The Mott Miniatures can be seen at *Knotts Berry Farm, Buena Park, CA 90620.*

*Miniature reproductions of 18th-century china exportware hand-decorated with a tiny brush. (Chestnut Hill Studio).*

*Dollhouse c. 1905, American—one of a collection of six hundred. Lithographed paper on wood. (Collection of the Margaret Woodbury Strong Museum, Rochester, New York)*

*Finished Miniatures and Unfinished Parts*, plus all the supplies and instructions to make it yourself (another fast-growing hobby) are available at Mini Mundus, New York NY 10021.

**THIMBLES** are a compact collectible offering great variety and fine detail. (Other small sewing tools are scissors, tape measures, needle cases, pincushions.) Made as souvenirs and promotional pieces and for special events, in every hard material: gold, silver, steel, brass, pewter, china, even bone with scrimshaw. Shown in a printer's drawer. *(Collection of Ann Tolstoi Wallach)*

Silver thimbles. *(The Sewing Corner)*

*Petite Picture Frames and Pictures.*

*Small Items for Sale—Matchbook Safes* for the safekeeping of non-sulfur-tipped matches; *Corkscrews, Scissors, Knives, Souvenir Statuettes. (Collection of Albert Mackles)*

*Miniature Portraits—This pint-size picture is one of 450 paintings of aristocrats collected by Greta Heckett. (Sotheby Parke Bernet)*

*Minatures* displayed in *Type Drawer (Collection Judith Liss, photograph by Leonard Speier)*

*Silver Salts, Baby's Cup, Paste Work Frames*
*(Collection of Mr. and Mrs. Robert Brown)*

*Netsukes*—Fasteners like a toggle for Japanese cord belts, these small-scale sculptures carved from bone and ivory are valuable collector's items. *(Collection of Jerry Cooke)*

## Mail-Order Miniatures

*The Miniature Mart*, 1807 Octavia Street, San Francisco, CA 94109 (catalogue $4)

*Mini Mundus*, 1030 Lexington Avenue, New York, NY 10021 (catalogue $3)

*Chestnut Hill Studio*, Box 907, Taylors, SC 39687 (catalogue $3)

*The Enchanted Doll House* Manchester Center, VT 05255 (catalogue $2)

*Miniature Doll House Catalogue*, Federal Smallwares Corp., 85 Fifth Avenue, New York, NY 10003 ($1)

*The Dollhouse*, 176 Ninth Avenue, New York, NY 10011 (catalogue $1.50)

## Publications and Organizations

*Collectors Circle Gazette*, 150–11 14th Avenue, Whitestone, NY 11357 (FREE sample issue)

*Nutshell News*, Clifton House, Clifton, Va. 22024, (monthly subscription $22)

*Miniature Collector*, 170 Fifth Avenue, New York, NY 10010 (bimonthly subscription $12)

*National Association of Miniature Enthusiasts*, Box 2621, Brookhurst Center, Anaheim, CA 92804 (membership $12.50; quarterly magazine *Miniature Gazette*). "We have Regional Houseparties in each of our 10 geographic regions and a National Houseparty once a year. We also have over 200 individual clubs across the United States and Canada who operate under our by-laws."–Naomi Doss, office secretary

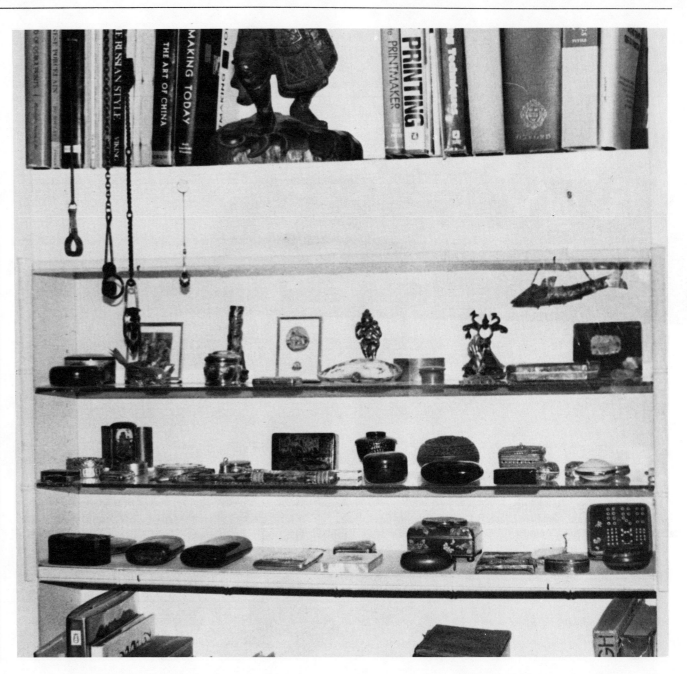

*Boxes, Cigarettes and Eyeglass Cases, Victorian Belt Clips* (hanging down, above—they held onto handkerchiefs, gloves and skirt trains). (Collection of Cecily Firestein)

# ADVERTIQUES

## Burdick Collection

## 306,353 Pieces of Paper Americana

Jefferson R. Burdick, 25 February 1900–13 March 1963

"Jeff Burdick impressed one by what he managed to do, but even more by the way he did it. Early in life arthritis began to stiffen his joints and warp his fingers until finally so simple an act as putting on his hat cost him a painful minute to contrive. Defying torture, he made his living at the Crouse-Hines Company in Syracuse by assembling intricate electrical connections for use in mines, flour mills, or wherever an open spark might set off an explosion. Illness probably prevented him from marrying. The energy that he might have put into making a home and bringing up a family, he poured instead into studying insert cards, into editing the Card Collector's Bulletin, and writing a series of books on the subject, until he had made himself into an expert whose opinion carried authority far and wide.

"Living in meager lodgings and spending little on himself, he threw his earnings as well as his energy into

Tobacco Insert Cards of Governors—"inserted" with a product as a sales lure to persuade a buyer to continue using it; made in series to be collected; the forerunner of today's baseball cards. Part of a collection of 136,670 insert cards. (*Metropolitan Museum of Art, Jefferson R. Burdick Collection*)

publishing books and acquiring the finest collection of American cards and of ephemeral printing in general. Then in time he had to decide what to do with his life's accumulation. One day in 1947 he brought this problem to me at the Metropolitan Museum. I told him that much as we would like to have his collection, he must look at other institutions that might care for it equally well and make it equally available to the public. After a week or so he returned to say that he had weighed everything and wanted to give his great collection to us. This honor brought responsibility, as we realized when the first of several annual shipments arrived that December. How could we keep these thousands of cards, labels, banners, etc. from being disarranged by public handling? How should we mount them to preserve them from damage? We tried one thing after another until Jeff was satisfied. But then we asked ourselves where we could get the patient, neat and intelligent hands to mount so many thousands of papers in their proper places? At that moment Jeff's health forced him to retire from his work in Syracuse, and he moved to New York to give his whole time to making his collection safe for public use. He brought his little art nouveau oak desk from home and installed it in the only available corner of the crowded print department, which at once became the American headquarters of cartophiles from everywhere. Many enthusiasts came to help him, the chief support being given by Fred

*Baum. We bought him more and more scrapbook binders, more and more pure rag pages, and more and more pots of paste.*

*"On first meeting, one felt sorry for this racked, frail man, with black-lashed eyes of a haunting gray violet, but pity quickly gave way to admiration—even envy—at his making so much of so bad a bargain. All in all, he triumphed more than many."*

*—A. HYATT MAYOR*
*(Directory of The Burdick Collection, Metropolitan Museum of Art)*

Boston Baked Beans: An Advertising or Trade Card given away free in the last decade of the 19th century to stores and customers. One of 65,994 advertising cards arranged in product groups—everything from shoes to soap—and stored in 30 albums and boxes. (*Metropolitan Museum of Art, Jefferson R. Burdick Collection*)

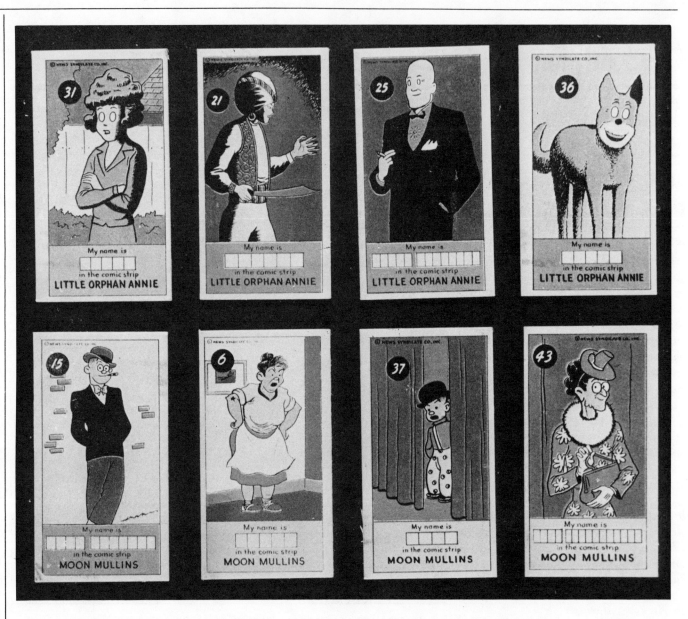

Puzzle Comic Character Insert Cards—packaged with Sugar Daddy candy, fifty in a series. (*Collection of Robert Lesser*)

# Coke Collectibles

*"We are doing some of the handsomest and most artistic advertising ever done in this or any other country. We are spending hundreds of thousands of dollars in telling people to go to your store for Coca-Cola.* –from a 1906 notebook for vendors of Coca-Cola

*"Its immediate and beneficial effects upon the diseases of the vocal cords are wonderful. By its use the husky voice can be made clear and natural, and all other affections of the throat be relieved. In periodic sickness, and the headache consequent upon it, its effect is marvelous, strengthening the system and relieving it of all impurities. Coca-Cola is endorsed by the medical profession for nervous and sick headache. Coca-Cola exhilarates and revives the drooping spirits, quenches the thirst, and cures headaches.* –from a booklet published in 1892 when Coca-Cola was promoted as a medicine called "The Best Brain and Nerve Tonic."

*The annual advertising budget of the Coca-Cola Company reached $100 thousand in 1901; $1 million in 1911, $10 million in 1941; and now runs over $100 million. The advertising material distributed in 1913 will give the reader an idea of the quantities produced: 1 million calendars, 1 million Japanese fans, 2 million serving trays, 5 million lithographed metal signs, 10 million match books, 20 million blotters, and 25 million baseball score cards. By 1924, two and a half million*

*Three Tin Signs (1927) at the top. Two Calendars (1914 and 1915) in the center. Three-Piece Wall Planter Set (1933).*

*calendars were printed. The old advertising campaigns depended heavily on giveaway items which means great collecting today.* –from "Coca-Cola Advertising," by William E. Bateman and Randy S. Schaeffer, in *Collectibles Monthly.* Theirs, they say, is one of the largest private Coke collections in the United States.

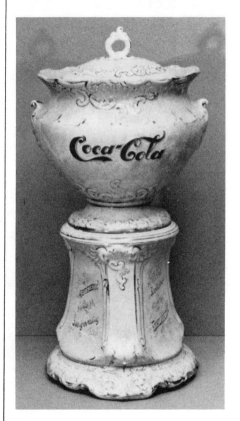

**Three-Piece Ceramic Syrup Dispenser c. 1895, 18 inches high. Says "Delicious, Refreshing, Exhilarating, Invigorating."**

*Free-Standing Cardboard Cutout Window Display* c. 1920.

All pieces on pages 47–49. *(Collection of William E. Bateman and Randy S. Schaeffer, C. C. Tray-ders)*

*Cardboard Window Display* c. 1920.

*"Bottle Tray"* c. 1902 shows the bottle used from 1900 to 1915. The only early serving tray that does not feature a woman. Note the paper label on bottle. An extremely rare item.

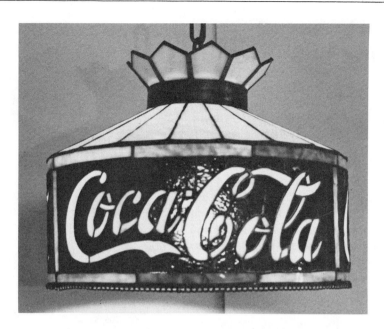

*Leaded-Glass Light Fixture* c. 1915. Red, green and white glass.

"*Topless Tray*" produced by the Western Coca-Cola Bottling Co., Chicago, 1907. Obviously a controversial item at the time for both the half-naked woman and the association with liquor. Intended for the bar trade.

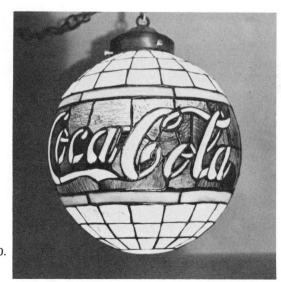

*Hanging Leaded-Glass Light Fixture* (white, red and green) from about 1920. Also extremely rare—fewer than six known to exist.

# Reflecting the Past: Mirrors

Before the sophisticated electronic media of today, advertising was limited to humbler forms. One of these, pocket mirrors, were produced and distributed from 1900 to about 1930. They appealed to Burt Purmell, an advertising art director, because of their excellent typography and graphics and their clever messages. They were also a natural extension of his other collections, folk art and advertising trade cards. Hard to find, most were purchased through classified ads in collectors' publications and mail-order auction houses. ''The advertising antique shows at Gaithersburg, Maryland, and Indianapolis are other good sources.'' Purmell says ''to avoid reproductions by examining for the look of real celluloid and the name of the manufacturer (on authentic old mirrors often printed on the rim), and by buying from an honest dealer.''

*Four Hundred Advertising Mirrors* hung with double-faced 1/16-inch foam tape on the walls of Purmell's small foyer.

# Advertising Signs

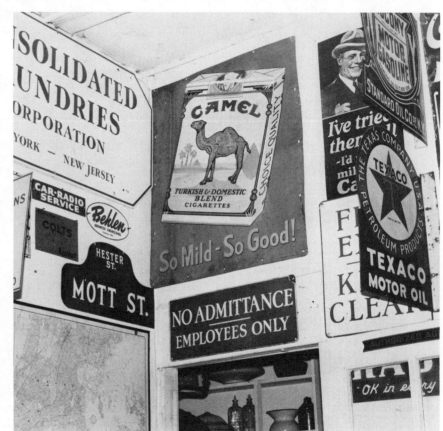

*Metal and Porcelain Advertising Signs* adorn bedroom walls of collector Leonard Schechter. (*Urban Archeology*)

*Old Rulers* on kitchen wall. *(Collection of Dr. Stephen Firestein)*

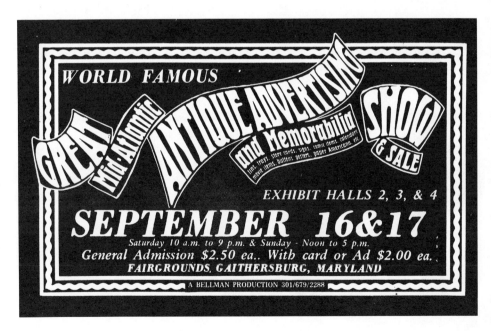

# CELEBRITY COLLECTING

## Smitten with Sinatra

*"Unlike many collectors, all Sinatra collectors—and most are men—want to share their collection. A local disc jockey who has a daily Sinatra program has an open invitation to borrow any of my material and I have most of the recordings that he made. Everyone asks me, would I like to meet the man? Yes, very much so; but more important than just meeting him, I would love to be invited to watch a recording session. To any Sinatra fan, seeing the man record would be a treat to end all treats."* –Stanley Komorowski, Warminster, Pennsylvania (NOTE: Mr. Komorowski, who is in the office cleaning business, now does a Sinatra show on a local community radio station.)

### Sinatra Society of America

Another fan is a single lady of 47—was "in love with Sinatra by the age of 14." Unlike Mr. Komorowski, she has met Sinatra and collected more than records. In fact, her entire three-room apartment is devoted to his relics: tapes (many collectors make their own, she told me, and then trade or sell them to other collectors), books, pendants, programs, T-shirts, posters, ticket stubs, matchcovers, hats, Tootsie Roll wrappers, a glass from Caesar's Palace, handkerchiefs and napkins he has used (she stops at cigarette butts), a pillow with his picture, thousands of photos (some from news services and his agents—"more than he has," she says). Although many of the items were free, the cost of getting them was high—traveling to golf matches, attending every concert and planning her vacations according to his schedule.

### Organizations

*Sinatra Society of America,* c/o Scott Sayers, Box 10512, Dallas, TX 75225 (membership $7; sample copy of monthly newsletter $1.50)

# Garlandia

Wayne Martin collected and catalogued her every move before he finally met her, from the time he was a teenager and she was child star Frances Gumm performing at the Chicago World's Fair. He became her number-one fan and in later years, her friend. Martin writes about Judy Garland:

*"A close friend the last five years of her life, she gave me what she had collected for my collection, which she called* our *collection. When she died, we were in the process of doing a book together, a pictorial, my photos, her captions."*

Martin lives alone, with his dog and his collection. His living room, which he calls Judyland, is filled to overflowing with the relics of his lifelong passion and her lifetime pursuits, beginning with her birth certificate and including: over 3,000 photographs (some are unpublished family candids and pictures of Judy with Wayne); practically every clipping published here and abroad; tapes from Judy's entire career; every phonograph record—78's, 45's, LP's, transcriptions, Armed Forces recordings, etc.; radio shows from the thirties on, live stage, TV backstage and home interviews; movie, TV and radio scripts and programs; audio tapes, including phone conversations; drawings, sketches, water colors; a pendant, letters, greeting cards from Judy to

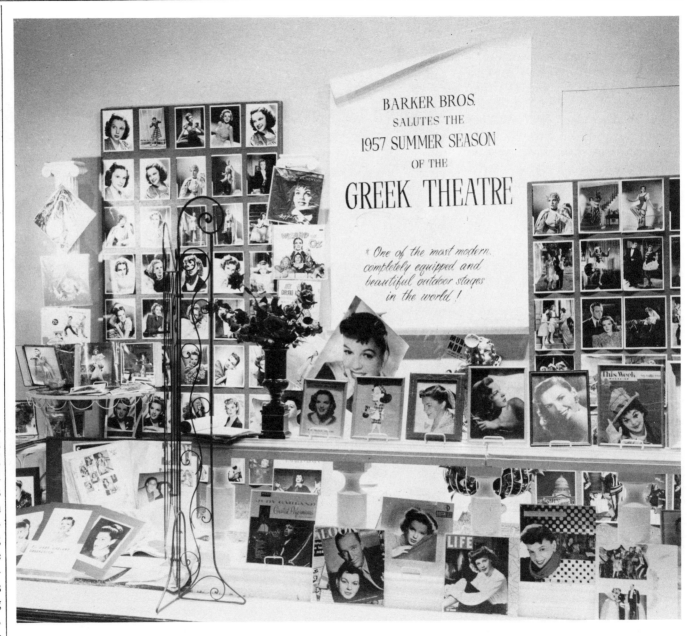

*On Display at Barker Brothers Store.*

Wayne; letters, tributes from other celebrities about Judy; all books and fan magazines about her; costumes—a black bolero from *A Star Is Born*, a beaded chamois from *Annie Get Your Gun*, a tramp wig from The Palace 1951 and two Mandarin jackets that her daughter Liza Minelli gave him after Judy's death. And the favor may be returned many-fold because Martin hopes to leave these remarkable mementos to Liza.

Dress worn in *The Wizard of Oz*, one of many costumes in the collection.

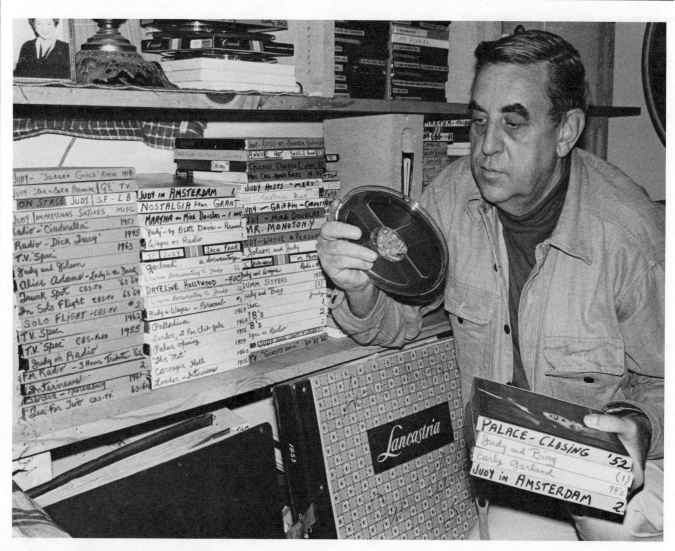

*Wayne Martin with Collection of Tapes* two days after Judy's death. (*Hollywood Citizen News*, photograph by Milt Fries)

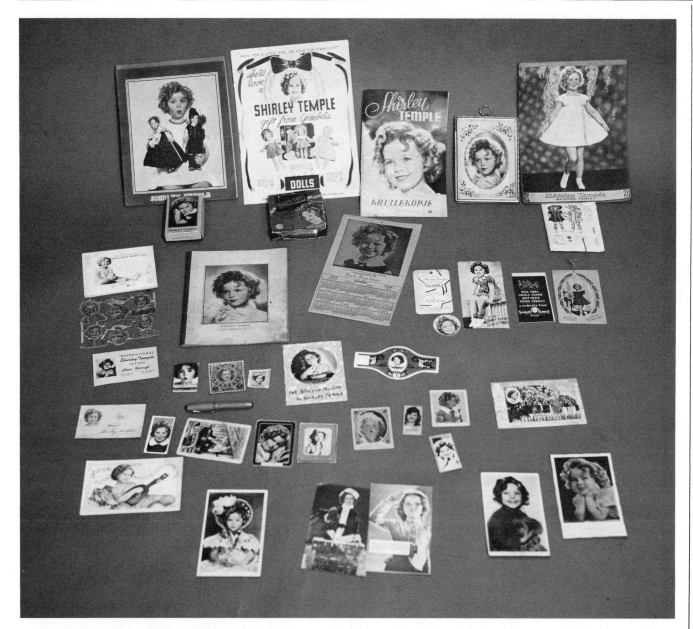

*Unusual Shirley Temple Collectibles*—tablets, catalogues, birthday cards, cigar bands, pen postcards, cigarette cards, calendars, films, patterns and playing cards.

# Shirley Temple

As all collectors agree, one fringe benefit is the people you meet; and the ultimate reward is to meet the star or subject of the collection. For Mrs. Earl Meisinger of Naperville, Illinois, meeting Shirley Temple Black "was a thrilling experience." She has practically every kind of Shirley memorabilia: jewelry, charms, bracelets, necklaces, a Shirley police badge and, of course, dolls.

*"I have several dolls in original boxes obviously never played with (one wonders why they were never used). I treasure a Shirley Temple trunk with an absolutely mint doll and several outfits that belonged to a girl who inherited it from her mother and was not allowed to play with it. When the girl died suddenly, her mother wanted me to have the doll in my collection. But the most important doll is a 35-inch vinyl, sought after by collectors and the one I gave my daughter in 1960 when she was three."*

## Organizations

*Shirley Temple Collectors' Club, Box 524, Anchorage, AK 99510. ". . . publishes a bimonthly newsletter at $4 yearly ($5 overseas), which lists new items available and also includes an ad section where members can buy and sell. I don't know of another ST club, but there may be one. Ours is not an official fan club, and isn't endorsed by Shirley Temple Black, but it's useful for collectors. We hold a mail auction nearly every year, with the proceeds going to the National Multiple Sclerosis Society in Shirley's honor, and have given over $1,890 in six auctions."–Jackie Musgrove, President*

*The Shirley Temple Collectors News (FREE sample issue with SASE)*

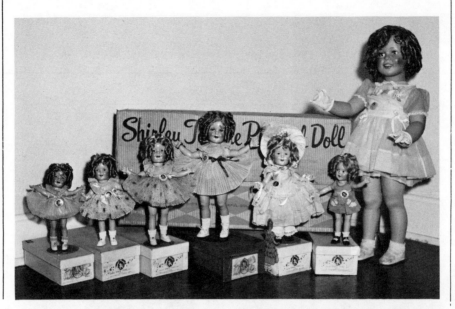

All pieces this page (Collection of Mrs. Earl Meisinger)

Original and Mint Shirley Temple Dolls and original boxes, all but the largest from the 1930s.

Shirley Temple Jewelry, Pinback, Buttons, Barrettes.

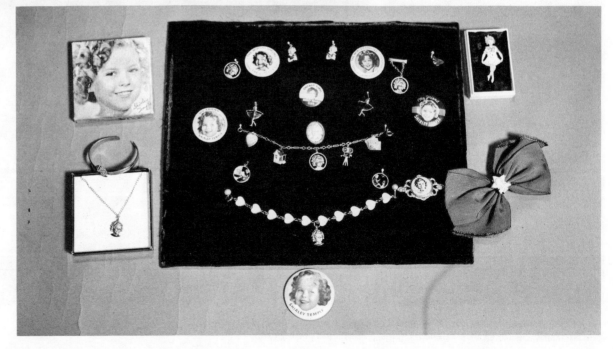

# Elvis the Idol: Presleyana

*"I went to a flea market in Memphis the week following Presley's death, and saw our first-day issue of August 17th, which carried a full color picture, on sale for $11.00. The market owner said people only wanted that issue, not the morning paper. That's a pretty good markup for something which sold for 15 cents."* —Circulation department staff member, Memphis *Press-Scimitar*

Since his death, Presley's home town of Memphis has had a hard time keeping Elvis Presley Boulevard signs from being stolen by the thousands of visiting fans who come to pay their respects.

As *Newsweek* reported, January 30, 1978: For Elvis zealots, no item is too trivial. Geissler (editor Harry Geissler, President of Factors Etc., Inc., who has the exclusive rights to produce and market all Elvis memorabilia) has already brought his Elvis line to shows in Memphis and Chicago and now plans to tour nationwide. Fans are offered the chance to pursue items ranging from 15-cent bubble-gum packs to solid-gold $850 medallions—or to opt for such middle-range exotica as Elvis Christmas-tree ornaments, Elvis dollar bills ($3.50 apiece), Elvis wrist-watches, gold-plated Elvis belt buckles and gold-plated replicas of the singer's army dog tag.

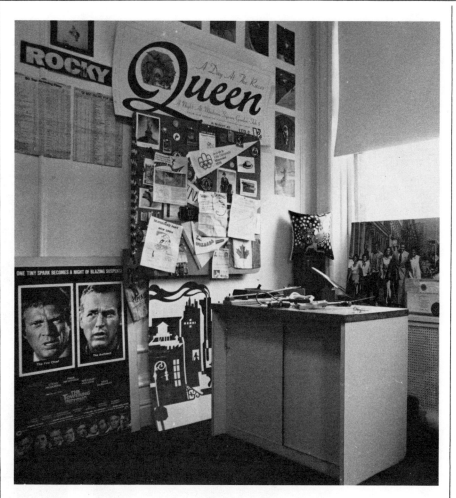

*Movie Posters* are ideal teenage decor. (Collection of Douglas Propp)

*Elvis Button—$2.50 in 1978. (The Martin Friedman Specialty Co.)*

Kenny Dwain, owner of Elvis Presley Boulevard Souvenirs, stood in front of his display of Presley's old bed, guitar and horseblanket, and stoutly defended the traffic in memories. "All these people here want something," he explained. "What are they going to do if they can't get it? Elvis is a saint, and these are his relics."

'Idolizing Him': Andy Kern would agree. The 25-year-old president of Elvis Unlimited, a 10,000-member fan club based in Houston, Kern began collecting Elvis memorabilia in his teens. Beginning in 1969, when his mother took him to Las Vegas to watch Presley perform, Kern saw him at every opportunity. "At first it was idolizing him," says Kern. "Then it was thinking maybe I could be like that—his life-style and his money, his personal charisma." Now, Kern has at least a piece of the mystique. His hobby has turned into a business, and he traffics full-time in Elvis jewelry, records, posters and carrying cases.

## Celebrity Auctions

At a recent auction of the estate of Joan Crawford, one collector bought 85 pairs of false lashes for $325, a carton of sheets and pillowcases monogrammed ''JC'' for $275, a leather-bound script of *Mildred Pierce* for $625, and a guest book filled with autographs of equally great stars for $2,800. This portion of the estate raised $42,500, almost five times more than expected.

## Mimicry Memorabilia

For his act as a TV, hotel and film comedian, Will Jordan collects material on the people he impersonates. And he also collects information about impersonators, particularly famous but forgotten mimics imitating forgotten stars.

Although he has books, records, photographs, magazine articles, tapes and a 1910 recording of Cissy Loftus (a well-known mimic at the turn of the century) imitating Caruso, he says,

*''It's the mimics I've interviewed, their biographies and clippings that are the real story. For example, did you know that there was no known mimic who liked to do his impersonations—they all wanted to be themselves.''*

*Gypsy Rose Lee's Gorgeous Gowns up for sale at Plaza Auction Galleries. (Photographs by Emily Liman)*

# Celebrities that Collect

Ali McGraw—antique clothing and ancient Japanese kimonos

Ernest Borgnine—stamps

Dustin Hoffman, Roosevelt Grier—photographs

Reggie Jackson—old cars

Charles Addams—armor

Pauline Trigère—turtles

Leo Lehrman and Eugenia Sheppard—lions

Joseph Cotton—antique Harlequins, and other Commedia dell'Arte figures (porcelain figures of actors made in 16th, 17th and 18th centuries)

Joshua Logan—19th-century Automata

Burt Stevelove—circusiana, miniature dictionaries

Ed Wynn and Fred Allen—one of the largest collections of joke books

Gavin MacLeod—kewpie dolls

Tony Randall—classical and operatic albums and tapes

Humphrey Bogart—pewter

Helena Rubinstein—French and American opaline

George Shearing—Steuben glass (although he cannot see it he can feel it)

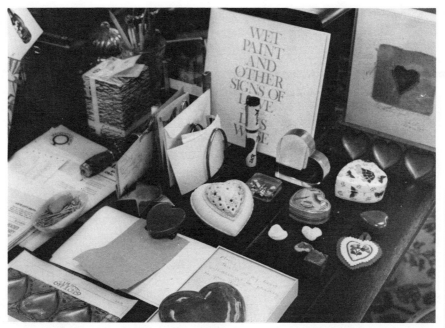

*Hearts*—Lois Wyse, the well-known poet who writes about love, collects hearts.

Kenneth Jay Lane—memento mori (skulls, skeletons, death mementos) such as this 17th-century German boxwood skull. *(Sotheby Parke Bernet. Agent: Editorial Photocolor Archives*

Maurice Sendak—Herman Melville and Mickey Mousiana

James Jones—belt buckles

King Farouk—coins

Betty Ford—plates

Mary Martin—porcelain hands

Truman Capote, Oscar Wilde, Colette, Empress Eugénie and Queen Victorian—paper weights

Barry Goldwater—kachina dolls

Stephen Sondheim—games

Jerry Lewis—clown figures

John Lennon—pianos

Andy Warhol—folk art, jewelry from the forties and fifties, junk mail, American Indian artifacts, gold coins, blue cobalt glass and Americana—architectural ornaments, pinball machines, cookie jars, copper molds for manufacturing dolls and toys—and more

# STAGE AND SCREEN

## Herb Bridges Has Scarlett Fever

Herbert Bridges, mail carrier in rural Georgia, has one of the world's largest collections of *Gone With the Wind* memorabilia. Most of it was purchased at flea markets, used bookstores and so forth. Although he keeps the collection in his attic (unless it is on exhibit at a museum, library or club) he hopes someday to house it in a permanent *GWTW* museum in Atlanta or Jonesboro, Georgia, the locale of "Tara" in the story. More than 500 photographs from his collection, as well as movie stills, costume changes and behind-the-scenes studio shots are published —many for the first time—in the book *Scarlett Fever: The Ultimate Pictorial Treasury of* Gone With the Wind *(Macmillan).*

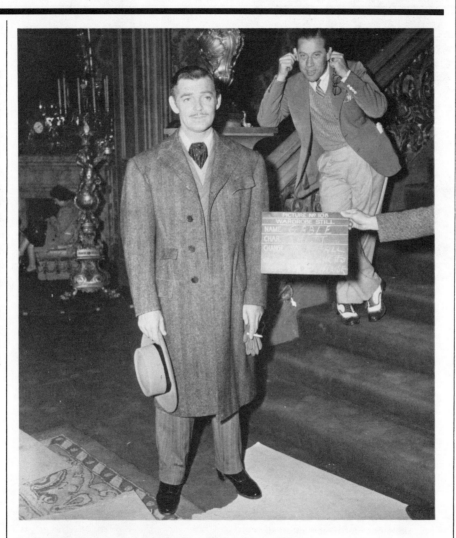

*Publicity Photos* (an unpublished still)—Clark Gable, as Rhett Butler, poses for a wardrobe still, while cinematographer Ernest Haller mimics the famous Gable ears.

Bridges with a rare edition of *Gone With the Wind*—Behind him are some of the hundreds of other editions that fill the bookshelves of his home.

# STAGE MEMORABILIA, COLLECTING:
## Promise Is Forever in the Air

**by WALTER KEER**—*The New York Times*

I've often felt guilty about not collecting, or just plain keeping, my theatrical playbills, those programs that are handed out by—or must be snatched from—ushers on opening night. Guilty because every once in a while I get a winsome letter from some ardent theater-buff in the hinterlands (from which I once all so innocently came) asking if I might just possibly have an "Oklahoma!" or a "Seven Keys to Baldpate" playbill (I don't know how old they think I *am*) to complete their otherwise perfect run of memorabilia. Could I just possibly find it in my heart to part with my copy? It would mean so much to them. . . .

I always feel I ought to be able to oblige, having spent so much of my time in the theater freeloading, getting not only my playbill but my seats courtesy of the management. I should be able to pass the courtesy, some courtesy, on. Unfortunately, I already *have* parted with my playbills, straight into the waste basket (I can hear my correspondents scream a little), for what seemed to me good and sufficit reasons. Naturally, I keep the program for a new show around for a few weeks, while I am still checking out minor bits of information (such as the name of the theater I was in night before last, a detail that ought to be easy to remember). Once I've dealt, well or ill, with the show in print, however, those booklets (leaflets?) must go. After all, I do have a complete run of the old Burns Mantle yearbooks, together with Otis L. Guernsey Jr.'s invaluable index, plus about 3,000 plays, in single volumes or anthologies, shelved to the ceiling. I can always find out who played what, when. And *something* must go before the floor or the side walls do.

### Obvious Passions

I sympathize with collectors, though, for two reasons. For instance, now that Christmas is over and I've got to start shopping for St. Valentine's Day, I realize that the easiest people in the world to buy gifts for are collectors. Collectors of anything. You know what they want, you can march off and get them one of whatever it is, and that done, you can turn your rattled attention to your other non-collecting friends who are probably never going to get any presents at all. Some people have obvious passions, and these can be satisfied; the others, poor colorless creatures, don't really deserve all the time, imagination, and tortured decision-making that would have to go into thinking of some suitable bibelot for *them*. Let them wait until inspiration strikes, or just suffer.

I admire passions. It doesn't matter for what: first editions, ticket stubs, Lalique glass, chessmen, postage stamps (expensive, especially the new ones), Meerschaum pipes, playbills. And I admire the good folks who are ruled by them, for what reason. Usually we think of buffs who spend half their lives accumulating memorabilia as people who like in the past. But that's it. They don't. They live in the future.

The collector's psychology isn't a matter of wallowing in nostalgia. The man who assembles a mountain of playbills or endless cabinets of ceramics or row upon row of 19th-century first editions is *not* a man who devotes himself to gloating over what he's got. He doesn't live in, on, or even very much around his hoard. After all, how much time can you spend, how much pleasure can you get, just leafing an album of already-collected stamps, how deeply can you delve into the times past that produced those holograph manuscripts, those faded photographs, those autographed baseballs, those matchbook covers? You're scarcely going to touch your manuscripts for fear of soiling, foxing or otherwise defacing them. And you are certainly not going to *read* your first editions; if, by any chance, you haven't read the book of which you own a limp-condition first, you are going to go out and buy a paperback for the purpose, leaving the original undisturbed—and, after a short time, unnoticed—in its lonely splendor behind glass. You may want to show *others* a few choice trophies of your long, long, hunt now and then. Otherwise you don't touch them, scarcely lay eyes on them. In a way, once they're yours, you're through with them.

### Always Another Rarity

And on to the next. What a collector really looks for is what he *hasn't* got. There's always an important, if obscure, item missing, there's always another rarity just around the corner, there's always the fish—lo, damned fish!—that got away. (Would you believe that I have spent 43 years looking for Stephen Crane's "Maggie" in the original paper? The only time I got close, it was gone before I could phone the bookseller.(Collecting is the open-ended life, the pursuit that can't be finished, the promise that tomorrow or tomorrow or tomorrow will nail the quarry.

And so the collector lives on tenterhooks, listening for phone calls, sorting the morning mail rapidly to see if there's anything *important*—such as a catalogue—in that mass of bills and billetsdoux. His body count is good: a prisoner of quivering expectancy, he must keep himself in trim, alert, eternally ready for the chase. Desire points forward; all satisfaction lies ahead; promise, unlike spring, is forever in the air; earlier triumphs count for nothing. If anyone is sure we should all be happy as kings because the world is so full of a number of things, it's the collector who hasn't collected all the times yet. He knows they're there, hiding out from him, held back by varlets who meanly keep them for themselves (they'll die, and his curse will help hurry the day) forgotten in attics, filed in the wrong drawers, waiting to be fished out of old shoeboxes; older barns. And he'll get them. If he has to live to be 100, he'll get them. You see? Future tense.

Having finished with my small paradox, I feel honor bound to report that I do have one playbill, framed. It's not a playbill, exactly; it's one of those fliers they used to put out in the 1920's advertising shows in several different theaters, and I've got a double spread. On the left side is the announcement that Francine Larrimore is appearing in a play called "Parasites" by one Cosmo Hamilton, and friends who come by wonder what Francine Larrimore—or, heaven forfend, Cosmo Hamilton—can possibly mean to me.

Then they look at the right hand side, which calls attention to the new "Laugh-A-Minute Revue" titled "I'll Say She Is." No one is starred. Just below the title, though, and in slightly smaller type, is the information that it is "with the Marx Brothers." Their first show; I never saw it; Chico doesn't look like Chico in the photograph; Harpo's curls are so close-cropped he seems positively nude.

No, you can't have it.

## House of Horrors

Robert Sherl says a movie collection should have a focus—a particular actor, a film genre, an Academy Award winner, etc.—and his is classic horror, gothic and fantasy films of the 1920s–40s. Among his 20,000 items are: lobby cards; the keybook to *The Cabinet of Dr. Caligari;* one sheet for Barrymore in *Dr. Jekyll and Mr. Hyde;* playbills going back to 1900 that belonged to Bela Lugosi; stills from films such as *Frankenstein,* and *Black Cat and the Raven;* and many original posters. He doesn't know why he collects, but he started at age 11 by keeping souvenirs of the films he saw. Maybe living in Hollywood had a subliminal effect. In any event, you can contact him there to trade and talk: Box 2712, Hollywood, CA 90028.

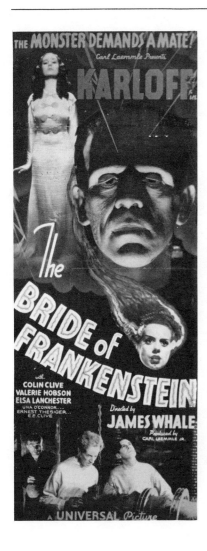

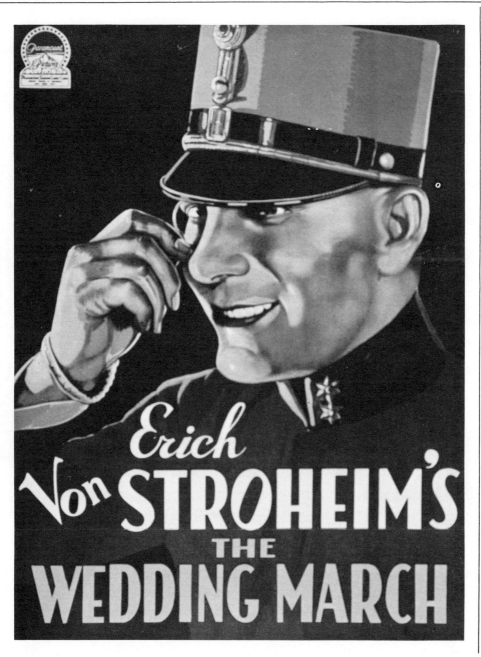

## Pictures: Moving and Still

This movie buff not only has autographed photos of Sinatra, Crawford, Lombard, Chaplin and many more, but the actual movies that many of them starred in: *Citizen Kane, Grand Hotel, Casablanca.*

He takes an autograph book along in case he crosses paths with someone famous, and provides his movie mogul friends with the stills to be autographed to him.

"*Collecting personal 16mm prints of the great feature films is a little bit tricky and the method of acquisition a bit hazy and somewhat expensive since elaborate equipment is necessary in order to enjoy them, but it is nonetheless a popular pastime; on the flip side, the cost of collecting autographs can be zero.*"

"*An extensive library of film books rounds out the collection. About 150 seems to be the number a buff needs at home to satisfy trivia needs (who played the doorman in 42nd Street?). They also provide cast listings and credits, biographical sketches, musical numbers, etc*".

# Prints and Posters

*Nineteenth-Century English Tinsel Prints* of famous actors. Tinsel refers to the sheets of foil that were cut out and glued on to embellish the picture. Detail at left. (*Collection of Peggy Cass*)

*Nineteenth-Century Japanese Prints of Actors*—actually advertisements in the form of handbills that were distributed free.

## Collecting by Mail

*Pin-up Posters*—An original Veronica Lake poster from 1941 will set you back $110; the catalogue ($1) from Yesterday, 174A Ninth Avenue, New York, NY 10011.

*For Anything Sherlock Holmes,* Father Francis Hertzberg, Our Lady's, 48 Shalmarsh, Hr. Bebington, Wirral L63 2JZ England

Circus Poster *(Collection of the Ringling Museum of The Circus, Sarasota, Florida)*

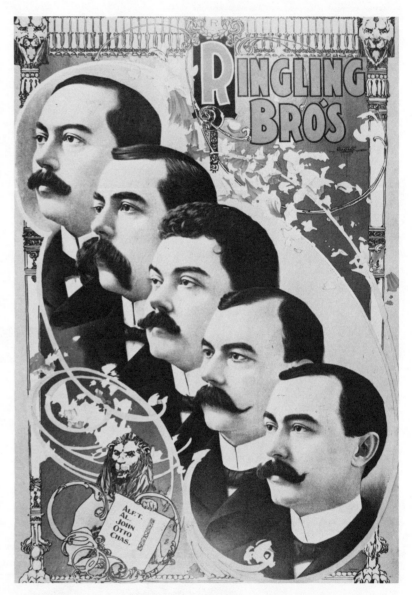

*Historic Circus Poster* printed in 1897 shows the five Ringling Brothers who were active in the circus: Alf T., Al, John, Otto and Charles. *(Permanent Collection of the Ringling Museum of the Circus, Sarasota, Florida)*

# Broadcasting

**HOWDY DOODY**  He has red hair but no freckles, fond childhood memories of watching the show in the fifties and in place of the baby brother he asked for, a Howdy Doody doll his mother gave him for Christmas 1952. Other than that there is no rational reason for Jeffrey Judson, a pharmacist, to have suddenly started collecting Howdy many years later at the age of 21. He may have over 500 pieces of the many Howdy objects that were manufactured; among them, toys, dolls, puppets, premiums, books, games, food containers, jewelry and watches. The most prized are two tin wind-up piano toys; a cookie jar; marionettes: Flub-A-Dub, Princess Clarabell and Mr. Buster; and, of course, the doll that may have started it all. "Howdy collectors are rare. I can think of only four crazies like me." But Judson would like to find more and start a Howdy Collecting Club. Anyone interested should write to him: Building 1, Apt. 5A, Prospect Hill Apartments, Flemington, NJ 08822.

*Howdy Doody Ads.* ( *photographs by Robert Allen Smith*)

## Organizations and Publications

*Actors Fund Bazaar,* 210 W. 44th Street, New York, NY, is a shop stocked with theatrical memorabilia (sheet music, playbills, posters, props from shows, costumes, etc.) donated by members of the theatre world and their friends. Proceeds benefit the needy.

Lincoln Center Public Library for the Performing Arts offers a wealth of well-priced theatre, opera, film, music and dance memorabilia.

*Film Collector's World,* Box 248, Rapids City, IL 61278 (bimonthly subscription, $6 for 12 issues; $10 for 24 issues; $1 for back issue)

*The National Film Society,* 7800 Conser Place, Shawnee Mission, KS 66204 (membership $10; bimonthly magazine *American Classic Screen*)

*Classic Film Collector* (sample issue $1.50)

*The Movie Collectors Catalogue* by Ken Weiss, Cummington Publishing, Inc., Box 466N, New Rochelle, NY 10801 ($6.45 postpaid). How to collect 8mm and 16mm movies, everything from *42nd Street* to *King Kong*; where to buy them, how much to pay; collectors' names and addresses; projectors and equipment; with 400 photos, articles and anecdotes.

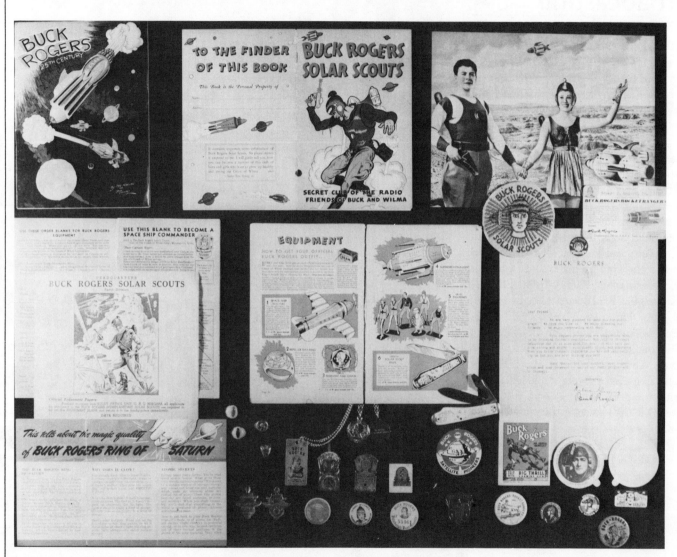

*Buck Rogers radio relics of premiums- badges, buttons, booklets, etc. (Collection Robert Lesser)*

*Robbie Robertson's Radio Collection.*
*(Photograph by Robbie)*

## What Other Collectors Collect

● *Premiums and Fan Club Material,* usually offered by cereal companies and honoring radio heroes like Captain Midnight, The Shadow, Tom Mix; rings, decoders, membership badges, manuals, etc.
● *Insignia* made to be worn by television network personnel

## Publications

*The TV Collector,* Stephen Albert, 132 Withington Road, Newtonville, MA 02160 (sample copy $1, subscription $5). A bimonthly publication by and for collectors of television films and memorabilia.

*Television and Radio Programs of the Past,* the most complete collection available to the public, can be seen and heard on these consoles at The Museum of Broadcasting, 1 E. 53rd Street, New York, New York.

# THE COMIC CRAZE

## Shazam

The craze is for comics, and the cost is up, up and away. Grown-up collectors are after the golden glamour issues of the thirties and forties: "Spiderman," "Superman," "Batman" and "Buck Rogers." They search for special, often rare and responsive editions—the first appearance of a famous character like Superman in the first (#1) issue of *Action Comics* (June 1938) or the first issue of a series like *Marvel Comics #1* (November 1939). These are reportedly worth over $4,000 in mint condition or for the elusive final issues to complete a series. While the prices aren't funny, those in less than mint condition—dogeared, with a loose staple, a missing page or, worse, a missing cover—can be almost worthless. Comics can be bought or traded (and read) at the usual sources and from comic dealers and at special comic conventions or fairs. "Some collectors may even go to the publisher's office," says James Warren, who should know because he publishes collector's comics like "Vampirella" and "Creepy." "When a new series is announced, they come here to buy copies of the first issue from the single sales department and often ask to have their copies autographed."

*Comic Art* covers the walls in Jerome Muller's home and office.

## Collecting Original Comic Art

Finally, it is not just the comic character who is seeing all the action. The creator behind him—and his artwork—are getting attention and, at last, good prices. Collectors, and even museums, are acquiring and preserving the work of cartoonists, whether it be a comic strip or an animation still (called "cels" because the picture was painted on thin celluloid). But it was not always so.

## THE CARTOON SHOW

*"Looking back, we can see what comics were, and are, and will be. Without putting too fine a point on it, or ever pontificating, they are modern mythology. They are first cousins to the Commedia dell' Arte, Punch and Judy and the vaudeville of our youth where our loves, despairs, agonies and elations were acted out with bangs on the head, swift hugs, fleeting kisses, incredible insults."* —Writer/Collector Ray Bradbury, in the catalogue for "The Cartoon Show"

Jerry Muller's collection of American comic art is so good that part of it is constantly touring the museum circuit. Dating from 1898, it includes animation cels by Disney, Walter Lantz and others, and syndicated features, comic book pages and magazine cartoons. Included are classics like R. F. Outcault's "Buster Brown," Frederick Opper's "Happy Hooligan," George Herriman's "Krazy Kat" and Milton Caniff's "Terry and the Pirates." Muller, a magazine editor and art director, started innocently enough with magazine cartoons acquired as gifts. But as a taste for the rarer and more expensive items developed, he was forced to buy: "After unearthing more material than I could afford, I became a dealer as well as a collector." According to Muller, "Comic art by re-

*The Muller Collection* at Bowers Museum, Santa Ana, California.

spected artists has in general doubled in the past five years, with the hottest area presently animation art with the emphasis on Disney studio items. The golden era in animation along with comic strip art is the thirties and early forties. By 1950 the quality of comic art and animation art declined rapidly and hence is less collectible on the whole. There are some exceptions, however: current 'Peanuts,' 'Broom Hilda,' 'Doonesbury' and 'BC.' ''

Muller advises keeping material dark, dry and locked (part of his collection is in antique oak blueprint files with 98 drawers, and some items are in a vault). He is always looking for material and can be contacted at Box 743, Costa Mesa, CA 92627.

*Comic Collectibles*—Robert Lesser's one-room multipurpose home museum/office/bedroom, filled to overflowing with comic character collectibles, toys, dolls, timepieces, radio, premiums, comic/artbooks, etc. etc., worth, he estimated in Spring of 1978, from $300,000 to $400,000. (The sheets, even the bathroom walls, are covered with comic strips.)

**CARTOONERVILLE** Dick Commer is an amateur collector of cartoon art turned pro; he represents cartoonists and sells their work by mail. Dick began collecting original comic strips, Sunday pages, political cartoons and gag panel cartoons in the late thirties when Walt Disney (a close personal friend of his dad) sent him an original painting of Mickey Mouse and Pluto. He then began writing to cartoonists and asking them for originals. In the thirties, forties, fifties and part of the sixties, it was possible to write to a cartoonist and ask for (gratis) original art. Most cartoonists were flattered by the requests and believed their originals had no monetary value (in fact for years, syndicates threw away tons of originals). Fans would trade and sell them, and the only one who didn't benefit from the transaction was the cartoonist. To do something about this injustice, Dick and his wife Karen founded Cartoonerville. Free catalogue (SASE). Cartoonerville, Box 445, Wheatley Heights, N.Y. 11798.

BILL HOLMAN/"SMOKEY STOVER".

THIS IS ONE OF THE EXTREMELY RARE "SMOKEY'S" FROM THE FIRST YEAR OF ITS RUN IN 1935. (19 x 12 1/2). 10/25/36...$475.

## Mickeymania

When a three-inch figurine of Mickey Mouse starts to look like the Statue of Liberty you know you're sick. One's sense of proportion can be distorted by this little mouse who made his debut in the first full-length talking cartoon, Disney's *Steamboat Willie*. Mel Birnkrant, a toy designer and chronic collector, says he has even seen an overinvolvement with Mickey break up marriages. He himself moved to rural New York to get away from the distraction of the city, other collectors and the excess activity the collection seemed to demand, "to be alone to carry on a dialogue between me and my stuff." The stuff he is so philosophical about is mostly three-dimensional: figurines, banks, a Michelin tire Mickey, thermometers and other gadgets, and things like party favors that would have been thrown away if he had not come to the rescue. (He considers comics at best just illustration; utilitarian objects like watches and spoons, uninteresting.)

Unlike other collectors who are motivated by nostalgia or jealousy (the act of possessing something someone else wants), he collects Mickey for his visual appeal and universal sculptural qualities. He enjoys the creative art of finding him—sometimes traveling all night to flea markets—and then the act of purchase, acknowledging Mickey as an object of value and protecting and preserving him.

*(Collection of Robert Lesser)*

Mickey Mouse tin bank *(Collection Jos. Trautwein)*

# Disneyana at Auction

Since the first auction in 1972, prices for comic collectibles have increased at an amazing rate. Here are some figures realized recently: $800 for a gold ring worn by and inscribed for Walt Disney; $525 for an early Mickey Mouse drum set and a toy Ferris wheel; $400 for a Mickey watch; $475 for a celluloid from *Sleeping Beauty*; $750 for a 1922 "Krazy Kat" comic strip; and $475 for a relatively new "Peanuts" comic strip.

Tin Wind-up Toy *(Collection Louis Marx, Photograph by Terry McGuinniss, Phillips, New York)*

*Atmosphere Study for* Snow White and the Seven Dwarfs, copyright 1936, Walt Disney Productions. *(Collection Jerome Muller)*

## Organizations and Publications

Museum of Cartoon Art; Comly Avenue, Rye/ Port Chester, NY 10573

*The Comics Journal,* Box 292, Riverdale, MD 20840 (subscription $4.50 for 10 issues, FREE sample issue with 50¢ handling)

*Comic Book Price Guide,* Robert M. Overstreet, 2905 Vista Dr. W., Cleveland, TN 37311 ($7.95)

*The Smithsonian Collection of Newspaper Comics,* Bill Black Beard and Martin Williams, editors ($12.50 paperbound, at bookstores)

*The Buyer's Guide for Comic Fandom,* Dyna Pubs Enterprises/15800, Rt. 84 North, East Moline, IL 61244 (weekly subscription $5 for 12 issues, $8 for 26 issues; sample issue $1). They say they are "the widest-read publication in the comic collecting field."

The Superman Movie-The First Photos!

the **COMICS JOURNAL**

No. 37    Dec.    75¢

Behind the scenes at DC:
Jenette Kahn and Martin Pasko!

**STAR WARS:**
The movie!
The comic!
The photos!

The collecting, buying and selling of comics has sparked an avalanche of small businesses—conventions, comic-book stores and even a do-it-yourself dealership.

# AMUSEMENTS: Toys, Banks, Dolls and Games

## Playthings of the Past

For the toy collector, every day is Christmas. He not only relives, but re-creates his youth, buying back the toys his parents threw out when he left home (making the surviving ones all the more valued and treasured).

"The toy-collecting world has increased rapidly, mainly since 1960," explains David Redden of Sotheby Parke Bernet in an interview in *Avenue Magazine*. "In the fifties you could buy these toys for almost nothing. Now there are a lot more professional people with the time and money to collect anything. Collectors aren't really interested in 18th-century toys, but in mass-produced toys from childhood, nothing before 1870, tin and cast iron, mainly. The number of toys in good condition is limited. That's why toys are so appealing to a collector's mentality—it's a limited edition mentality, a limited item but not one of an item." Of present-day toys, he says, "Any kind of space toys will be collectible and so will the new ones based on television series. Plastic does not necessarily hold up, but they're collectible if they're in excellent shape."

*Charlie McCarthy Mechanical Benzine Buggy*, by Marx, c. 1938. From the collection of toy manufacturer Louis Marx, it was sold in 1978 by The Phillips Gallery in New York City for $400.

**CHARACTER TOY COLLECTOR**

Robert Lesser once hired a taxi to go from Atlantic City to New York because he had no other safe way to transport his precious purchase—a Gene Autry bicycle. Nothing will stop him, and he believes "only fanatics accomplish something." Not surprisingly, Lesser equates collecting with the joy of the "hunt"; the "kill" to beating out other collectors; and the "trophy" to the spoils—the collection. But since you can't hunt white whales in mid-Manhattan, he hunts instead for comic-strip tin wind-up toys (and related collectibles: timepieces, radio premiums, original comic art). It has paid off. Lesser's collection of character toys is one of the most comprehensive in the country. He buys for cash because he feels it gives him an advantage over other collectors, and trades in person or by phone all over the country. However, he rarely is successful at shows where he feels the better toys are sold ahead of time. A prized possession is a pre-World War II Popeye tin wind-up toy which he says is now worth around $6,000. With competition in this field so fierce—Disney Studios is in the contest too, buying up for its archives and shops—many collectors refuse to show or talk about their collections. One middle-aged man, allegedly with the biggest collection of all, started at age three, is still at it, and still lives in his same childhood bedroom!

# Toys by Eve Propp

*Tin toys from an earlier age*
*sitting silently shelved, unwound*
*no sound of children's glee.*
*Coal carrier, donkey cart and stoves abound,*
*horse-drawn fire engine,*
*trolley car, and train, friction car,*
*no fraction moving,*
*no longer looking for a toy block station.*

*Gaily striped, wildly painted in faded colors*
*wrought iron playthings scratched but whole,*
*eons have passed since they played their role.*
*Still bank, mechanical bank, no longer collecting but*
*    collected now*
*musical merry-go-rounds, missing parts, making*
*    music still*
*at the onlooker's will.*

*On glass shelves in my collection.*
*This age and that, someone's joy is the connection.*

*Horse-Drawn Toys*, more than any others, evoke America's past. Fire apparatus, circus wagons, pleasure and commercial vehicles such as this stage coach are of painted tin, mid-18th century. *(Collection of Katherine Prentis Murphy*, courtesy of the New York Historical Society).

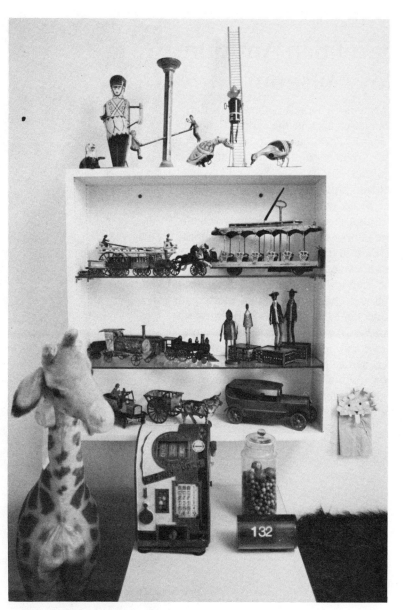

Cast-Iron and Tin Toys. (Collection of Eve Propp)

# Perelman Antique Toy Museum

"Mine is the largest collection of Early American toys in the world," boasts Leon J. Perelman. It is so large, in fact, that it is housed in its own museum (270 S. Second Street, Philadelphia, PA 19106). Three floors are filled with tin and cast-iron toys: locomotives, carousels, circus wagons and horse-drawn carriages, games, folk-art toys, novelty cap pistols, early automotive toys, automatic toy dolls, the famous collection of mechanical and still banks. Perelman started to collect in 1958 and opened the museum in 1969. His objective has been to preserve and pass on a form of American heritage to present and future generations, which indeed he has, both in the museum and in a book of the same name he has written about it ($5.95).

(Collection Edwin H. Mosler, Jr)

## What Other Collectors Collect

- Toys made of Wood (early 20th-century Schoenhut), *Glass* and *Paper.*
- Squeak and *Cracker Jack Toys; Magic Tricks; Cap Pistols, Kites.*
- *Friction, Surprise* and *Shudder Toys (i.e., Jacks-in-the-Box); Puppets, Whistles; Tops; Snow Shakers or Sand Toys* (activated by poured sand); *Pull and Motor Toys,* and *Toys Mirroring Domestic Activities* of the time (furniture, stoves, sewing machines, etc.).

## Collecting Clues

- Never repaint, remove paint or paint over an old toy, and do not even brush off flaking paint. Dust, wax and polish, or wash with great care.
- Be wary of fakes.
- The original box or packaging instructions, catalogues and other "go-withs" add to value. So does condition. Ironically, the less a plaything has been played with, the better.

## Publications

*Antique Toy World,* 4419 Irving Park Road Chicago, IL 60618 (sample issue $1)

*Miniature Truck News,* Miniature Truck Association, Ferdinand H. Zegel, 3449 N. Randolph Street, Arlington, VA 22207 ($4.50 per year, $1.50 per issue; FREE sample copy with SASE and 25¢ handling charge)

# Magical Mechanical Banks

To instill in them the virtue of saving their pennies, our ancestors gave their children ingenious mechanical banks. While Mosler safes have undoubtedly held more than pennies, it may have been his association with the company, as grandson of the founder and former chairman of the board, that was the catalyst for Edwin H. Mosler, Jr.'s, bank collection. In 25 years he has amassed a truly amazing accumulation (subjects depicted range from Biblical and historical events to children's games, sports and circus acts). And he is still improving it—trading up, adding to it. There is not just one of almost every mechanical bank made since 1867, but several variations of each, with no two banks exactly alike. It is a valuable reference collection—probably one of a kind—enabling him to answer questions about authenticity like: is it fake (and many are); did this bank have rivets; has this base been changed? Genuinely interested in meeting with and helping other collectors (there are over 5,000), he has installed his collection in his office to make it more accessible to them.

The quality and condition of the banks he buys must be mint. He advertises in trade journal want ads this way:

Girl Skipping—This key-wind bank is a favorite of collectors and symbol of the Bank Collectors Association.

Watchdog Safe—When you put a coin in, the dog's mouth opens and closes, a bellows is activated, and a sound like barking is made.

Punch and Judy—two variations of the same bank with large and small lettering.

**MECHANICAL BANKS WANTED.**
Private collector interested in mechanical banks in good operating and paint condition. No reproductions, repairs or repaints.

The competition for good banks is keen. Many are acquired through barter (sometimes with cash added), and relatively few come on the open market. When they do, the prices can be astronomical—over $7,000 was realized at Sotheby Parke Bernet in 1978 for a 50-year-old tin bank called Snake and Frog; $18,000, a world record for a cast-iron bank, was bid for a very rare (only three or four exist) Jonah and the Whale on a pedestal.

*Tammany Bank U.S. c. 1873. (Collection of Ellie Nadelman, courtesy of the New York Historical Society)*

*(Collection Edwin H. Mosler, Jr.)*

*Uncle Sam*, a famous symbol seen often in advertising, teaches thrift as the money goes into a carpetbag.

*Independence Hall Tower Bank* c. 1875 *(Collection of the Henry Ford Museum, Dearborn, Michigan*

# Dollologists

When a bisque-headed boy made by Kammert Reinhardt sells in 1978 for a record $7,372, you know dolls are no longer child's play. Old dolls may, in fact, be returning to their original status as luxurious playthings exclusively for the rich.

## COLLECTING BETTY BOOP

Among the top-quality American dolls are those designed by Joseph Kallus. And one, Betty Boop, made in the thirties and modeled after the popular cartoon character, is particularly sought after, especially by collector Helene G. Pollack. She even wears a pin that says "Wanted: Betty Boop" when she shops at antique shows and flea markets. All the dealers call her "Betty" and save items for her. In addition to dolls, Helene has other "Betty" collectibles, among them umbrellas, necklaces and candy boxes.

*"If you start collecting Betty Boop you have to be very careful,"* advises Helene Pollack. *"Few people and dealers know the real Betty and most of the items quoted to me are so-called Betty Boop 'types.' The only way to recognize the real thing is by the number of curls and knobs on her head. The older Betty has 16; the newer Betty, 10."*

*Antique Doll* with bisque head, kid body, human hair and original clothes

*Betty Boop. (Collection of Robert Lesser)*

*Celebrity Dolls*—Scarlett O'Hara, Kate Greenaway—by Madame Alexander; *(Collection of Mrs. Earl Meisinger)*

*Lauren Peery* with some of the more than 4,000 American and foreign dolls in her collection. Collecting runs in the family; her grandfather has a vast collection of boats in bottles. *(Photograph by Larry Lettera)*

**BARRY GOLDWATER COLLECTION OF KACHINA DOLLS** The kachina cult is the religion of the Hopi Indians of Arizona. They believe in kachinas, supernatural beings whose powers influence relationships with nature, life, death and fertility. The dolls, symbols of what each kachina looks like, are ceremonial gifts to Hopi girls, who are meant to preserve the tradition.

*"I am probably the world's worst collector, or maybe not the worst but the most prolific. I collect books on the history of my state and northern Mexico; I collect guns; I collect model airplanes; and I had the world's largest collection of Hopi kachina dolls, which I have given to the Heard Museum."* —Senator Barry Goldwater of Arizona, April 1978

*Peddler Doll*, wax.

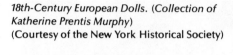

*18th-Century European Dolls. (Collection of Katherine Prentis Murphy) (Courtesy of the New York Historical Society)*

*Fortune-Telling Doll*—The skirt is made up of many fortunes written on folded paper such as: "You are loved for your amiable and good qualities." English.

*Queen Anne Doll*—jointed wooden doll gessoed and painted.

*Fashion Doll* used as model, N.Y. World's Fair. 1939 *(Collection The New York Historical Society)*

**DOLLS OF MANY COUNTRIES** In Dr. Howard Rusk's office at The Institute of Rehabilitation Medicine, New York University Medical Center, there is a collection representing gifts from grateful students and patients around the world, a veritable United Nations of dolls. These priceless possessions include: a pair of peasant dolls from Asia, the gift of the mother of the Dalai Lama of Tibet; from Brazil, a double identity doll that becomes either rich or poor when turned upside down; a hobo from Australia that doubles as a music box; a bridal doll dating from before the Civil War; an exact replica of the human body from Taiwan, complete with acupuncture needles and the places for insertion marked.

## PLAYING WITH PAPER DOLLS

Anne Tolstoi Wallach collected paper dolls as a child and now, many, many years later, she is at it again—only seriously this time. Currently an advertising executive and an active "paperdollar," she was attracted to paper dolls this time as documents of historic interest, changing fashion ("they're great on the development of underwear"), advertising, printing and color techniques. "Paper dolls are flat and small enough not to take up room (she keeps hers in a large ring binder with acetate pages); cheap enough so that you can't get cheated with reproductions; and limited enough in production time, 1850 to 1950, so that it is easy to become an instant expert."

Her extensive collection seems to include the most important categories: celebrities (Shirley Temple, Jackie Kennedy, the Dionne quintuplets); royal families; men (Rock Hudson, J.P. Morgan, Albert Einstein); dolls that were printed in magazines; paper dolls that were advertising premiums given free with purchases (1900 to 1925); and fine early European examples.

Mrs. Wallach says that uncut paper dolls are preferred, but if you have cut-up pieces there are I.D. books, similar to blank stamp albums, that help identify the wardrobes of important dolls. Also, paper dolls can be discovered in unexpected places: between pages of old magazines (shake and a doll may fall out), or in boxes of old junk.

Dolly Dingle, Johnny, and the Story of Fido

*Drawings by GRACE G. DRAYTON*

FIDO PLAYS TENNIS

went to his
and got a
bag of
Then he went to a
store and bought a
and then
he bought some
and a
But then when
he was all ready to
play he had
nobody to play with
So he asked
to play with him
She got her
and away they
went. Neither of
them could hit
a ⭕ Until all
of a sudden
hit one
bang!
and it struck
right in
her 👁
Kitty says
she won't play
with again
was wrong!
LISTEN WHY.

MORAL

Be a sport
and take your
knocks with a
smile!

Dolly Dingle

Dolly's Tennis Costume

Johnny on the Jump

Dolly's Hat Cut on Dotted Line

Cut Base of Figures and Insert Stands

## What Other Collectors Collect

- *Kewpie Dolls; Rag, Corn Husk,* and *Pincushion Dolls: Teddy Bears;* original *Doll Clothes* and *Doll Clothes Patterns*

## Organizations and Publications

*International Rose O'Neill Club* (originator of the Kewpie), Box 668, Branson, MO 65616 (membership $3; FREE copy with SASE, *Introduction to Rose O'Neill and the Rose O'Neill Club*)

*Midwest Paper Dolls and Toys Quarterly,* Janie Varsolona, Talesberg, KS 66740

## Collecting and Repairing by Mail

*Dolls Part Supply Co.,* 5–06 51st Avenue, Long Island City, NY 11101 (FREE catalogue)

*Standard Doll Company,* 23–83 31st Street, Long Island City, NY 11105 (catalogue $1). Supply house of dolls, parts, patterns, furnishings, books for doll-crafters.

*Doll Repair Parts, Inc.,* 9918 Lorain Avenue, Cleveland, OH 44102 (FREE catalogue)

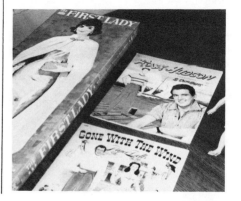

**THE FUN HOUSE** Composer/lyricist Stephen Sondheim plays the games he collects:

*"With Sondheim's increasing extracurricular activities of late, he has had less time to work on his best of all possible hobbies: the creation of homemade puzzles and games, though his Turtle Bay townhouse (which he purchased after the movie sale of* Gypsy) *does not denote a deficiency in its penny arcade-like ornamentation. The walls of the lower level of his home are covered with nineteenth-century game boards, and about the room are such artifacts as a Skittle-Pool table, obscure puzzles, a slot machine, jackpot games of various sizes, a gigantic chess set, antique ninepins, a ship's telegraph, a harmonica (an 1820s set of tuned glasses), and a bicycle (Sondheim's favorite form of transportation), creating the illusion of a museum hijacked from Coney Island. His lodging of all-encompassing amusements inspired Anthony Shaffer to write* Sleuth *after the playwright spent several evenings of game playing at Sondheim's home. And Sondheim's penchant for games (not to mention word puzzles—he's reputedly one of the world's fastest anagram-crackers) inspired yet another friend, director Herbert Ross, to persuade Sondheim to turn a party entertainment, a murder game, into an original screenplay for one of the most mind-boggling motion pictures of 1973,* The Last of Sheila.*"*
—Craig Zadan, in *Sondheim & Co.* (Macmillan, 1974)

# Games

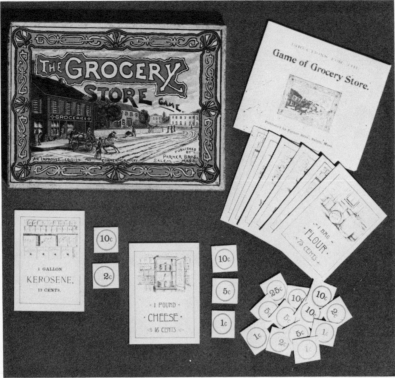

The Grocery Store Game, c. 1883 (Collection Parker Brothers)

Innocence Abroad Game, c. 1888 (Collection Parker Brothers)

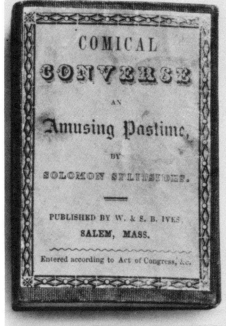

*What say you to a trip on the fantastic toe ?*

*I'll think about it.*

*Do you admire my wig?*

*Will you marry me ?*

*This music charms to move your gentle breast ?*

## Playing Cards

*SNAP, a Children's Card Game, published in 1917. (Metropolitan Museum of Art, Jefferson R. Burdick Collection)*

A WHIP SNAP

GINGER SNAP

*Comical Converse*, an adult card game, consisted of cards with questions asked by men, and cards with answers given by women; the amusement in the game was created in the matching (or mismatching) of questions to answers when piles of each were turned up. *(Metropolitan Museum of Art, Collection of Lincoln Kirstein, 64.629.23)*

# Marble Mania

With names like Candy Core, Clearies, Micas, Solid Core, Candle Split Core, or Lobed Core Swirls, Banded Luts, Peppermint Indian Swirls, this hobby has to be fun. In addition to glass, marbles are made of cobalt, onyx, carnelain, jade, jasper (and glass and tin-glazed stoneware imitations). Sulfides are balls of glass with figures, animals or, more commonly, swirled-glass filigree imbedded within.

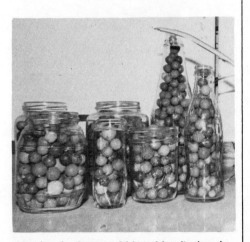

*Handmade, Opaque Old Marbles displayed in jars. (Collection of Eve Propp)*

## What Other Collectors Collect

- Early hand-painted or woodblock-printed *Cards* with advertising
- *Souvenir or Commemorative Cards* such as those featuring a place or a politician
- *Educational Cards*
- *Jokers*
- *Card Boxes* that are decorative and are special sizes

## Organizations

*Playing Card Collectors' Association*, 1511 W. 6th Street, Racine, WI 53404 (free sample copy of quarterly bulletin)

*International Toy Buffs Association*, 25 W. Walnut Street, Room 306, Pasadena, CA 91103

*Marble Collectors Society of America*, Box 222, Trumbull, CT 06611 (membership $10)

# THE PAPER CHASE: Literary Collectibles

Eliot, Gertrude Stein, Dreiser, Joyce, Virginia Woolf, Conrad, Dickens, Thackeray and D.H. Lawrence.'' – Salvatore J. Iacone, English teacher, author of *The Pleasures of Book Collecting*.

## Books

Highly touted as a hedge against inflation, with phenomenal new price levels reached daily (recently a Gutenberg Bible sold for $2 million, a record for a single volume), book collecting is not just a rich man's hobby. There does seem to be something for everyone, and popular specialized fields are: first edition fiction; children's books; science and medical books; detective and mystery books; books on natural history and art; books on travel, cooking, wine; dictionaries, atlases, almanacs; miniature books; Bibles, prayerbooks.

*"I originally became interested in collecting rare books and first editions as a result of my interest in literature. I find great pleasure in acquiring copies of works by my favorite authors in their original published form. Preferably the books should be in the finest obtainable condition, and in their original bindings. While the novels and tales of Henry James have remained the central focal point of my collection, one of my most prized books is an inscribed first edition of* The Better Sort *(1903) presented by James to George Meredith. Other authors included Hemingway, Fitzgerald, T.S.*

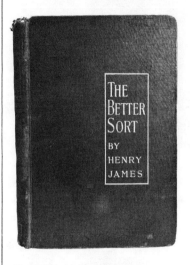

First Edition of *The Better Sort* with inscription on front end paper.

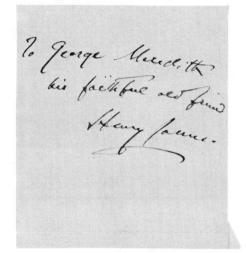

First Edition (published in Paris 1932) *Matisse, Picasso and Gertrude Stein* endpaper with inscription: "For Mrs. Duez—A cook does not mean that there is cooking" Gertrude Stein. *(Collection of S.J. and Renee Iacone, photographs by Daniel Langdon).*

MATISSE PICASSO
AND GERTRUDE STEIN
WITH
TWO SHORTER STORIES

BY
GERTRUDE STEIN

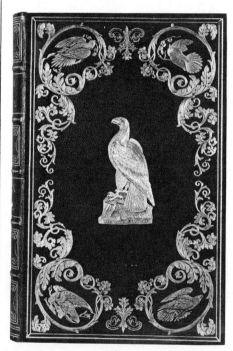

1840 Edition of an *Audubon Book (Collection of Sotheby Parke Bernet)*

## Collecting Clues

- The rules for buying books could fill a book. First, they do not have to be that old to be valuable, but they must be in good condition. A first edition (first printing or impression) of a recent modern classic, like *The Great Gatsby* by F. Scott Fitzgerald (published in 1925), in poor condition might be worth $25; in mint condition with a dust jacket, $200. And a copy with Fitzgerald's signature brought $4,250 at an auction in 1977.
- Books that are in an uncompleted form, such as unbound versions, printer's galleys, original manuscripts and excerpts from magazines—especially if they have some form of author's signature, notation, inscription, etc.—are quite valuable, as are books with printing errors.
- Beginners could consider buying the books of authors who are not overpublicized and overcollected—living authors, perhaps, who are popular and have potential. (Authors love to autograph their work. If the book is a current best-seller, the author may be on an autographing tour in the area; or try sending the book to him for his signature.)
- As in other areas of collecting, the sum is greater than its parts, so that a collection concentrating on one subject or author, all other things being equal, will have greater value; on the other hand, it is better to have a few books of quality than a big collection of junk. Books can be underpriced, found in unexpected places (like tag sales where sellers may not know what they are selling, or the remainder shelves of retail bookstores).
- Dealers in fine books are important to the collector who knows what he wants because the dealer can find it. Many publish catalogues, an important guide to current prices as well as to what is available. To get a FREE list of dealers, send a SASE to Antiquarian Booksellers Association of America, 50 Rockefeller Plaza, 630 Fifth Avenue, New York, NY 10020.

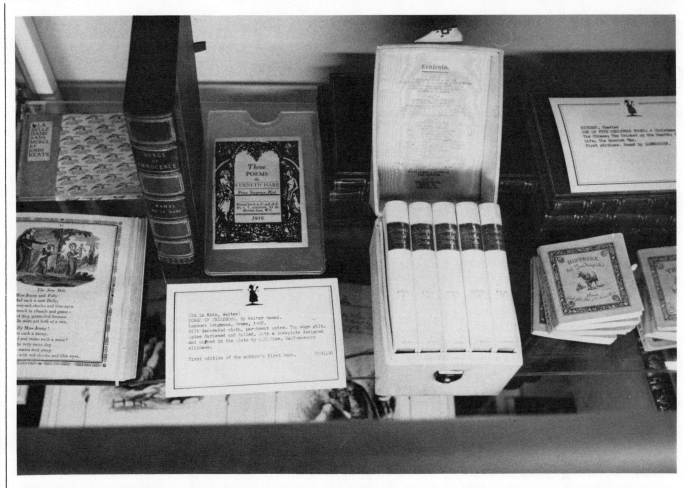

Miniature children's books including hand-colored nursery rhymes, and a set of almanacs illustrated by Kate Greenaway. *(Collection of dealer Doris Frohnsdorff)*

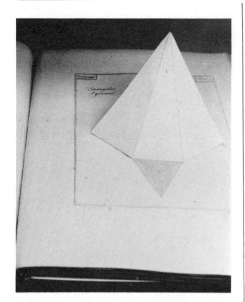

Eighteenth-century Euclid—Drawings are cut and folded to illustrate particular propositions.

The Berg Collection of Rare Books and Manuscripts—15th to 20th century. (English and American Literature at the New York Public Library)

Hearst and Angela Davis, and those dating as far back as Mary Queen of Scots (and other British trials), a 1650 treason trial, and an argument by John Q. Adams before the Supreme Court.

## Institutions

*The New York Public Library, New York, NY 10018*

*Henry Huntington Library, San Marino, CA 91108*

*The Pierpont Morgan Library, New York, NY 10016*

## What Other Collectors Collect

- Baron Philippe de Rothschild has a *Library on Wine and Food* that complements his wine collection.
- The Dreppard Collection at the Metropolitan Museum of Art consists of *Art and Drawing Instruction Books* printed in the United States from 1792 to 1876.
- Allstalr Cooke's collection of *Books on Geography* are arranged geographically on his bookshelves: Maine is high to the right, Florida low down on the right.
- Stephen Wolf, owner of S. Wolf and Sons, paint store, has a collection of *Rare Books on Paint, Dyes, Tints and Lacquers*.
- Lawyer James Brosnahan collects *Trial Transcripts*. He has over 400 volumes, including contemporary trials like those of Patty

Rare Maps and Prints from dealer W. Graham Arader are on sale at an antique show and also through their bimonthly catalogue ($4): 1000 Boxwood Court, King of Prussia, PA 19406.

# Autograph Hounds

Like bottle caps and shells, autographs can be free collectibles, available for the asking. But for the less-than-casual collector who is not satisfied to wait patiently for his path to cross with a celebrity, autograph collecting—or philography, as more serious collectors call it—can be as expensive and extensive a hobby as one's budget and interest permit.

Collecting can be a matter of nerve. One collector's long vigil outside a Washington courthouse paid off recently with autographs of Watergate defendants Haldeman, Ehrlichman and Mitchell. He had them sign under their pictures in his copy of *All the President's Men.* And in response to a woman who wrote to Abraham Lincoln (one of many that hounded him) for his autograph and a sentiment, came this priceless letter: "Dear Madam, When you ask from a stranger that which is of interest only to yourself, always enclose a stamp. There's your sentiment and here's your autograph. A. LINCOLN."

For those collectors who do not acquire their autographs first-hand, a dealer's or auction house's assurance of authenticity is important, particularly in light of the many forgeries and facsimiles—for example, documents signed mechanically with a gadget called an autopen. Dealers sell by catalogue and on approval.

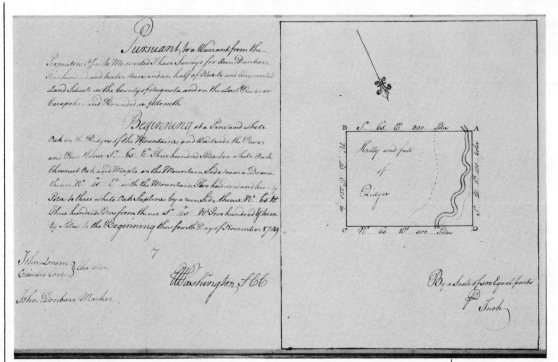

Land Survey by George Washington (autographed manuscript)—one of the earliest known, executed 4 November 1749, when he was 17. (Sotheby Parke Bernet)

## THE VALUE OF AUTOGRAPHS

*The valuation of autographs depends on many factors, but among the chief determinants of price are demand, rarity, and the content of the document. Signatures (S) alone are the least expensive, as they are the least satisfying, to acquire. Letters signed (LS), where only the signature is in the hand of the signer, and autograph letters signed (ALS) generally cost more, as do documents signed (DS). Nevertheless, values vary widely with the popularity of the signer or the field of activity or historical period represented, along with the relative scarcity of the signature. Collectors of sets of signatures may care little about the* content of the documents involved, but those who collect the letters of an individual will be much more concerned with interesting content. In the case of a manuscript (MS) of a famous author, the content is all-important. Autographs of Presidents of the United States are fairly common, but letters concerning great events in which they participated will be valued more highly than those approving routine appointments. The length of the letter is also important, and age may be a factor, although by itself it will not mean high values unless an American document dates before 1675, or a European one before 1400. Autographs may very well appreciate in value if they are held for a number of years, yet most collections are acquired solely for the emotional, intellectual and aesthetic rewards that come from owning samples of the handwriting of persons who have shaped our history. –from *An Introduction to The Manuscript Society*

# The Sang Collection

Mary Benjamin, the well-known dealer, wrote in her publication *The Collector:*

". . . Mr. Sang was our customer for many years, and we were not the only dealer from whom he acquired his treasures. I can safely say, however, that in my opinion he was among the

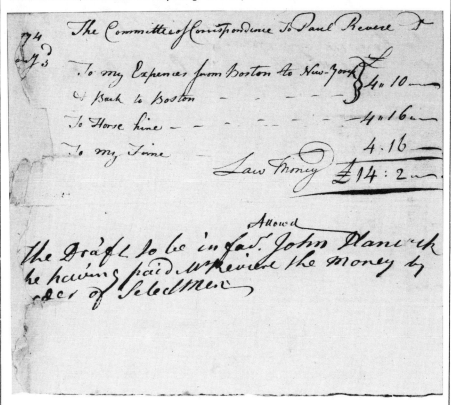

*Paul Revere's Bank Account*—Malcolm Forbes, publisher of *Forbes* Magazine, set a record for a handwritten American document sale at auction when he paid $70,000 for this document *(Collection of Philip Sang, Courtesy of Sotheby Parke Bernet)*

greatest collectors of the 20th Century. There will be ample proof of this in the forthcoming catalogs the Galleries will issue; their advance release mentions such items as John Alden, Peter Stuyvesant, Major André, Casimir Pulaski, Haym Salomon, Joseph Smith, Peter Zenger and others. Also mentioned are Paul Revere's autograph bill to the Committee of Correspondence in Massachusetts for expenses incurred during his ride from Boston to New York; Washington's letter to Benjamin Franklin introducing Lafayette; a complete set of Signers of the Declaration of Independence, all the Presidents, of course, and many others. While none of the items listed in the publicity release happen to include the astounding material our firm added to his collection, we know that Mr. Sang was extraordinarily generous to institutions all over the country, and some of his finest items may have been donated and therefore will never appear on the open market.

"Mr. Sang was the kind of collector a dealer dreams about. With the wealth to humor his hobby and the taste to desire only the absolute best, the type of item he sought had to give one chills. Just one more letter of fine contents would not do. Only when an item's superlative dramatic interest stirred his emotions would he consider it.''

## What Other Collectors Collect

- *Signatures* of Supreme Court justices, Nobel Prize winners, composers (with bars of their music), kings and queens, Civil War generals, explorers, astronauts, French Impressionist artists, famous children and infamous villains (Hitler, John Dillinger, Lee Harvey Oswald, often more valuable than others)
- *Love Letters* and *Diaries*
- Malcomb Forbes has a collection of telegrams sent by Russian royalty at the turn of the century.

**HIGH SCHOOL HOBBY** Charles Hamilton, the well-known dealer in fine documents and autographs, began collecting at the age of 12 when he wrote for and got Rudyard Kipling's signature. Jack Luks seems to be on the same track, although he went public at a much earlier age than Hamilton (who was 40 before he began to sell his collection and became a full-time dealer):

*"Last summer, my parents were trying to interest me in tennis camp but summer camp was no longer for me, so I went to a nearby regional shopping center and asked a coin dealer if I could rent a showcase in his store to sell autographs. He agreed and I turned my hobby into a successful business. When high school reopened in the fall, I changed my business operation to mail order. I have about 2,500 signatures—politicians like Humphrey and Ted Kennedy, entertainers like Groucho Marx, and sports figures, many baseball cards or magazine pictures or programs. I know a lot about the players; when I have their autographs I feel closer to them in a way."*

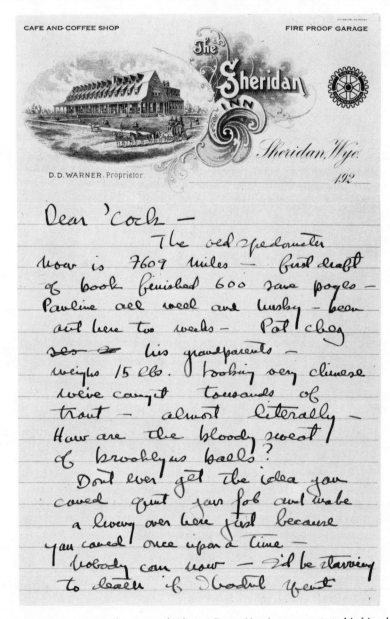

Hemingway Letter—one of a group of 19 letters Ernest Hemingway wrote to his friend Guy Hickock; estimated value $18,000 to $24,000. *(Collection of Jonathan Goodwin, Sotheby Parke Bernet).*

His price list of autographs that range from 50¢ to $18 for Mickey Mantle, is available by sending a SASE to him at: 868 Greenwood Road, Teaneck, NJ 07666.

## Collecting Clues

- To make a signature more meaningful, have it written on a related item: a program or movie still for someone in the performing arts; a menu or news photograph or clipping for a politician speaking at a dinner (and try to get an extra one for trading).

## Publications and Organizations

*The Autograph News,* 7606 Charlotte Drive, Huntsville, AL 35802 (monthly, $6 per year; FREE sample issue with SASE)

*American Society of Bookplate Collectors and Designers,* 429 North Daisy Avenue, Pasadena, CA 91107 (membership $7.50; sample issue of quarterly publication $2; *Bookplates in the News* $2)

*Successful Autograph Collecting,* Henry Mazlen, Memorabilia Americana, 1211 Avenue I, Brooklyn, NY 11230 (FREE booklet with 50¢ handling) *Manuscript Society,* c/o Audrey Arellanas, 1206 N. Stoneman Avenue #15, Alhambra, CA 91801 (membership $10, student $4; sample issue of quarterly magazine $4, applicable to membership fee)

*Universal Autograph Collectors Club,* Box 467, Rockville Center, NY 11571 (membership $9)

*Pen and Quill* (FREE sample newsletter 50¢ handling)

*The Jimmy Carter Philegraphic Study* ($3) identifies secretarial, printed, autopen and authentic Jimmy Carter signatures.

*The Collector,* catalogue and magazine of Walter R. Benjamin Autographs, Inc., Box 255, Scribner Hollow Road, Hunter, NY 12422 ($10 bimonthly)

*King George Autographs,* 86 King George Rd., Poughkeepsie NY 12603 FREE catalogue

# American Paperback Cover Art

A Dutch architect, Hans Oldewarris, has 3,000 American paperbacks from the major publishing houses dating from 1939 to 1955. He says, "The main reason I collect is for the cover art, but a second reason is that I will have a good impression of what titles interested the general American during this period." He is trying to get complete sets for each publisher and would like to hear from other collectors. His address: Honingerdijk 245, 3063 NA Rotterdam.

Two Ace "double" novels

An American jacket and the same cover stolen by a Dutch publisher

A Dell cover and the same cover "censored"

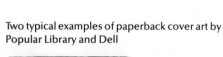

Two typical examples of paperback cover art by Popular Library and Dell

# Deltiology: Postcard Collecting

Sending and collecting *cartes postales* emerged as a social phenomenon in Europe and North America at the turn of the century; almost everyone was involved in the hobby, and postcard manufacturers published actively and imaginatively to keep up with the demand. Today, the serious collector of old cards is the beneficiary of this energetic output, and he can specialize in one or more of the hundreds of possible categories: advertising; political propaganda; historical events; presidents and royalty; vanishing American scenes; railroad stations; trolleys; World Fairs; old hotels and court houses; holidays; novelty cards—woven silk or embroidered, with mirrors and records attached; and handwork cards with real hair, feathers or cloth, and animals covered in bits of real fur.

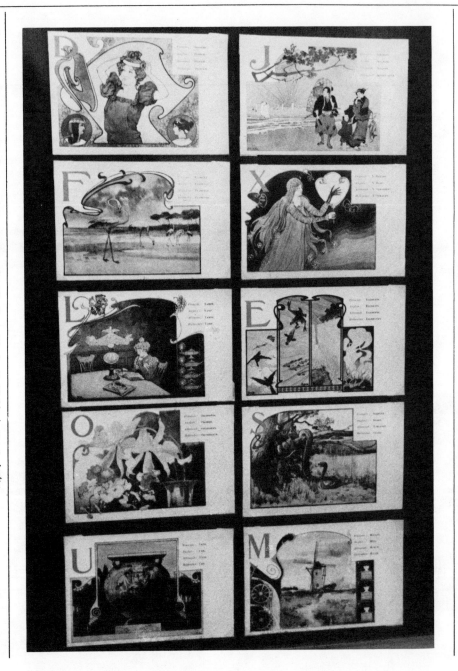

**A PASSION FOR FRENCH POST-CARDS** Although it is limited in time (1889 to 1919) and place (France), the collection of Leonard Lauder, a serious deltiologist for 30 years, is notable for its scope. The postcards commemorate events of the period such as the inauguration of the Eiffel Tower, 1889; the International Exposition of 1900; the early years of aviation; World War I and the Japanese War; and socio-political events including the Dreyfus Affair and labor demonstrations. They range from real photographs of contemporary events or persons of all occupations and backgrounds—Queen Victoria, the Tsar, Mata Hari, Sarah Bernhardt, Clemenceau—to fantasy cards prevising the surrealist movement (multitudes of babies riding on butterflies and ogres envisioned against mountainsides). Designs by the best turn-of-the-century artists include some by Alphonse Mucha, Jules Cheret, Raphael Kirchner and Toulouse-Lautrec. The collection also includes sets of "continuity" cards which together form puzzles, "hold to light" cards revealing another design when held against a strong light, and "pop-up" cards.

French Art Nouveau Alphabet Postcards c. 1901, sold in sets of the 26 letters of the alphabet; the message would then be spelled out with the cards.

*A Day at the French Seashore*—turn-of-the-century postcard.

*(Collection of Leonard Lauder all cards pages 102–103)*

French Surrealist Picture Postcard with a bizarre image of babies emerging from shells.

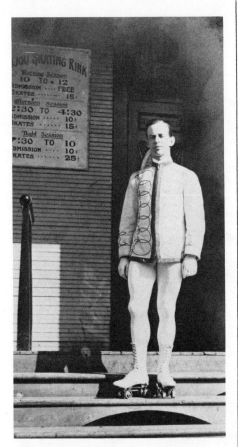

Skating and Christmas Cards: Junkinsville, U.S.A.—a unique collection of 540 uncolored photo views chronicling every phase of American life in the first decade of the century. *(Metropolitan Museum of Art, Jefferson R. Burdick Collection)*

## Magazines and Newspapers

The discovery of a stack of old papers in a closet started Charlie Smith collecting historic newspapers. That closet has long since been emptied but his other closets are full, as is the rest of his home, with over 10,000 papers. They range from a copy of *Mercurius Politicus 1650,* a broadside issued in 1661 reporting the coronation of King Charles II, to more modern events such as the Battle of Gettysburg and Lindbergh's flight. He generously shares his expertise through lectures; a traveling exhibit he has organized for schools, libraries and other institutions; and the International Newspaper Collectors Club, which he founded. He also shares his advice:

*"Put away a few local paper front pages as you go along, it won't cost anything. Get a number of copies of anything real good, huge headlines or very historic events (moon landing, Kennedy assassination) for swaps. . . . Old papers should not be folded, so newspaper-size shelves should be built."*

And if you send an SASE and description of a paper (but not the paper) he will gladly reply with a *free* appraisal of value.

*The Abdication of King Edward. (Collection of Charlie Smith)*

For FREE sample issue (SASE) of *The Newes* (club publication) and a FREE newspaper facsimile of the first U.S. paper of 1690 (35¢ handling), write: Box 7271, Phoenix, AZ 85011.

**Numb: 1.**

# PUBLICK OCCURRENCES

### Both FORREIGN and DOMESTICK.

*Boston, Thursday Sept. 25th. 1690.*

IT is designed, that the Countrey shall be furnished once a moneth (or if any Glut of Occurrences happen, oftener,) with an Account of such considerable things as have arrived unto our Notice.

In order hereunto, the Publisher will take what pains he can to obtain a Faithful Relation of all such things; and will particularly make himself beholden to such Persons in Boston whom he knows to have been for their own use the diligent Observers of such matters.

That which is herein proposed, is, First, That Memorable Occurrents of Divine Providence may not be neglected or forgotten, as they too often are. Secondly, That people every where may better understand the Circumstances of Publique Affairs, both abroad and at home; which may not only direct their Thoughts at all times, but at some times also to assist their Businesses and Negotiations.

Thirdly, That some thing may be done towards the Curing, or at least the Charming of that Spirit of Lying, which prevails amongst us, wherefore nothing shall be entered, but what we have reason to believe is true, repairing to the best fountains for our Information. And when there appears any material mistake in any thing that is collected, it shall be corrected in the next.

Moreover, the Publisher of these Occurrences is willing to engage, that whereas, there are many False Reports, maliciously made, and spread among us, if any well-minded person will be at the pains to trace any such false Report so far as to find out and Convict the First Raiser of it, he will in this Paper (unless just Advice be given to the contrary) expose the Name of such person, as A malicious Raiser of a false Report. It is supposed that none will dislike this Proposal, but such as intend to be guilty of so villanous a Crime.

THE Christianized Indians in some parts of Plimouth, have newly appointed a day of Thanksgiving to God for his Mercy in supplying their extream and pinching Necessities under their late want of Corn, & for His giving them now a prospect of a very Comfortable Harvest. Their Example may be worth Mentioning.

'Tis observed by the Husbandmen, that altho' the Withdraw of so great a strength

from them, as what is in the Forces lately gone for Canada, made them think it almost impossible for them to get well through the Affairs of their Husbandry at this time of the year, yet the season has been so unusually favourable that they scarce find any want of the many hundreds of hands, that are gone from them; which is looked upon as a Merciful Providence.

While the barbarous Indians were lurking about Chelmsford, there were missing about the beginning of this month a couple of Children belonging to a man of that Town, one of them aged about eleven, the other aged about nine years, both of them supposed to be fallen into the hands of the Indians.

A very Tragical Accident happened at Water-Town, the beginning of this Month, an Old man, that was of somewhat a Silent and Morose Temper, but one that had long Enjoyed the reputation of a Sober and a pious Man, having newly buried his Wife, The Devil took advantage of the Melancholy which he thereupon fell into, his Wives discretion and industry had long been the support of his Family, and he seemed hurried with an impertinent fear that he should now come to want before he dyed, though he had very careful friends to look after him who kept a strict eye upon him, least he should do himself any harm. But one evening escaping from them into the Cow-house, they there quickly followed him found him hanging by a Rope, which they had used to tye their Calves withal, he was dead with his feet near touching the Ground.

Epidemical Fevers and Agues grow very common, in some parts of the Country, whereof, tho' many dye not, yet they are sorely unfitted for their imployments; but in some parts a more malignant Fever seems to prevail in such sort that it usually goes thro' a Family where it comes, and proves Mortal unto many.

The Small-pox which has been raging in Boston, after a manner very Extraordinary is now very much abated. It is thought that far more have been sick of it then were visited with it, when it raged so much twelve years ago, nevertheless it has not been so Mortal. The number of them that have

*Old Magazines* are collected for their illustrations (fine engraved and colored fashion plates in 19th-century publications); editorial content (a first printing of a famous literary work); nostalgic ads; paper doll cutouts; and covers by famous artists. Technical periodicals such as medical journals might be collected for research purposes, college humor magazines for fun.

# MOBILE MEMORABILIA:
## Transportation

## Vintage Vehicles

Interest in old cars—"antiques" (pre-1930), "classics" (1925–48) and postwar "milestone models" (1945–64)—has increased to such an extent that major financial publications like *Forbes* write about them as investments similar to stocks and bonds. Until recently, a 10-year-old car might have had only scrap value; now when it gets to be around that age, it stops depreciating, provided it is in mint condition. And that's a big proviso. Car collectors caution that authentic restoration—although for many, part of the fun—can easily cost $10,000 to $20,000 if you can't do it yourself. All collectors advise studying up on prices and makes before buying (read *Hemmings Motor News*); purchasing a low-price vintage car that can be fixed (perhaps an unrestored 15-year-old high-quality car with a milestone classification potential—75 American cars have so qualified); working on it while attending club rallies and car shows; then trading up if you decide you like the hobby.

According to *Businessweek* magazine, there are 750,000 vintage car buffs who do like the hobby, among them businessman Peter Morgan of

*1908 Thomas Flyer Race Car,* the winner of the longest race in history from New York to Paris in 1908.

*1929 Miller Race Car.*

*3 Cars (Harrah's Automobile Collection)*

*1911 Simplex 4 Passenger Tour-About.*

Morgan Construction, who got into car collecting because his grandfather kept a Model T fire engine on their farm. Morgan bought his own fire engine about 20 years ago and adds, "I've been collecting ever since. I even have a 1929 dump truck." Or Richard Teaque, of American Motors Corporation, who owns 12 real cars (and a collection of toy cars) and likes the romance of brass headlights and beautiful machinery. But it is not necessary to be a car owner to participate in the activities of vintage car clubs, and many members collect related items only: literature, hubcaps, lamps, horns, radiator emblems and ornaments.

**HARRAH'S AUTOMOBILE COL-
LECTION** Cars require both cash and
space, especially if you have 1,500 of them
(the collection needs about 60 more to be
complete). So William Harrah built a 13-
building complex for his collection on 10
acres in Sparks, Nevada, complete with
pristine workshops for restoration and a
research library, itself a virtual collection
of trade journals, automotive publications
and service manuals, some meticulously
compiled by the staff as they worked on the
cars. (Authentic restoration is so important
that when Harrah's acquired the famous
Thomas Flyer race car it aged the finish on
the car, to simulate the wear of the race, by
driving it through the sagebrush of the
Nevada desert.)

*Wall-to-Wall Antique Automobiles. (Harrah's Museum)*

**THE HOUSE THAT WHIT BUILT—
OF LICENSE PLATES** Whit Nesbit
was so successful at collecting license
plates that he ran out of room to put them.
So he shingled the playhouse behind his
home with around 2,000 of the extras. And
since some plates were red, white and
blue, it seemed only logical to use 200 of
them to form the American flag. Even the
inside of the playhouse is covered with
beautifully preserved plates—retouched
when necessary—and then hung on
boards. There are thousands from every
state, but most are from South Carolina.
After years of searching, he is proud to say
that he now has the complete run issued,
including the very first plate made in 1917.

Whit Nesbitt doesn't believe in paying
for plates; they have value only to collectors. Trading by mail across the country
with 1,300 fellow members of the Auto
License Plate Collectors Association is
one way to build a collection, but he finds
his best sources are people he talks with on
his travels as an insurance salesman. Old
barns, pack houses, trees—anyplace a
plate might have been tacked up and in that
way preserved—are also good hunting
grounds; but contrary to popular opinion,
junkyards are not (plates there are too
quickly corroded).

*Playhouse Covered with License Plates,* some forming the American flag.

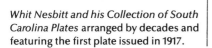

*Whit Nesbitt and his Collection of South
Carolina Plates* arranged by decades and
featuring the first plate issued in 1917.

### Organizations

*Spark Plug Collectors of America,* Box 2229,
Ann Arbor, MI 48106 (membership $4; FREE
sample issue of information flyer and newsletter (with 25¢ handling and SASE). Bill Bond,
founder and director, writes:

*"As we go into our third year we have over 150
members in the United States, Canada,
England and Australia. Our basic object is the
collection of spark plugs and related material.
Early ads give some idea of the odd types of
plugs—and there were hundreds of manufacturers and over 2,000 different brand names
prior to World War II. Unlike coin or stamp
collecting, in which you 'fill in the blanks,'
knowing exactly what exists, in spark-plug collecting new names and variations are constantly turning up. The only listing of companies and their brand names is one that our
club is now preparing."*

**AUTOMOBILE EMBLEMS** "... I had my first ride in a 1903 one-cylinder Cadillac with wicker baskets on the sides that made the Detroit streetcars look like they were standing still." That seemed to have set off Harry Pulfer's love affair with cars. "I used to collect old cars, and what a headache to even store them, yet I have friends that collected double-decker buses." So he turned to something small—car emblems and name plates. He has 5,000 mounted on 61 display boards, including plates from motorcycles, bicycles, airplanes and buggies. To Pulfer, who has worked in many phases of automotive dealing and selling, the history of an automobile is intertwined with their emblems.

Other related collections are: automobiles stamps from around the world; tax stamps and A-ration stickers for cars; license plates and over 100 "nickel novels" with cars on the cover. If anyone has an emblem they cannot identify, Harry Pulfer will help. Just make a rubbing of it (better, he says, than a photograph) and send it to him at: 2700 Mary Street, La Crescenta, CA 91214.

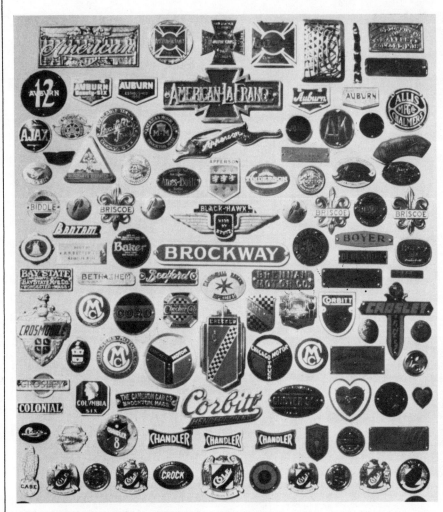

*Car Name Plates,* including several racing cards

*Ad for Early Lincolns.*

Hubcap Collectors Club, c/o Dennis Kuhn, Box 54, Buckley, MI 49620 (FREE sample issue of newsletter with SASE). Excerpt from newsletter:

*The unofficial annual meeting of The International Amalgamated Society of Searchers for Rare, Greasy, Dirty Old Hubcaps," otherwise known as The IASOSFRGDOH (for short) was held at 4:00 P.M. Friday, October 7th, 1977; under cloudy skies on the green grass at the entrance to the World's Greatest Display of Antique Automobiles and Automotive Bits and Pieces (sometimes known as junque). All respected members displayed the required signs of a true "Hubcapper" by a show of greasy hands and a bag-full of ancient well worn grease caps. There being no minutes of the last annual meeting—the reading of the minutes was dispensed with.*

*The members all displayed great ability to tell tall stories and lies (without cracking a smile) as to where they found the hubcaps and how they purchased a $25.00 cap for $10.00. These tall stories were flying in all directions and it was difficult for this Secretary to properly record the minutes and sift the grain from the chaff.*

(Collection Frank Miller)

*Denis Kuhn Boasts Over 900 Caps* in his collection, with around 300 different makes, some from foreign countries and some from early carriages and buggies.

**HOOD ORNAMENTS** Once radiator caps were prominently displayed on hoods in the form of symbolic sculptures of wings, women, birds and mythological figures. Ornaments were often quite beautiful and sometimes costly—the Bugatti Elephant was rumored to have been made of silver. (*Collection of Harrah's*)

*Isotta Fraschini, 1922*

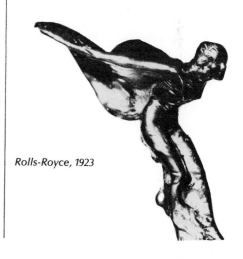

*Rolls-Royce, 1923*

## What Other Collectors Collect

- A member of the National Military Vehicle Collectors Association collects World War I tanks, jeeps and half trucks.
- *Military Police Harley Davidson Model 1917* at Rodney C. Gott–Harley Davidson Museum, York, Pennsylvania

*Postcards of Motorcycles.*

## Organizations

*Auto License Plate Collectors Association,* c/o Gary Kincaid, 207 Springdale Ave., Beckley, WV

*The Society of Automotive Historians,* National Automotive History Collection, Detroit Free Public Library, 5201 Woodward Avenue, Detroit, MI 48202 (membership $10)

*Antique Automobile Club of America,* Governor Road, Hershey, PA 17033 (membership $8.50, bimonthly magazine *Antique Automobile* $7.50, free with membership)

## Publications

*Hemmings Motor News,* world's largest antique, vintage and special-interest auto marketplace—paid subscribers, over 156,000 (sample $1, monthly subscription $6.75); *Special Interest Autos* (sample $1.50, bimonthly subscription $7); *The Vintage Auto Almanac* (annual $5.50). All available from *Hemmings Motor News,* Box 256, Bennington, VT 05201.

*Cars and Parts Magazine,* Dept. G0006, Box 482, Sidney, OH 45367 (free sample issue)

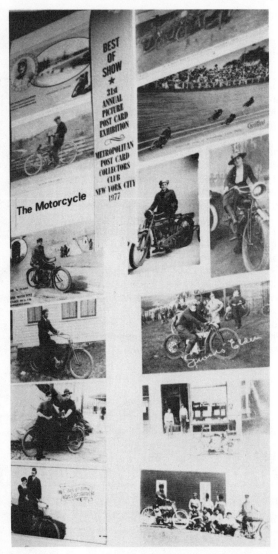

# Railroadiana

**STARTING OUT ON THE RIGHT TRACK** "At the age of three, with photos to prove it, Seth Bramson was scampering (with the aid of his father) all over the big steam engines in the Florida East Coast Railway's Miami (Buena Vista) yard. Serious collecting began at the age of 11, and now Bramson is recognized as the foremost authority on the history of the FEC Railway as well as commercial transportation in Florida in general. He has the largest collection of FEC and Florida transportation memorabilia in the world, and one of the largest rail and trolleyana collections in the country. It includes the oldest piece of marked railroad memorabilia (U.S.) known to be in existence—the ribbon commemorating the laying of the cornerstone of the B & O Railroad by Charles Carroll, last surviving signer of the Declaration of Independence. Seth Bramson comments:

*"Interestingly enough, the rail buffs were a 'lunatic fringe' of collectors until only a few years ago, when, with the coming of the Bicentennial, the whole country turned around and realized there were very few graphic portrayals of the golden age of the railroads, including views of the cities in which they operated. Suddenly, as if mysteriously and on command, the railroad buffs emerged from the closet to the brightness of daylight. It seems they were the only ones with photos of Podunk station (or Key West or Memphis or Lunch-*

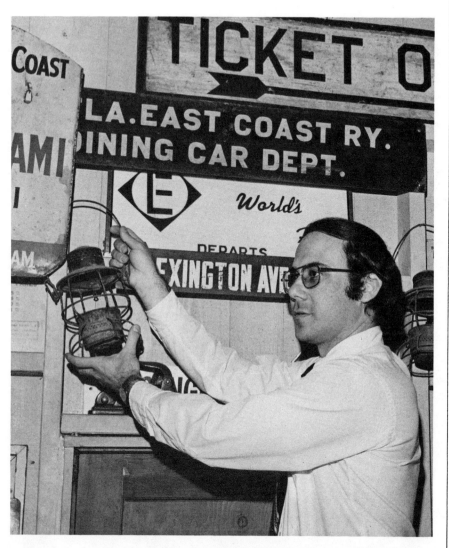

*Seth Bramson's Utility Room* is filled with fabulous old railroad memorabilia. The ticket office sign is from the FEC Railway's now demolished Miami station, while the Dining Car Department sign came from St. Augustine, Florida. The "E" in the diamond is a sign from the now abandoned Dearbone Station in Chicago, and the world "Local" completes the sign with the words "Lexington Ave" visible. The Lexington sign is from a division of the New York subway system. *"One of my real collector's prizes is this sign from New York's lamented 'old' Penn Station."* Other railroad memorabilia surrounds owner-collector Seth Bramson.

*burg or Walla-Walla, for that matter) and they had old timetables with classically beautiful graphics, memorabilia, lanterns and the like. Additionally, the great American trolley car, all but forgotten except in a handful of cities, had been preserved on film by the trolley buffs. Amazing! And suddenly railroadiana was legitimatized. The hobby with its many branches, from collecting old toy trains to building live steam engines in miniature to collecting lanterns, became something that was no longer 'silly.' The railroad buffs are here to stay!"*

*French Art Deco Railroad Posters*—A.M. Cassandre, "Etoile du Nord," 1927.

*The Henry Ford Museum* in Dearborn, Michigan, has an important collection of trains. Shown in the foreground: the *Dewitt Clinton* of the 1830s contrasts sharply with the mightly *Allegheny* of the 1940s.

Pierre Masseau, "Exactitude," 1932. Both posters (*Collection of Mr. and Mrs. Leonard Lauder,* shown at The French Institute/Alliance Française)

*Railroad Insignia.*

## What Other Collectors Collect

- *Items Related to Streetcars in Scranton, Pennsylvania:* photographs, transfers, tickets, etc.
- *Trolly and Steamboat Timetables*

*Timetables*

*Lanterns.*

*Maine Central Dinner Service*

# Air and Space Travel

## What Other Collectors Collect

- *Patches* from different space missions
- *Collection of Zeppelin Memorabilia* that includes stamps, baggage labels, schedules, menus, even fabric from the *Hindenburg*
- *Collection of Pocket Watches* that commemorate flights, including those of the zeppelin
- *Memorabilia commemorating the solo flight of Charles Lindbergh* across the Atlantic in 1927
- *Bi-Planes*

## Organizations

*Antique Airplane Association* (full membership $25, associate membership $12.50); *International Airplane Digest,* quarterly publication, Box H, Ottumwa, IA 52501

# Maritime Memorabilia

**THINGS FROM THE SEA** In his bay-front den, Leo Kelmensen, advertising tycoon and sometime sailor, is surrounded by water and a very seaworthy collection. Some of it is strictly for show: on the mantle, ship models made when he was a boy; and all over, anchors, decoys, tide clocks, barometers, a diver's helmet, a ship's telegraph, old signs, scrimshaw, steamship souvenirs (a pocketbook and ashtray from the last voyage of the *Queen Mary*) and more. Other objects have been made into furnishings: taffrail logs become bookends; lanterns become lamps; driftwood, ship's wheels and a compass become tables.

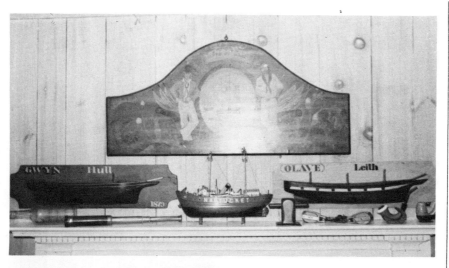

**NAGLER'S NAUTICALS** A childhood admiration for Chris Craft wooden boats of the thirties coupled with a stint in the Navy may have been the stimulus for Robert Nagler's collection of nautical and marine "art" dating from the turn of the century and up to the present time. It includes: brass instruments, signs, gauges, compasses, navigational aids, diver's helmet, unusual photos, paintings, ship fittings, scrimshaw, lights, a wheel and a captain's bridge. Most have been purchased.

*"Price is an important consideration. Much of the fun is in snooping and finding bargains. All acquisitions must be museum quality after restoration. Objects are then hung on walls or carefully mounted on bronze, wood, brass, slate or plexiglass bases. Mounting costs often exceed the cost of the item. I have major non-wood mountings prepared in London to my design by a fine workshop whose principal work is for museums and large private art collections."*

*(Collection Leo Kelmensen)*

*Naval Jugs. (Collection of Arthur J. Sussel, C. G. Sloan & Co., Inc.)*

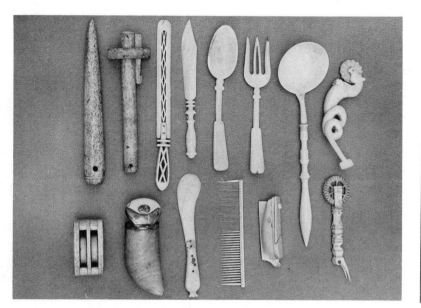

*Scrimshaw Kitchen and Other Tools* that belonged to Douglas Fonda. A book dealer in New York, he specialized in nautical books, eventually moved to Nantucket and amassed an important collection of whaling artifacts and memorabilia. *(Richard Bourne Galleries)*

*Nineteenth-Century Carved Wooden Figure* probably stood outside a nautical instrument maker's ship or chandler's shop. *(Collection of Mystic Seaport Museum and Village, Mystic, Connecticut)*

## INSTITUTIONS

Peabody Museum, Salem, Mass.
Suffolk County Whaling Museum, Sag Harbor, N.Y.

*Fine Snuff Boxes. (Collection of Arthur J. Sussel, C. G. Sloan & Co., Inc.)*

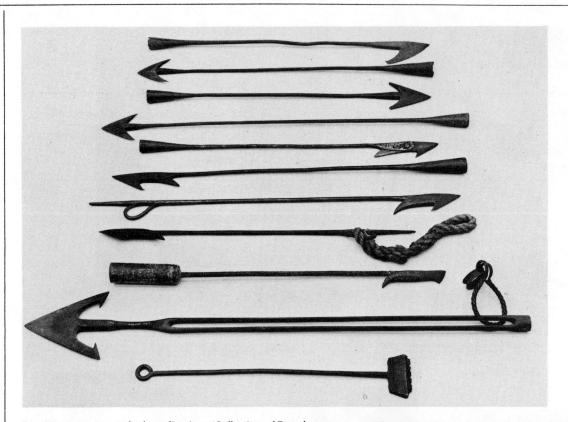

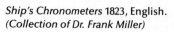

*Rare Harpoons* except for branding iron (Collection of Douglas Fonda). *(Richard Bourne Galleries)*

*Ship's Chronometers* 1823, English. *(Collection of Dr. Frank Miller)*

# MEMORIES

## Personal Mementos

In olden days our ancestors hand-crafted quilts, sewed samplers, painted birth certificates to help recall the past; today, our personal mementos are likely to be products of modern technology, such as photographs and newspaper clippings.

*Framed Family Pictures*—A lover of antique frames, this collector matches the subject and time of a picture—for example, her grandparents' wedding—to the style of the frame prevalent then, Art Deco. *(Collection of Judith Liss, Photograph by Leonard Speier)*

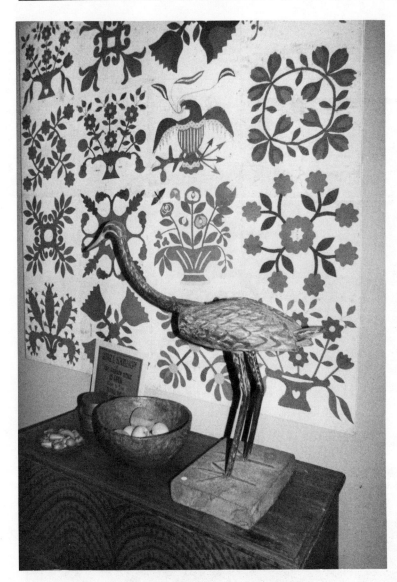

*Friendship Quilt*—so called because each panel was appliquéd by a friend. *(George Shoellkopf Galleries)*

*Early American Birth Certificate.*

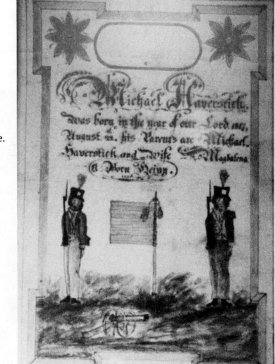

*Merit Card 1814. (The Metropolitan Museum of Art, Jefferson R. Burdick Collection)*

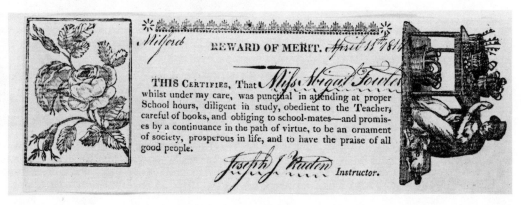

*Articles of Achievement*—Framed clippings line walls of hallway in the home of designer Eleanor Brenner.

*Wall Collage*—golf balls, license plates, locks, dishes and old radio, telephone and doll, each with special significance. *(Collected and created by Richard Gibbs)*

*Picture Collage* of photographs and other memorabilia, collected and made for a birthday gift. *(Morton Hamburg)*

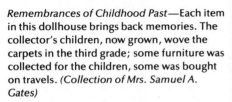

*Remembrances of Childhood Past*—Each item in this dollhouse brings back memories. The collector's children, now grown, wove the carpets in the third grade; some furniture was collected for the children, some was bought on travels. *(Collection of Mrs. Samuel A. Gates)*

*Dolls from Around the World*—All were bought by the collector on her travels, with the exception of the dolls from Syria which were purchased for her by a friend, Wendell Willkie. *(Collection of Mrs. Samuel A. Gates)*

# Travel Souvenirs

There are many ways to remember. Photographs, postcards, flyers, road maps, soap wrappers, soda bottles and caps with foreign names are common keepsakes; but some travelers select more unusual souvenirs. One well-known designer looks for and buys (or trades for her own) exotic hats. These are used back home in fashion shows and afterwards hung on the walls of her home. An ambulatory golfer fills his basement with all the scorecards and pencils of the courses he has played.

Purists will collect objects that are only from their own travels and not others given to them as gifts. "Moral" collectors may help themselves to what is clearly there to be taken—matches, swizzle sticks—while others collect "contraband" such as silverware and room keys. Keys are actually one of the most sought-after souvenirs and are particularly popular among travel agents. Some will stop at nothing. To avoid embarrassing encounters at check-out time, one collector removes the key from someone else's door, when he arrives. However, this practice has its drawbacks. Once, when this collector wanted to have his room changed to a more desirable location, the manager was unable to do so because the one available room had a missing key. Poetic justice.

*Souvenir Banners*

*Meals Worth Remembering*—To discourage theft and probably to make a little money, some establishments will sell their ashtrays. *(Collection of Barbara Kalmensen)*

*Keys* from the great hostelries of the world decorate guest bathroom.

*"Do Not Disturb" Signs*—a legal alternative to keys.

*Souvenir Road Sign* found knocked down at the intersection where James Dean was killed. *(Collection of Henry J. Stern)*

# An Impressive Event: The World's Fair

Vicki Nobel is a collector of "anything and everything from the 1964–65 New York World's Fair." How did it start? Vicki explains, "My mother took me to the fair as a baby every weekend to feed me. The music and excitement kept my mouth open, and my mother was handy with a spoon. After that exposure, it was easy!"

Visiting the '39 fair had a slightly different effect on Edward Orth. It led him not only to his avocation; but with its stimulating advanced architecture, to his vocation as a city planner. He says that his collection and library are a permanent hobby, not a speculative investment, and he hopes one day to donate the New York World's Fair 1939–40 material to a New York museum or World's Fair organization. In addition to almost 2,000 postcards (the first ones bought at age 12), he has World's Fair memorabilia in just about every category. "I may be narrow-minded as to subject but everything except the kitchen sink is collected, classified according to the section of the fair, and further classified by pavilion, including advertisements, banks, books, bookends, bookmarks, bottles, boxes, building models, cameras, catalogues, clocks, clothing, coins,

Tray from the World's Fair 1939 (photographs by *The New York Historical Society*)

Radio (*Collection of Larry Zim*)

color slides, dishes, electric shavers, exhibitors' literature, Fair Corporation publications, first-day covers, flags, furniture, games, glasses, hats, heat pads, invitations, jewelry, kerchiefs, letter openers, magazine articles, maps, matchbooks, menus, meter slogans, motion pictures, newspaper articles, novelties, paperweights, pencil sharpeners, pennants, photographs, pillow covers, pinbacks, pitchers, plaques, plates, playing cards, posters, postage stamps, prints, programs, radios, salt-pepper sets, seals, sheet music, silverware, stamps, tablecloths, thermometers, tickets, toys, trays, Trylon and Perisphere replicas, viewbooks and watches."

## Organizations

Orth is an organizer of ECHO (Expo Collectors and Historians Organization; membership $6) and editor of their bulletin. For information, write: 1436 Killarney Avenue, Los Angeles, CA 90065.

*World's Fair Collectors Society, Inc.* 148 Poplar Street, Garden City, NY 11530 (membership $5). The 800 members, dedicated to the preservation of the heritage of World's Fairs past, present and future, issue a bimonthly newsletter called *Fair News* (FREE sample copy with 24¢ in stamps or coins).

Michael Pender, one of the organizers of WFCS, was already interested in expositions and a collector of World's Fair medals, tokens since 1851 and elongated coins, when he went to work as an engineer for the New York World's Fair of 1964–65. Long after the fair ended its influence remained, as Mr. Pender and other alumni expanded their collections and formed the organization to help others with the hobby.

# CITYANA

## Rubbings of New York

*"Rubbing—the craft of reproducing the surface of a design by rubbing a piece of paper or cloth with waxes, inks or graphite—offers the opportunity to explore the architecture, history and peculiar art forms of any city . . . rubbing helps to keep a record of some beautiful objects that might otherwise be forgotton."* –Cecily Barth Firestein, in *Rubbing Crafts*, p. 11 (Quick Fox)

Collection of Sewer Covers, Architectural Trim and Gravestone Rubbings by Cecily Firestein — sewer cover from the Mott Haven historic district in the Bronx (above); sewer cover from historic Hunters Point, Queens, New York (right).

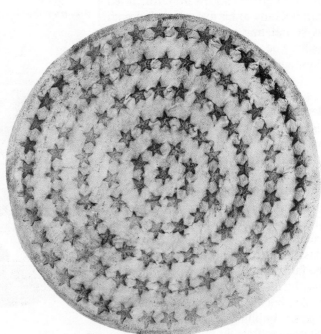

Art Deco decoration from the Bronx County Court House
and rubbing from gravestone in the Trinity Church
graveyard, Wall Street, New York.

Art Deco decorations on a panel of an elevator door in the
lobby of the Waldorf Astoria Hotel in Manhattan.

# Urban Archeologist

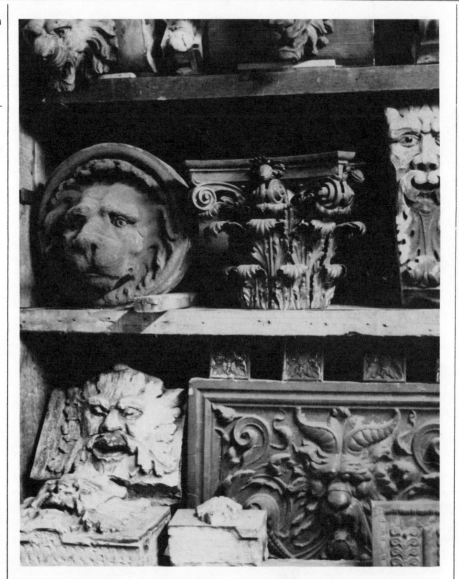

Lenny Schechter deplores the waste in the destruction of fine old buildings and feels an emotional commitment to at least save their embellishments—cast- or carved-stone figures of animals, grotesques, men, women, foliage. He is so well-known now that demolition companies call *him,* and he has opened a shop to sell his salvaged prizes. Mr. Schechter advises that these architectural ornaments, though heavy, can be hung on walls by inserting an angle iron into the piece and into the wall.

Photographs courtesy of Urban Archeology, 135 Spring St., New York.

**SMALL SOUVENIRS OF OLD BUILDINGS** The demolition site can be the source for collections of carved balustrades from a staircase, and for other interior architectural embellishments: ceramic tiles from walls or floor and around fireplaces, even decorative hardware nails and screws.

*Classified Advertisement* to sell pieces of 1871 Nevada State capitol.

Back

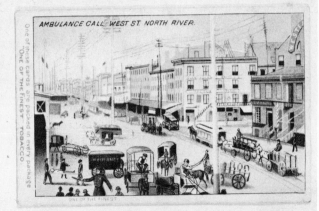

*Cityana*, 16 E. 53rd Streeet, New York, NY 10022. Memorabilia sold in this shop.

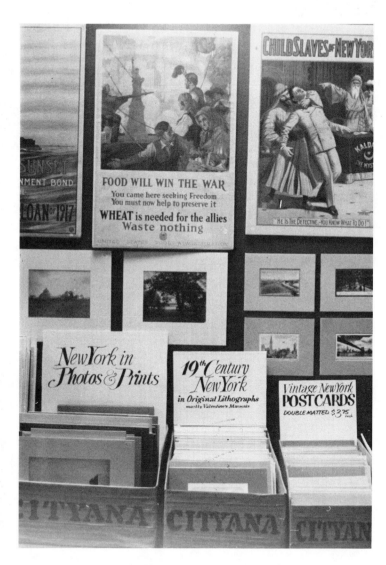

*Scenes of New York City* on tobacco insert cards. *(Metropolitan Museum of Art, Jefferson R. Burdick Collection)*

# New York Academic

Professor Leo Hershkowitz of Queens College:

*"My interest is basically academic— illustrative materials, books, maps, prints, Staffordshire and manuscripts relating to New York City. They are as important to me as a knife to a surgeon or paint to an artist because I write and teach about the city. Collecting for collecting's sake has little interest to me. It is only when esoterica becomes part of history and has value as such that collecting takes on meaning."*

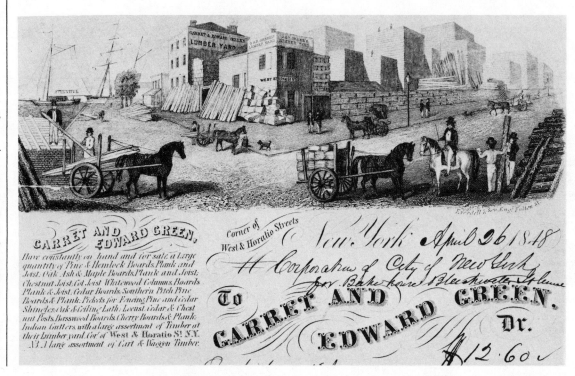

*Early Trade Bills of New York City (Historical Documents, Collection of Paul Lapper Tehan, Queens College, Reproduced by permission of The Magazine Antiques).*

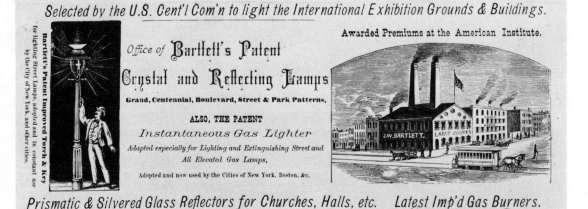

ASTOR HOUSE.

New York, *Nov 15 1849*

M *Common Council*

To COLEMAN & STETSON,............Dr.

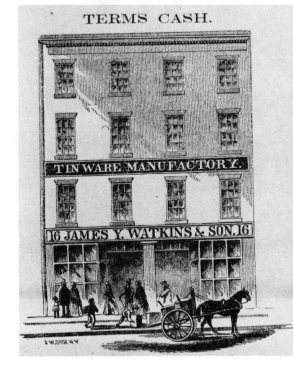

TERMS CASH.

TINWARE MANUFACTORY.

16 JAMES Y. WATKINS & SON. 16

ESTABLISHED 1830.

New York, *June 23* 185 7

*With the Corporation of the City of New York*

*Bought of* JAMES Y. WATKINS & SON,

MANUFACTURERS OF TINWARE,

IMPORTERS AND DEALERS IN

HOUSEKEEPING HARDWARE, CUTLERY,

SILVER PLATED & BRITANNIA WARE,

BRUSHES, MATS, &c. &c.

No. 16 CATHARINE ST., near Chatham Square.

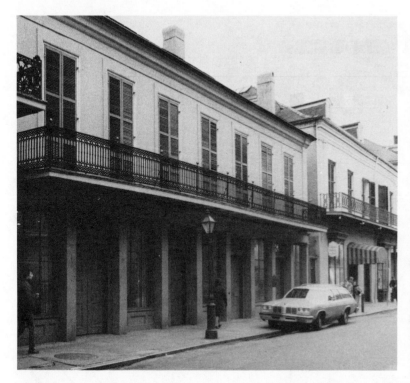

*The Historic New Orleans Collection—"I have bequeathed to the trustees my entire interest in a valuable collection of historical items pertaining to Louisiana, along with the property bearing numbers 527–533 Royal Street, New Orleans, Louisiana, in which at least the major part of such collection is housed" (will of Kemper Williams).*

Documents, prints, engravings and maps.

# FESTIVAL FAVORS

## Valuable Valentines

Eveline Pulati has a large personal collection of cards commemorating St. Valentine's Day and a year-round occupation. She runs the National Valentine Collectors Association and a collector's shop that specializes in paper Americana including antique valentines. She writes:

*"The club was started by me as a labor of love to pass on information . . . the only books on the subject are out of print and most collectors who come in are not very knowledgeable. . . . I buy three or four or more collections each year to replace my stock and since I constantly give talks to civic groups and do displays in libraries and banks, I am always looking for fresh material to display, as well as for my own collection. After a piece has been shown a few times, it ends up in the store for sale—except for my pets that I treasure and would never sell. . . . The two most important things for collectors to remember about preservation is to try to keep their valentines (and all paper collectibles) out of the sunlight and to try and use acid-free paper behind them when mounting in frames or albums—and never laminate between plastic."*

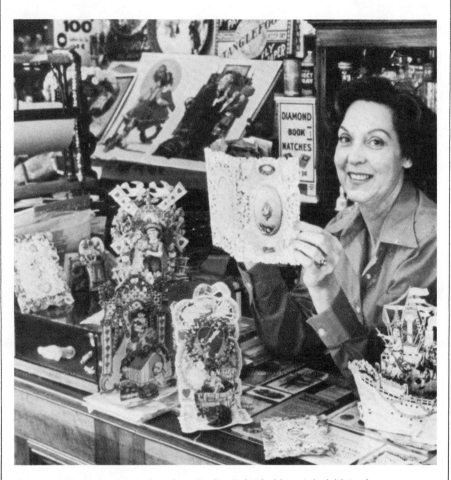

Surrounded by valentines in her shop, Eveline Pulati holds a triple-fold *Kershaw Mid-19th-Century Sachet Valentine.*

Cameo-Embossed Lace Paper Valentine by Mansell, London, England, c. 1845–50. Verse taken from it:

> The Blushing rose that hangs it's head,
> Or meets the sun with shrinking dread,
> Lo, have I loved; but some strong spell,
> Forbids my heart it's love to tell.
> Here, take these simple flowers and feel,
> The love my life dare not reveal,
> And if your heart beats love to mine,
> Oh! then I'll be your Valentine.
> As limpid streams reflect the azure sky,
> See mirrored here their own bright beaming eye"

Comic Character Valentine Postal Cards. (Collection of Robert Lesser)

Sachet Valentine — Verse and ribbons are satin.

## Organizations

*National Valentine Collectors Association E. Cubbon, Santa Ana, CA 92701 (membership $10 a year, sample issue of quarterly bulletin $1—each issue specializes in a different kind of valentine)*

# Louis Prang in the Hallmark Cards Historical Collection

A commercial and aesthetic success when he first introduced them in 1875, and now highly sought-after collector's items, Louis Prang's Christmas cards chronicled quaint customs of the 19th-century Christmas. One of the earliest examples of high-quality mass-produced art, the lithography and use of color was exceptional for the times. The world's largest collection of Prang Christmas cards (60,000), as well as other antique greeting cards, is housed in the Hallmark archives, Kansas City, Missouri.

*Christmas in the 1880s* is portrayed in this Christmas card.

*Late 19th-Century Greeting*—Pansies, roses and robins were the most popular designs on early Christmas cards.

# In Celebration of Christmas

"I'm always looking for a glass peacock and the particular clown I grew up with—most collectors are constantly trying to find ornaments from the Christmas trees of their youth." Luckily the search has been somewhat eased for Philip Snyder, who inherited his grandfather's tree ornaments. They formed the nucleus of a collection of many thousand pieces, including three-dimensional cardboard ornaments covered in gold and silver paper (Dresden, Germany 1880–1910)—the house and the shoes held candy—and glass Santas from Lausha, Germany.

When his ornaments are not decorating his Christmas tree, they are stored and displayed in a 98-drawer English apothecary chest and an old oak map chest. Ironically, as collector demand has increased, so has the supply. Dealers and others who might have passed by or disposed of these seemingly worthless and fragile ornaments now recognize their fine workmanship and current market value (although Snyder adds that the Dresden ornaments are so rare that most dealers have never seen them, let alone passed them by). Written material on the subject is also scarce. One of the few books is *The Christmas Tree Book: The History of the Christmas Tree and Antique Christmas Tree Ornaments* by Philip

*Collection of Christmas Ornaments* hung from evergreen branches and covered with lucite boxes. (From a Christmas exhibition, Gotham Book Mart, New York, New York)

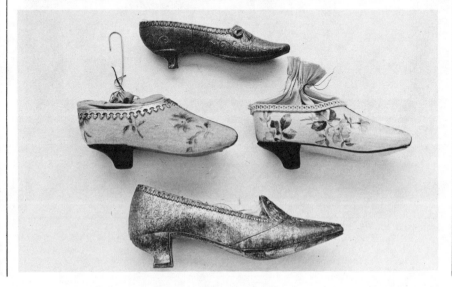

Snyder (Viking $10.95, Penguin $4.95). He wrote it in self-defense: "I finally researched and wrote the book that as a collector I had waited 15 years for somebody else to write." This, it seems, is a rather common occurrence among collectors. Snyder collects other Christmas memorabilia like Santa Claus figures, ornament molds, and figural light-bulb ornaments.

*(Collection of Philip Snyder)*

*Ancient Chanukah menorah.*

## Collecting Clues

- Old greeting cards can often be found in old books or albums. Their value is determined by age, condition, the printer or publisher and the design, and is enhanced if they are part of a large collection.
- Snyder says not to wash old ornaments with water—even a damp cloth may harm the finish. Just dust with a soft cloth.

## What Other Collectors Collect

*Halloween Masks; Christmas Seals*

# EATING

## The Councilman Who Collects Campbell's Soup Cans

When Henry Stern goes on vacation he spends a lot of time in the supermarket searching for new additions to his large collection of Campbell's Soup cans. And while many are from trips or from traveling friends who bring them back to him as gifts, the array also includes those bought locally—in fact, every Campbell's Soup can ever made, in all its variations.

There are obsolete soups and special soups (like Man-Handlers). There are soups in different size cans: large economy, restaurant, single portions. And there are the same soups with different labels, modifications in type or in artwork (changes in chickens or Campbell kids), or in slogans ("Mm-mm Good" or "Chicken Flavor"). He groups the cans on shelves; one area is for chicken soups or tomato soups; one for French soups or Spanish soups. Not only has Henry Stern collected all these cans, but he has tasted all these soups. He generally buys two

cans, one to sample and evaluate (pepper pot was the worst, he says) and one unopened can to collect (the soup does not seem to affect the can and only tomato bisque burst, Stern says, but not violently). (*Collection of Peggy and Henry J. Stern*)

## Antiques of Its Industry: The Campbell Museum's Collection of Soup Tureens

The Campbell Soup Company provided the original funds to establish this remarkable monument to soup. Famous the world over, the Campbell collection of soup tureens and accompanying accessories—ladles, spoons and soup plates—reminds us of the once sumptuous service and elaborate presentation of this humble dish.

One guiding principle in the acquisition of this collection was that objects identified with important persons be included. So there are pieces that belonged to royalty—Tsar Nicholas I and Queen Elizabeth II, among others. The museum also has a delightful collection of animal and vegetable tureens. The Campbell Museum is located at Campbell Place, Camden, New Jersey.

_Tureen_ with stand c.1760, hard-paste porcelain, China, Ch'ien Lung period, for beef soups.

_Tureen_ with stand c. 1770, tin-enameled earthenware (faience), Denmark.

_Tureen_ with stand, 1783–84, silver, Paris, France, Jacques Charles Mongenot.

**ORANGE CRATE LABELS** Bill Power not only has a personal collection of crate labels, but also a mail-order company called Pacific Label Archives which sells authentic California fruit box labels printed between 1900 and 1950. The catalog ($1, Box 5445, Santa Ana, CA 92705) offers original, rare and out-of-print labels and gives the following information: Originally these labels were purchased by the fruit packers who intended to paste them on the ends of their wooden shipping boxes.

Just after World War II the wooden crates began to increase in cost until suddenly they were just too expensive. Cardboard boxes with pre-printed designs rapidly replaced the wooden boxes and paper labels. This sudden change-over left the fruit packers with limited numbers of unused labels. In most cases, the remaining lots were burned or dumped over a period of years.

Recognizing their artistic and historical value, we systematically located the remains of these packing houses and purchased the labels represented in this catalog. This effort took us through the entire state of California, over an eight-year period.

Our first catalog contains 90 labels from California and 10 from the state of Florida. They were all printed by a now obsolete printing process, unique to label printing. Their vivid colors are a result of quality ink and the fact that the colors were generally hand separated. Our second catalog contains 64 more labels of the same quality.

SPECIALIZING IN ORIGINAL, RARE AND OUT-OF-PRINT LABELS
P.O. BOX 15445, SANTA ANA, CALIF. 92705

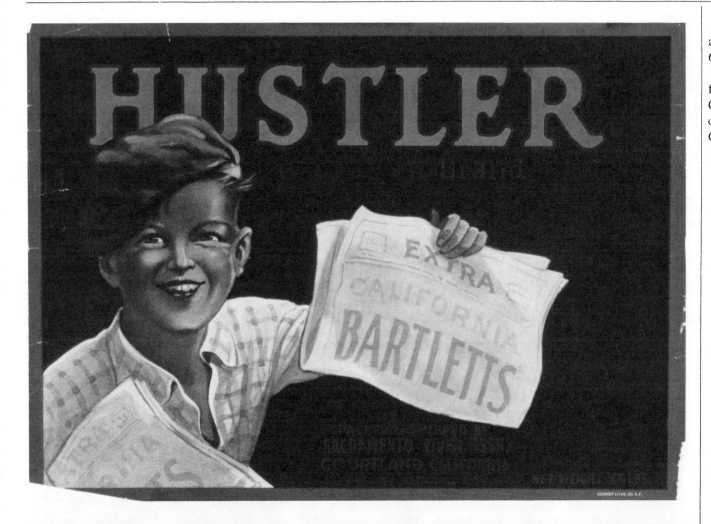

In addition to this, some fine graphic artists were hired to illustrate them over the 60-year period they were used.

These historical, artistic and technical facts, combined with the fascination of old California, explain the growing popularity of fruit box label collecting.

Categories of labels as follows:

California Orange Box Labels
California Lemon Box Labels
California Pear Box Labels
Florida Orange Box Labels
California Apple Box Labels

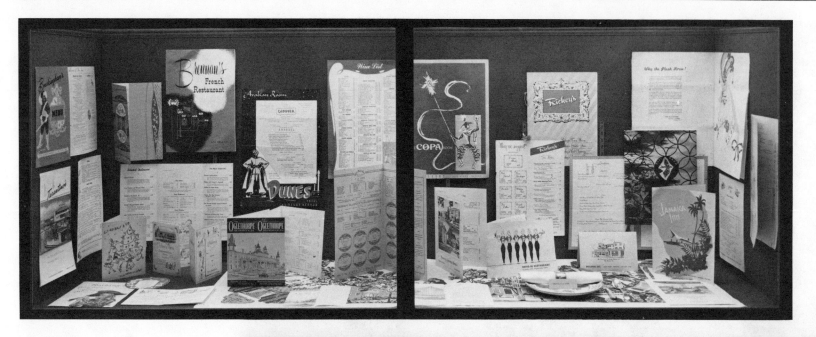

*The Shircliffe Menu Collection*—Historic and souvenir menus, as well as children's, foreign, train, plane and hotel menus, are popular categories for collectors. (*New York Historical Society*)

*Dried Herbs in Jars*

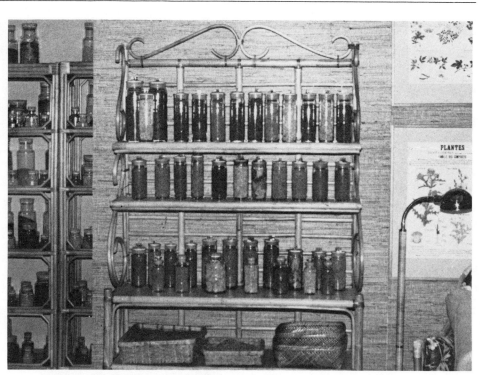

Menus decorate kitchen walls, bringing back mouth-watering memories of culinary adventures. (Collection of Ann and Bob Shanks)

*Gum Wrappers. (Collection of and photograph by Doug Liman)*

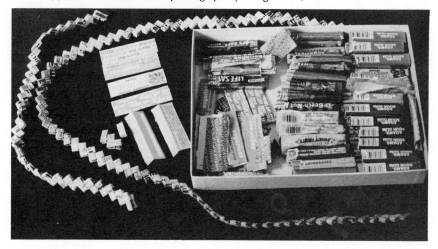

# Kitchen Collectibles

The molds of yesterday that transformed the simplest foods—butter, ice cream, pudding—into fancy forms are actively collected and used in today's kitchens.

**WOODEN BUTTER MOLDS** Paul Kindig and his wife (right) examine their collection of butter prints and molds, which they recently gave to the museum at Michigan State University. Since there is little written information on butter molds, Mr. Kindig is now devoting his efforts to filling the void. "The gift to the museum offered or opened up an opportunity to work with their specialists in folk art, to try and develop a book on this subject, an interesting retirement project. They have even presented me with the fancy title of *Adjunct Specialist–History.*"

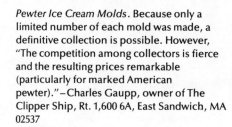

*Copper Molds.*

*Pewter Ice Cream Molds.* Because only a limited number of each mold was made, a definitive collection is possible. However, "The competition among collectors is fierce and the resulting prices remarkable (particularly for marked American pewter)."—Charles Gaupp, owner of The Clipper Ship, Rt. 1,600 6A, East Sandwich, MA 02537

*Unique Banquet Eagle Mold, $850.*

*Portrait Bust Mold of Admiral Byrd*

*Portrait Bust Mold of Thomas Jefferson*

*Banquet Mold from the Queen Mary*

**ABOUT EGG-BEATERS, APPLE PEELERS, CHERRY PITTERS** *"My first encounter with old cooking implements came over 20 years ago when I found a mechanical cast-iron apple peeler at an antique shop in the Catskills. I rushed home, clamped the machine to a table, impaled an apple on the prongs, and turned the handle. The moment the spring-operated blade met the fruit and began to send a spiral of thin peel towards the floor I became a collector. At that time most antique dealers and kitchenware collectors concentrated on handsome wooden burl bowls, graceful copper skimmers and decorative wrought-iron 18th-century utensils. Tin cream whippers and sifters, patented egg beaters, wooden cabbage choppers lay neglected in old baskets or piled on dusty shelves. Before long, the apple peeler was joined by a wooden lemon squeezer, a flour sifter and a cast-iron doughnut shaper. . . . As the collection grew so did my curiosity. Was that maple double-handled rolling pin a rarity, or the pancake-turner machine hand stamped? How did they cook in an open fireplace? . . . The records of the United State Patent Office, established in 1790, offer a panorama of the fanciful and the practical . . . egg beaters, first patented in the 1860s, come in infinite varieties and shapes, as do can openers, corkscrews, string-bean slicers and ice scrapers. Gadgets that have working, movable parts and those that are dated and identified by manufacturer are particularly desirable and consequently more expensive. Prices can range from 50 cents for a simple can opener to $30 or $40 for an unusual cherry*

Assorted 19th- and 20th-century Egg Beaters. (Collection of Meryle Evans, photograph by John Gruen)

*pitter."* –Meryle Evans, in "Yard Sale Treasure Hunts," *(Food & Wine, July 1978)*

Old Spatulas, Cookie Cutters and Molds.

English *Wine De-Corker and Apple Corer* on kitchen counter. (Collection of Eve Propp).

**AN OIL DEALER WHO SAVES STOVES** Three cast-iron 19th-century American stoves and a Shaker stove c. 1800 from a collection of 300 in the private Museum of Antique Stoves, open by appointment. (*Collection of Carleton L. "Bus" Mendenhall, East Quogue, New York*)

# Tableware

*Pewter* for dining and drinking (mugs and teapots). *(Thomas and Constance Williams, Litchfield, Connecticut)*

*Silverware for Sale*—A collection of odd but similar pieces will be the talk of the table—unusual and less expensive than a comparable matching set.

*Salt and Peppers* are practical as well as pretty. One shop that specializes in "open" salts from $1 to $1,400 is The Salt Lady, Demarest, NJ.

*Sterling Silver 19th- and 20th-Century Place-Card Holders* collected from all over the world by Phyllis Girard, a professional party planner from Palm Beach. She likes to entertain for pleasure as well as for profit, and at her own dinner parties she matches the guest (for example, a home body) with the holder (perhaps a house or fireplace).

*Souvenir Spoons*, mementos of events, people and places, shown on a spoon rack. (*Collection of Raquel R. Levin*)

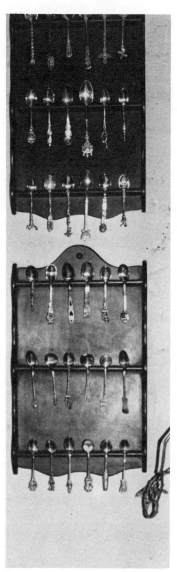

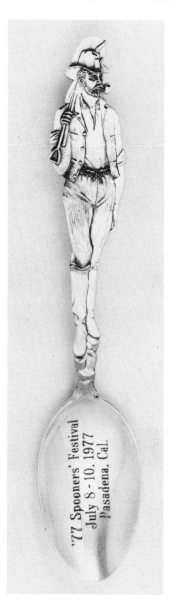

*California Miner Souvenir Spoon* made from a turn-of-the-century mold to commemorate a spooner's festival. (*Collection of Bill Boyd*)

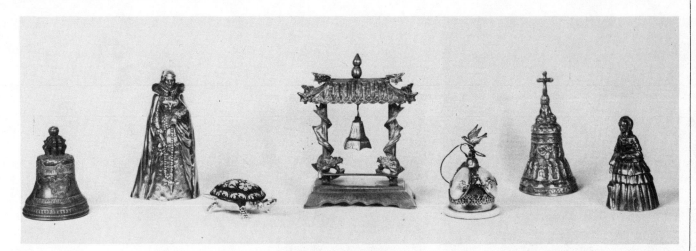

(Left to right) Replica of bell of Moscow Czar Kolokol; Mary Queen of Scots; turtle bell from Spain; Japanese gate; oval shells; copy of saint Peter's bell in Rome; Carrie Nation (?), well-known for her repugnance toward liquor; and below, The Battle of Sennacheribs; Mandarin button bell from China; prayer wheel carried by Tibetan women; elephant "tap" bell; and French bell.

# DuBois' Dinner Bells

Bernice DuBois is a tintinnabulist (a bell collector). She was attracted to bells because like so many other collectibles, they are interesting historically and they offer variety in shape, size and material (china, glass, porcelain, bronze, brass, wood, etc). They also sound good. There are 3,000 bells in her collection, all bought. She recommends the American Bell Association for further information. RD 1 Box 286, Natrona, PA 15065.

## What Other Collectors Collect

- *Candlesticks* and *Candlesnuffers*, *Victorian Napkin Rings*
- *19th-Century Mustache Spoons* (spoons with a guard to hold back a mustache and prevent it from getting wet) and *Monkey* (or liquor) *Spoons*
- *Other Kinds of Bells*—sleigh bells, animal bells (cow or camel bells), dancing bells, candleholder bells, saddle bells, doorbells and bicycle bells
- *Tea Balls* and *Tea Ball Stands*

## Organizations and Publications

*Spooners Forum,* Bill Boyd, Box 814, Temple City, CA 91780. Published monthly for souvenir spoon collectors ($7.50 per year; FREE sample issue with SASE and 30¢ *postage).*

# DRINKING

## Beer Can Fans

One of the few pastimes that is carried
on exclusively by trading is beer-can
collecting. Ever since the first can was
made in 1935, literally thousands of
variations have been produced, differ-
ing not only in decoration but in size,
shape and metal. Surprisingly, although this fast-growing hobby is
dominated by children and teenagers,
the experts are often adults. Among
the best sources for cans are dumps and
garbage cans along interstate high-
ways, although a rare can might be
found hiding in the back of a supermarket stack.

**THE BASEMENT BAR**  Collector and
real-estate appraiser Ken Zent has filled his
basement with 2,600 cans, souvenirs of his
travels abroad and around the United
States. Among his gems are a can manufactured for the inauguration of Prince
Charles, and a set of rare and scenic
Japanese cans.

In 1956, Rheingold Breweries of Orange, New Jersey, put the pictures of contestants in their famous Miss Rheingold Contest on their cans. Few mint examples are known today.

In 1964, the National Brewing Company of Phoenix, Arizona, tried to cash in on the James Bond craze and test-marketed James Bond 007 Special Blend. The brand was a total failure and the can is today much sought after by collectors.

*American* and *Foreign Cans. (Collection of Ken Zent, Photograph by Fort Wayne News Sentinal)*

**BREWERIANA OF WILLIAM CHRISTENSEN**   This collection numbers over 7,500 different cans from 58 countires; he started it in kindergarten. It includes the first beer can made by Kruegers of Newark, two different commemorative cans for the Coronation of King George VI in 1937, special cans for the New York World's Fairs 1939 and 1964, for the Brussels and Tokyo World's Fairs, and the two cans shown to the left.

**CASHING IN ON THE CENTENNIAL CAN**   The town of Grafton, Iowa (population 254), has found a unique way of raising money. According to *Time* magazine, the town fathers ordered 48,000 special cans of beer and 12,000 empty souvenir cans to celebrate their centennial. Thanks to ads in two collector's magazines, the cans have become a valuable municipal asset. While most of the full cans were sold at $1 apiece, the price of the empties rose to $5 in the collector's black market. Grafton is now holding onto its remaining cans in the hope that their value will continue to rise.

*Beer Trays*

*Beer Cans. (Collection of Rick Swearer, photograph by Randolph Swearer)*

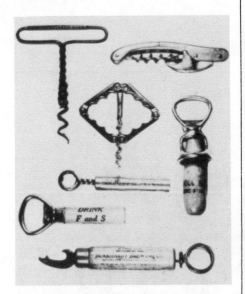

## Organizations and Publications

*Stein Collectors International,* Box 16326, St. Paul, MN 55116. As early as the 16th century, beer steins were manufactured in Germany, and with them was launched one of the most popular areas of beer collecting. Beer steins were designed to keep the beverage fresh and cool, and were made out of glass, stone, clay, porcelain and pewter.

*Beer Can Collectors of America,* 747 Merus Court, Fenton, MO 63026 (membership $17). The foremost club for the collectors of beer cans, it boasts over 15,000 dues-paying members all over the world. Special features include a news report (a page from the bulletin with collectors' calling cards shown here) every 45 days, a club roster and a checklist of beer cans. Conventions (labeled CANventions) are held annually.

*Beer Advertising Openers* by Donald Bull. (120 pages, $8.95). Mr. Bull is also co-author of *The Register of U.S. Breweries 1876–1976* ($10.95). Both can be obtained by writing to: 21 Frelma Drive, Trumbull, CT 06611.

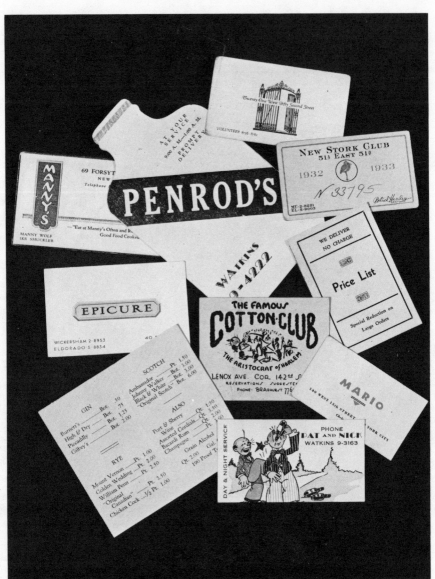

*Speakeasy Cards, Liquor and Price Lists (Collection of Museum of the City of New York)*

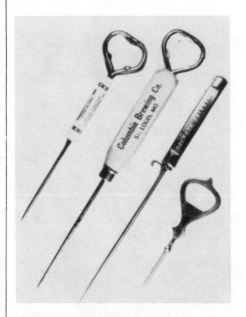

*(from Beer Advertising Openers by Donald Bull)*

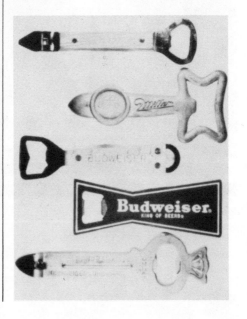

# Calling Cards

B.C.C.A. #3207
E.C.B.A. #274

BEER CAN COLLECTOR
DOMESTIC & FOREIGN

## Frank Vazquez

I DRINK UM · COLLECT UM · AND ADOPT UM

(914) 338-5004

RISELEY STREET
SUNRISE PARK
KINGSTON, N.Y. 12401

---

*Your BCCA Friend*

BILL HELSLEY

# 193

Phone
717-545 3158

129 Shell St.
Harrisburg, Pa. 17109

---

THE CONCORD COLLECTOR

Randy R. Boerst

16 Pershing Avenue
North East, Pa. 16428

BCCA #16064

814/725-3396

---

*I'll Go Almost Anywhere*

BCCA 12399

*For A Beer Can*

JIM LUBY

939 MAPLE STREET

SCRANTON PA 13505

PHONE 717 343 4994

---

GREG KURCZEWSKI
BCCA #12166

Collector of Grade 1 Beer Cans, Any Size, Any Age

member of Badger Bunch

1640 Osage Trail
Brookfield, Wisconsin 53005
(414) 784-4898

Trades Welcome Anytime

---

2312 Keystone Rd. Parma, Ohio 44134

Bill Weeber BEER can collector

---

A Full Can "Turns Me On."

JOE BRADAC
B.C.C.A. # 11656
113 Owsley St., Masury, Ohio 44438

---

Mark Sheremeta

BCCA 10460

---

OBSOLETES · ALE · FLATS · BEER · QUARTS · BOCK · GALLONS · DRAFT

CURRENTS · CROWNS · LIGHT · LITE

"BEER CANS ARE BEAUTIFUL"
**LARRY Y. WOFFORD**
BCCA No. 15375
Beer Can Collector
*"DON'T KICK THE CAN"*
100 FOOTE AVE      BELLEVUE, KY 41073
(606) 491 7980

CONES · MALT LIQUOR · TABS

· STOUT · RING TOPS · MALT LAGER · DOMESTIC · FOREIGN · GRADE ONE ·

---

COUNTRY CANMAN
COLLECTOR OF BREWERANIA

105 PORTSMOUTH AVE., APT. #25
EXETER, N.H. 03833

JOHN H. CRESSY, JR.
BCCA #3580

---

BEER CAN COLLECTORS OF AMERICA
#14387

**DAVID CALDWELL**

COLLECTOR OF BEER, BOCK
MALT LIQUOR, ALE CANS

CAPITAL CITY
CHAPTER

6616 BAY TREE LANE
FALLS CHURCH, VA. 22041

---

Compliments of
**THE BEER CAN MAN**
TED ROBINSON
FOURTH AVENUE
ABSECON HIGHLANDS, N.J. 08201
PHONE (609) 652-1421

**This is a Free Ticket**

──○○○──

It's Not Good For Anything

It's Just Free!

---

THE JACKSON
CAN MAN
Monitors CH.  19

Dale Fisher
1108 Donnely Rd.
Jackson, Mich.
49201

Beer Can Collector,
Trader, Drinker and
Rooter.
BCCA #7771

---

MEMBER OF THE RAINIER CHAPTER

Buy Local Beer - Keep'em Brew'in

GREG ERWIN
BCCA #12649

"Keep on
Collect'in"

(206) 588-5682

8214 Bridgeport Way
Tacoma, Wa. 98499

# Wall of Wine Labels

Every year, Baron Phillipe de Rothschild commissions a famous artist such as Marc Chagall, Robert Motherwell or Andy Warhol to design the label for Chateau Mouton Rothschild wine. While they may not have any of these works of art, Sandra and Victor Friedman do seem to have collected almost every other kind of label from wines that they have enjoyed at home and abroad. In 20 years, they have amassed several thousand labels—practically every bottle they have shared, except those wines too bad to be remembered. The labels are pasted on the kitchen walls and arranged by type—Pouilly Fumé and Pouilly Chablis to the right, red Burgundy to the left—and by country: South America, Australia, Greece, Italy, Germany and, of course, France. To avoid carting around empty wine bottles, they ask the restaurant to remove the label for them (by soaking the bottle in warm water) while they finish dinner. The Friedmans use white glue to paste the label on the wall, and after the label has aged on the wall a few weeks, they cover it with a thin protective layer of plastic.

# SMOKING

## Save Them, Don't Smoke Them

Dr. Robert E. Kaufman believes cigarettes should be collected, not smoked. He has approximately 7,130 different kinds from 167 different countries, stored in corked, plastic or glass tubes (bought by the thousands from a manufacturer of tubes he found through the Yellow Pages), and installed in homemade racks that are all over the walls. The cigarettes are grouped according to country of manufacture and catalogued alphabetically by country.

Among the unusual cigarettes are many closed at one or both ends; old ones marked 1885 to 1900; several brands that light by striking the end of the cigarette pack; and those wrapped in rice paper, flax, straw or tendu leaf. He has prisoner-of-war cigarettes and cigarettes that belonged to Emperor Karl of Austria and King Farouk of Egypt. He has many mentholated, some perfumed and a few medicated to "relieve" asthma; brands flavored with cola, honey, rum, coffee, lemon and cloves. The smallest is 1¼ inches long. The longest is an 11-foot cigarette that was made to save excise tax, intended to be cut into four cigarettes. Dr. Kaufman almost missed out on this

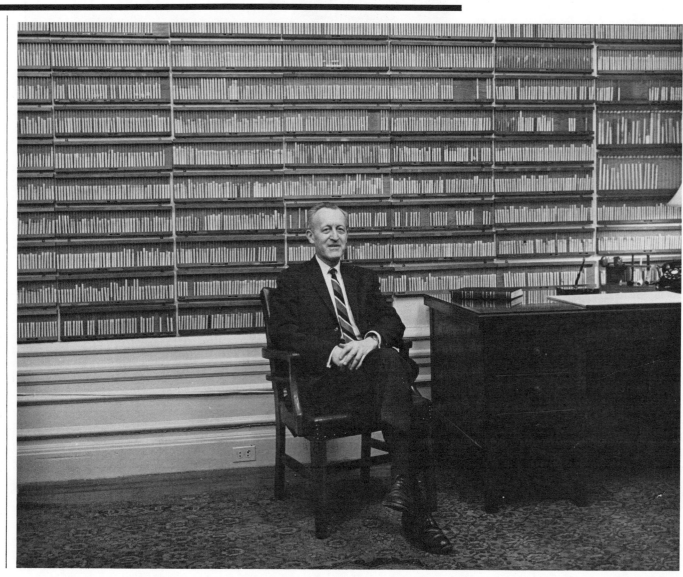

one. He didn't acquire the cigarette when it first became available and had to wait 20 years for another chance; this he got at an antique shop where he finally found one inside its pack. More packs survive than cigarettes, so there are more pack collectors than cigarette collectors. He trades with one such collector in Denmark—cigarettes for packs. He also obtains cigarettes by writing to governments and cigarette companies.

How did this madness start? With a college joke 50 years ago. Someone asked how many American cigarettes there were, he started looking around, went to Europe, found a few there, and so it went, ending with a collection so unique that it is mentioned in *The Guinness Book of World Records.*

# Phillumenia

Whether it's covers from Chinese restaurants or Holiday Inns, jewelites (covers that sparkle) or matcharamus (covers with full-color photos), collecting matchbooks is a hot hobby. The true followers, as opposed to the gatherers who save matchbooks mostly as souvenirs, call themselves phillumenists. They avidly trade at local club meetings and national conventions, worldwide and through the mail. Standard-size books or covers have 20 (regular), 30 (aristocrats) or 40 (royal flash) strikes or matches.

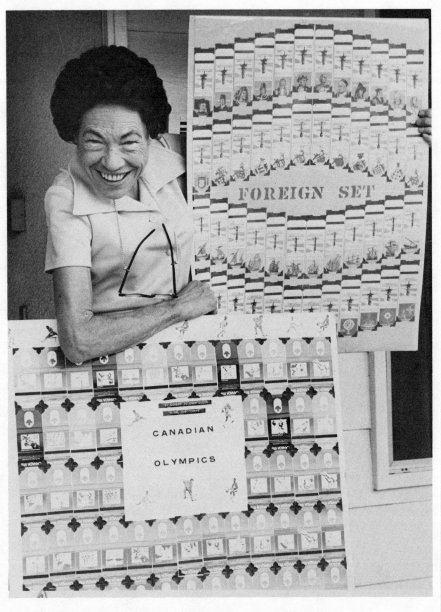

(Photograph by Ignacio Nanetti, *The Register*, Santa Ana, California)

Scarce, and thus sought after, are the odd strikers (the striker is in an odd place) and the odd sizes (''midgets'' made in the Depression to cut costs, smaller in length and with only eight matches).

**MITZI BRADBURY, PRESIDENT,**

The Golden Orange Matchcover Club (and a member of 11 others) holding two sets from her collection, one foreign and the other consisting of 105 Canadian Olympics covers (21 covers in each of five colors). The club included this in their bulletin about Mitzi: ''When Ted and I were first planning marriage, he said the matches must go. The women's lib movement started then and there. I still have my matches and Ted is becoming a full-fledged collector . . .'' The majority of the club's members are under 16. For information, contact Mitzi at: 1457 Westmont Drive, Anaheim, CA 92801.

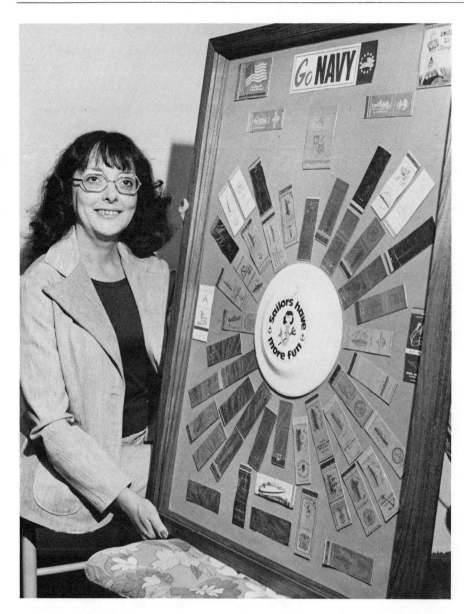

*Award-Winning Collection of Navy and Early Ship Covers.*(Member of Golden Orange Matchcover Club)

**THE FLAME OF POLITICS** John Larsen's collection includes covers from Presidential planes, helicopters and yachts like *Air Force One, The Independence* (Truman), *The Julie* (Nixon) and *The Honey Fitz* (J.F.K.). He also has inaugural and campaign covers, including those for Presidents when they were running for lesser office, and some from the White House itself. One bears the inscription "Stolen from the desk of FDR." But his most prized is an advertising, special-event cover with a photograph of Harry Truman and Richard Nixon together, arm in arm. This was made by Steinway for the Washington, D.C., National Press Club "Roast" in 1956. It says: "Harry S. Truman and Richard Nixon bury their hatchets in a Steinway, official state piano to the White House since 1908." Truman was furious and had the matchbooks recalled immediately by the F.B.I., but an avid collector managed to rescue and pocket two of them.

*Card from Long Beach Matchcover Club* lists typical categories of covers that are collected.

| Last (Please Print) First | | ☐ I am a General Collector. | |
|---|---|---|---|
| Name _____ | | My "Specialities" are checked below: | |
| Address _____ | | ☐ All types ☐ Sets ☐ Features, intact | |
| City _____ | | ☐ Full books ☐ Ten–strike ☐ Regular | |
| State _____ | Zip Code _____ | ☐ 21–30 ☐ Royal Flash ☐ 200–240 | |
| ☐ Airlines | ☐ Diamond Quality | ☐ Knot holes | ☐ Small towns |
| ☐ Americana | ☐ Elks | ☐ Matchoramas | ☐ Souvenir |
| ☐ Banks, Trust, S & L. | ☐ Embossed | ☐ Midgets | ☐ Sports |
| ☐ Best Western | ☐ Fairs | ☐ Navy Ships | ☐ Transportation |
| ☐ Bowling Alleys | ☐ Foilites | ☐ Odd Strikers | ☐ Travelodges |
| ☐ Cameo | ☐ Foreign | ☐ Patriotic | ☐ Trucklines |
| ☐ Chinese Restaurants | ☐ Fraternal | ☐ Pearltone | ☐ V.A. Hospitals |
| ☐ Christmas | ☐ Full length | ☐ Personalities | |
| ☐ Classiques | ☐ Girlies | ☐ Political | Printed by: |
| ☐ Colleges | ☐ Group One | ☐ Radio & TV | Long Beach |
| ☐ Contours | ☐ Hillbilly | ☐ Railroads | Matchcover Club |

(Collection U.S. Tobacco Museum)

## Institutions

*The U.S. Tobacco Museum*, 100 W. Putnam Avenue, Greenwich, CT (adjacent to the company's corporate headquarters). Open to the public, this museum houses all kinds of tobacco-related artifacts, from snuff boxes to spittoons as well as over 1,000 rare pipes, including examples of African pipes and Oriental opium pipes; and pipes crafted from clay Meerschaum, jade, silver, wood, Staffordshire and other china.

*The Arents Tobacco Collection*, New York Public Library. Consists of printed works, manuscripts and other rare materials from 1507 to the present, concerned directly or indirectly with the history of tobacco.

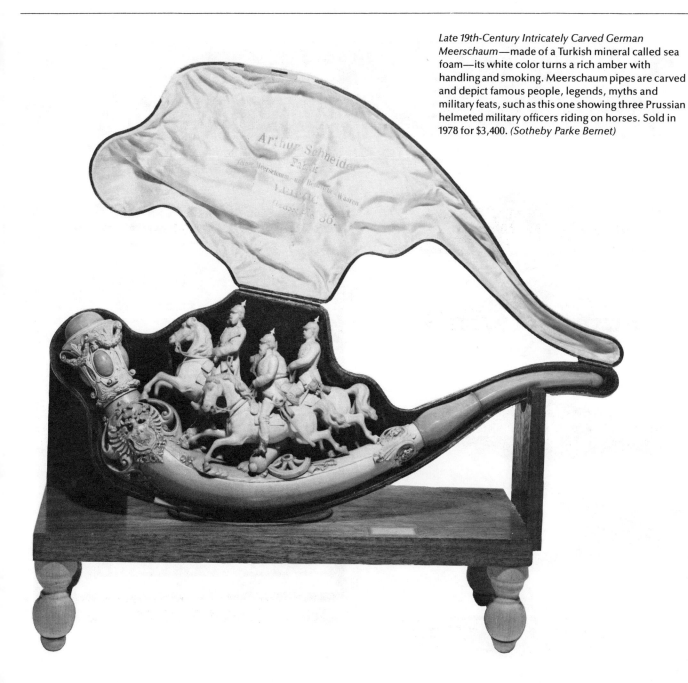

*Late 19th-Century Intricately Carved German Meerschaum*—made of a Turkish mineral called sea foam—its white color turns a rich amber with handling and smoking. Meerschaum pipes are carved and depict famous people, legends, myths and military feats, such as this one showing three Prussian helmeted military officers riding on horses. Sold in 1978 for $3,400. *(Sotheby Parke Bernet)*

## Collecting Clues

- A beginning collector should have several of the same cover—"dupes" for trading.
- To store matchcovers, carefully remove the staple, leave the striker, flatten under a heavy book, then put in scrapbooks—either a store-made album especially for covers or a homemade version—with paper or cellophane pages slit near the corners of the cover. Covers can also be attached with photo corners, but never use glue (it will ruin the text on the underside and it is too permanent; covers should be removable for trading).
- Sort according to size or style, alphabetically according to place, or any combination of these.

## Organizations

*Rathkamp Matchcover Society,* c/o Esther Rancier, 1312 E. 215th Place, Carson, CA 90745. The largest club. (Membership $5; FREE sample issue of newsletter *Voice of the Hobby* with SASE and 50¢ handling.)

*Empire Matchcover Club,* 3131 Knights Road, Building 1, Apt. 15, Cornwall Heights, PA 19020 (membership $3). Current president Bill Holman collects convention, foreign, Bicentennial, souvenir and political covers. He particularly likes old and rare covers; he has some that advertise long-forgotten cigarette brands of the twenties and the only cover, he believes, made for a dinner given by New York City to honor the first three flyers to cross the Atlantic, dated May 1, 1928.

# Cigar Band and Brand Box Labels

An early start paid off for Myron Freedman. His collection of 60,000 bands and 1,000 labels was begun in the 1930s when he was in grade school, and now it is so complete that only a few extremely rare items are missing. It is stored and displayed in three-ring loose-leaf binders, mounted in the same manner as stamps. Freedman is secretary of the International Seal Label and Cigar Band Society. Its members come from all over the world, he says, and collect and trade labels from beer, wine, liquor, cheese and matches, among others. Write to him at: 8915 E. Bellevue Avenue, Tucson, AZ 85715 for a free sample issue (with SASE) of the newsletter (include 50¢ for handling).

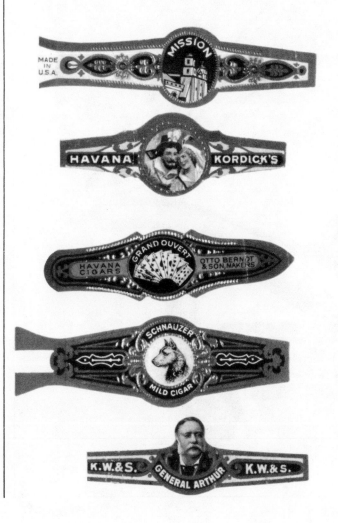

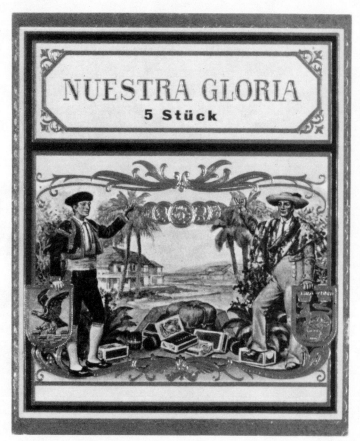

*Phillip Morris Standing Ashtrays.*

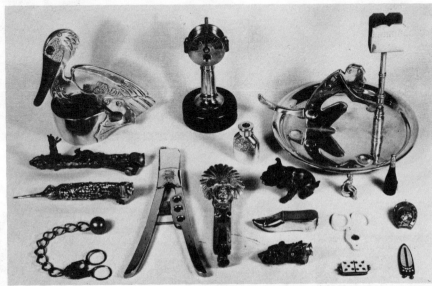

*Cigar Cutters,* 19th century. *(Collection of jewelry designer Lucy Feller and M. Richard Feller)*

*Cigar Vending Machine*—Coin is inserted which activates the mechanism in the center; this goes back and forth, then pierces and delivers the selection.

## Publications

*The Pipe Smoker's Ephemeris,* 20–37 120th Street, College Point, NY 11356. Published by The Universal Coterie of Pipe Smokers, this is an "irregular quarterly for pipe smokers and anyone else who is interested in its varied contents" (articles on cigar store Indians, clay pipes, cigar bands, tobacco tins appeared in a recent 30-page issue). Publication costs are absorbed by editor-publisher Tom Dunn, assisted by any contribution, financial or otherwise, that readers wish to make.

*Cigarette Pack Collectors Association,* 61 Searle Street, Georgetown, MA 01833 (bimonthly newsletter *Brandstand,* subscription $5, FREE sample issue with SASE)

*Assorted Tobacco Tins* and other packaging, some attached to the wall with two-sided adhesive or displayed in a restaurant supply pie case. *(Collection of Conrad Firestein)*

*Display of Packs* at National Textile and Tobacco Museum in Danville, VA, during CPCA convention.

# BURIED TREASURE

## Nuts About Date Nails

Nails with dates forged on their heads, or date nails, were used by railroad and later by utility companies between 1910 and 1940, to record the age of the ties they were driven into. Believe it or not, there are over 5,000 people who collect date nails and one of them, Glenn Wiswell, has almost that many nails in his collection. He personally discovered each one by hunting along the abandoned railroad beds and tracks of this country, Canada and Mexico.

A born accumulator, he collected coins, soda bottles and matchbooks early on. Then he literally stumbled into nails when he accompanied a friend on a search for insulators. While the friend looked up (to the top of telegraph poles), he looked down and discovered the date nail. Although he is New York corporate executive, he has a blossoming mini-business as an outgrowth of his hobby. Wiswell has co-authored the definitive guide *Date Nails Complete;* its table of contents, shown here, indicates the breadth of the book and the subject. Copies are $15 postpaid from WESIS Publications, 29 Meadowbrook Lane, Cedar Grove, NJ 07009. But for openers, Mr. Wiswell will send you a free copy (with SASE) of his booklet *A Brief Look at Date Nails*. To those planning to try the hobby, Wiswell gives this word of warning: "Anytime you walk on railroads you are trespassing—it's private property but it's almost never enforced. However, collectors may want to get permission before starting out."

DATE NAILS COMPLETE

by

Glenn Wiswell    and    John Evans
TDNCA #361           TDNCA #421

### TABLE OF CONTENTS

*The Union Pacific Railroad used a nail to show the length of ties at switches.*

*Some utility companies would drive in a nail to show the height of the pole.*

*The Illinois Central Railroad used a different shaped head for each year in case the numbers became illegible.*

Date Nails Mounted on a Board. (Collection of Glenn Wiswell)

*Buffalo, Rochester & Pittsburgh RR* Steel, round indent
*P-pine, RO-red oak, M-maple*

*Maryland & Pennsylvania Railroad* Aluminum, round indent

## Organizations

*Texas Date Nail Collectors' Association,* 405 N. Daugherty Street, Eastland, TX 76448 (membership $7.50)

Personalized Date Nail Plaque of Harlan (H) B. (B) Freyermuth (F), wife Doris (D), 1917, his birth year (17), 1926, her birth year (26), his birth month, September (9), her birth month, October (10).

**A COMMITTED CANAL BUFF** Harlan Freyermuth, the man who got Wiswell started "Mrs. Wiswell may not appreciate this—may, in fact, sometimes want to shoot me!", collects canal spikes, other canal collectibles and information on how canals operate, and he believes his hobby is unique. Mr. Freyermuth, a chemist by training, obviously likes to dig up dirt. At first he collected insulators. This led to collecting date nails which, in turn, led to collecting canal spikes (forged spikes and cut nails that held the gates of canals). He searches for spikes along the towpaths and among the debris of the rotted remains of locks and cribbing—mostly at the Lehigh and Delaware Canals in eastern Pennsylvania. Even though they are very rusty and 125 to 150 years old, he likes the patina of age and doesn't believe in cleaning them (which can be done with hydrochloric acid).

**BRICKS** Harlan Freyermuth also collects bricks by hunting around New York City, northern New Jersey and eastern Pennsylvania. He has found building, paving and fire bricks with the names and/or locations on the face or edge. (In the 19th and early 20th centuries, local factories often had the name of the maker, city or state incorporated into the design of the bricks.) Freyermuth suggests keeping this collection outdoors unless a fireplace will be built with them.

*Canal Buff Harlan Freyermuth* with some of the more than 180 different canal spikes in his collection.

# Glass Insulators

The Plains Indians were the first collectors of insulators, those colorful round glass shields that protect the wiring on telegraph, telephone and utility poles. They believed an evil force lived in the poles, so they frequently pulled down the poles and destroyed them. But they kept the insulators, which became a symbol of the enemy, the white man, and the object of their war dances. Today, insulators are collected for far different reasons. There are over 3,000 different types, many of which are quite valuable. Insulators are made in glorious colors: aqua, emerald green, amethyst and amber, as well as clear glass; and in assorted shapes, named for their appearance: beehives, coolie hats and hot cross buns. While insulators can be bought, it is more common to look for them in fields (on or around fallen poles) or along abandoned railroad lines, by digging, and even by illegally scaling telephone poles (one such scavenger is considerate enough to replace the stolen insulator with a duplicate from his collection). As they grow in popularity as collectibles, glass insulators become harder to find. Now that most lines are going underground, fewer insulators are made—adding to the challenge, say collectors.

*Glass Insulators. (Collection of Harlan Freyermuth)*

# Indian Artifacts

While Mr. Freyermuth is off at the canal, Mrs. Freyermuth is hunting at home, along the Delaware River, for local Indian artifacts left thousands of years ago by the Leni-Lenape tribe. Her collection consists of several thousand pieces: arrowheads, spear points, pottery, stone drills, scrapers, axes, celts, pipes, mortars and pestles, ceremonial objects, and stone tools and implements, all carefully catalogued according to sites and mounted in frames. Her interest has expanded from just collecting to excavating In-

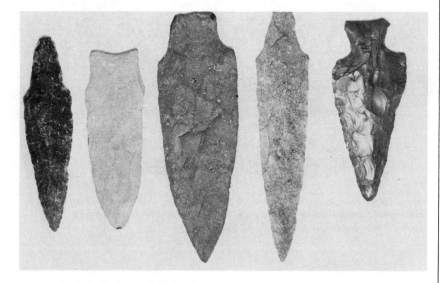

*Artifacts from the Freyermuth Collection.*

dian village sites in the area, and she belongs to the Society for Pennsylvania Archeology, local chapter 14. Joining an archeological group is important, Mrs. Freyermuth says, because not only does it make a collection more meaningful and scientifically valuable, but it also provides a source of further study through letters, publications and organized chapter digs. Surface hunting is simple and cheap: "You just 'go over' a plowed field softened by rain," she says, but there can be risks:

*"One day while I was surface hunting for Indian relics in a sand and gravel pit, a very polite state trooper came over to me and said, in a very quiet voice, 'Are you lost?' I said, 'No, I was just looking for Indian artifacts.' He said softly, 'You are?' I knew he was about to escort me out in a straitjacket and I could hardly keep from laughing. Again, in an unbelieving voice he said, 'Have you found any today?' 'Oh, yes,' I said, 'I found two hammerstones' (these look just like stones but show signs of battering from hammering). Well, I did finally convince him but I do suppose that I looked very odd climbing around in the pit examining rocks. However, in that same place, some months earlier, I found my 'first grooved axes.'"*

Hazards aside, both Freyermuths enjoy collecting Indian relics because of the fresh air, the anticipation of a treasure hunt and the constant education, and because they feel that they are contributing in some small way to the history of their area.

## ARTIFACT HUNTING CLUBS

Hunting for coins, bottles and other buried treasures is such a popular pastime that many clubs exist for the purpose of sponsoring group shoots. Armed with metal detectors and screwdrivers, members can pursue the hobby almost anyplace, and afterwards sit down to a convivial dinner with fellow shooters (in some clubs, new members get a free dinner and club patches for their jackets).

*Grooved stone axe head.*

### Publications

*DIG* (subscription $5). A newsletter about collecting Indian artifacts; everything about the hobby, including an article on "How to Start and Organize Your Own Home Museum" in a recent issue. Published by the Indian Shop, ·Box 246, Independence, KY 41051. Mr. von Hillard, the publisher, who also sells old authentic artifacts, publishes a catalogue and a wholesale book list, and will send a large packet of introductory literature for $1.

THE INTERNATIONAL
# BARBED WIRE GAZETTE
FOR THE BARBED WIRE COLLECTOR AND FRONTIER HISTORIAN
COW PUDDLE PRESS — SUNSET, TEXAS 76270
COPYRIGHT 1971

*Cover of Gazette*—Lyle Linch with a ball of barbed wire 5'6" in diameter, 17 feet in circumference and weighing 1,690 pounds. It can be seen at his Echo Barbwire Museum, 406 E. Butler Drive, Phoenix, AZ 85020.

# Barbarians

**A SHORT HISTORY OF BARBED WIRE** Three inventions are usually mentioned as having "Won the West": the revolver, the repeating rifle and barbed wire.

With a scarcity of trees, stones and other native materials, another cheap source of fencing was needed on the western prairies. "Bobbed Wire" was the answer—not, however, without a measure of violence.

Although many have claimed to have invented barbed wire, we must rely on patent application dates to determine who was first. In 1867 William D. Hunt of New York was the first applicant to receive a U.S. patent for barbed wire. Although Lucien B. Smith of Ohio received a patent prior to Hunt, the date of his application was later than Hunt's. Neither Hunt's nor Smith's wire was put into production, however.

In 1868 Michael Kelly patented his "Thorny Fence." Although not produced until eight years later, it was the earliest effective barbed wire and the first patent to have two strands of wire twisted together. In 1871 Lyman Judson received a patent on a flat hoop wire; however, it was too impractical.

The barbed wire revolution was triggered in 1873 by H. M. Rose's display at the De Kalb, Illinois, County Fair of his newly patented wooden rail with short wire points or spikes extending outward.

Three men, Jacob Haish, Isaac Ellwood and Joseph Glidden, all from De Kalb, saw the display and within months had patents on separate types of wire fencing with barbs, and a new industry was born. The three, along with John "Bet-a-million" Gates, a salesman for Ellwood and Glidden, became the first of the barbed wire millionaires. By 1900, more than 400 U.S. patents had been issued on barbed wire fencing as others tried to "cash in" on this new industry.

Barbed wire was first used to fence in farmland to keep cattle grazing on the open range *out*. Settlers blocked off a lot of the best grazing land and water holes which were needed by both the farmers and the cattle ranchers. The result was range wars and hardship until the mid-1890 when barbed wire was accepted and used by the cattlemen to keep their livestock *in*.

The best history on barbed wire is probably Henry D. McCallum's book *The Wire That Fenced The West*, (University of Oklahoma Press), and is recommended as a fantastic story—of big stakes, high tempers and patched fences.

*Reprinted from California Barbed Wire Collectors Association brochure)*

*Illustrated page from The Barbed Wire Bible V.*

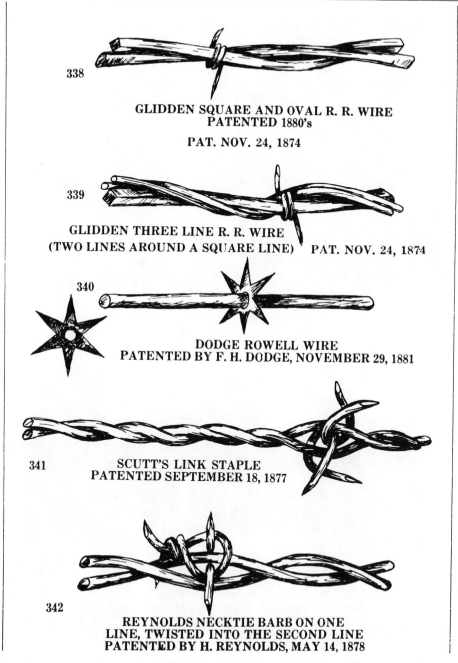

338 GLIDDEN SQUARE AND OVAL R. R. WIRE PATENTED 1880's
PAT. NOV. 24, 1874

339 GLIDDEN THREE LINE R. R. WIRE (TWO LINES AROUND A SQUARE LINE) PAT. NOV. 24, 1874

340 DODGE ROWELL WIRE PATENTED BY F. H. DODGE, NOVEMBER 29, 1881

341 SCUTT'S LINK STAPLE PATENTED SEPTEMBER 18, 1877

342 REYNOLDS NECKTIE BARB ON ONE LINE, TWISTED INTO THE SECOND LINE PATENTED BY H. REYNOLDS, MAY 14, 1878

## Collecting Clues

• Dan Sowle of New Mexico is an experienced collector who has over 1,600 different pieces valued at 25¢ to $400 each. "Barbed wire is bought sold and traded mostly through the mail, but some is acquired at barbed wire shows held by 12 different associations in 11 states, all west of the Mississippi. Trading is the most fun. Someone can find a roll or two of old wire in a dump, identify it, chop it into 18-inch pieces and have something to trade. (A collectible piece of wire is 18 inches with the barbs equal distances from the ends of the lines so that the wire will look uniform when displayed, usually on a board 2′ × 4′.) The value of wire is determined by the quantity produced, not the age. Metal detectors may uncover a buried piece while the remnant of a fence might be found hanging from an old post."

Members of the *California Barbed Wire Collectors Association* with winning entries. Charles Sawyer, Los Banos, California (above) first-place winner and William Pereira, Riverdale, California (above right), second-place winner (*Photographs by Glenn Winner*)

Charlie and Rosie Dalton of Sequin, Texas with portion of extensive collection.

## Publications

*The International Barbed Wire Gazette*, Jack Glover, Sunset Trading Post, Sunset, TX 76270 (monthly subscription $7.50, FREE sample issue with SASE)

The Barbed Wire Bible V: *An Illustrated Guide to Identification and Classification of Barbed Wire* (Cow Puddle Press, $7.95 postpaid; address above).

*National Barbed Wire Trader*, c/o Vernon Allison, 2912 Loraine, Ft. Worth, TX 76106 (subscription $7.50)

## Organizations

*California Barbed Wire Collectors Association*, c/o Ellwyn Carlson, 1046 N. San Carlos Street, Porterville, CA 93257 (membership $5, initiation $2.50)

*New Mexico Barbed Wire Collectors Association*, 108 Camino Crucitas, Santa Fe, NM 87501 (membership $5; bimonthly bulletin, *Wire, Barb & Nail*, sample copy 75¢)

*National Insulator Association*, 3557 Nicklaus Drive, Titusville, FL 32780

*Howard Nelson with a Wormley Cane* valued at $1000.

# SPORTS SOUVENIRS

Sports have been the nation's favorite recreation for the past 200 years, but only in the last 10 years have collectors of sports memorabilia organized and lifted the hobby from the elementary school playground to large conventions where thousands of dollars change hands. Within just a few years, two major publications and numerous clubs have been formed to service these collectors. Although trading cards have always been the favorite collectibles, objects ranging from hockey jerseys to programs and including autographs, team glasses and baseball caps, are now avidly collected.

## The Baseball Broker

Among the millions of children and adults who collect baseball cards is George Lyons, a Wall Street stockbroker. His collection would be the envy of the kids who gather around the local candy store after school. In a feature story in *Americana* magazine, he said, "Most people don't understand how anyone can pay so much for a baseball card, but when you're a

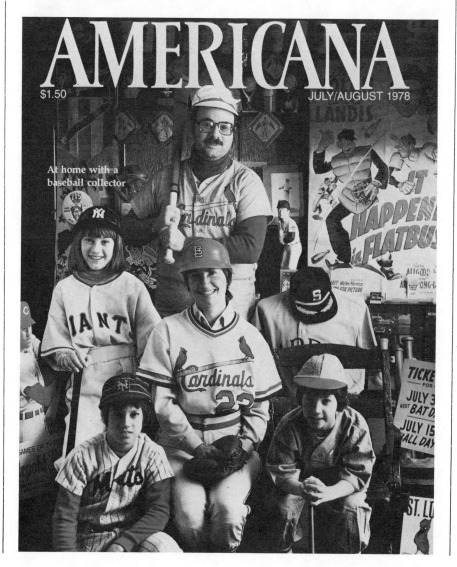

fan—and I mean a knowledgeable fan—cards like these come to life, they carry meaning. I've been a fan since I was a kid, and my first card convention was like my first burlesque show—I went crazy." George Lyons has branched out into other areas of baseball collecting. He has a baseball signed by Babe Ruth and a cap worn by Cy Young, in addition to many uniforms and other autographs.

*George Lyons and Family* pose in their suburban New York home surrounded by assorted baseball memorabilia from Lyons' collection. The stadium seats are from Sportsman's Park in St. Louis. The poster behind Lyons is for the 1942 film *It Happened in Flatbush*, which was about the old Brooklyn Dodgers. *(Americana, photograph by Bill Ray)*

## The Most Valuable Baseball Cards

Though new cards can be bought for pennies, older and rarer cards can cost hundreds and even thousands of dollars, particularly those recalled or with errors.

**1910 HONUS WAGNER**—Its rarity (only 12 were released) derives from the fact that Wagner demanded the recall of the card (published by the tobacco company Sweet Caporal), which made it seem as though he endorsed cigarette smoking. Today, in good condition, the card can bring $3,000 or more.

**1910  EDDIE PLANK**—Printed by Sweet Caporal, the plates for this card broke during production, making it worth around $1,900.

**1934  NAP LAJOIE**—Issued as a special edition in 1934 by the Goudey Gum Co. when several collectors complained of Lajoie's omission the previous year. It is worth approximately $1,500.

**1977  LOU PINELLA**—Age and skill of the player does not always determine value. In 1977, when a picture of the Yankees was taken, Pinella was the only player missing. The owners of the team protested and insisted that a separate card of Pinella be issued. It now sells for about $20.

*Baseball Cards and Autographs*—Collector Bruce Levy trades by mail to improve his collection, bypassing dealers. He acquires autographs by haunting ball parks and the hotels where teams stay. He stores his collection of over 1,900 items in photo albums with acetate sheets, in card file "boxes," and generally "all over the house."

**BOB VEACH**
OUTFIELD, DETROIT AMERICANS

**HARRY HEILMANN**
OUTFIELD, DETROIT AMERICANS

*Rare Baseball Cards. (Metropolitan Museum of Art, Jefferson R. Burdick Collection)*

*Rare Candy Insert Card. (Metropolitan Museum of Art, Jefferson R. Burdick Collection)*

## Collecting Clues

- As is the case with most collectibles, cards are more valuable when collected in sets. Thus, the 1910 card of Honus Wagner, which is part of a valuable set, is worth more than many far rarer cards issued as singles.
- One collector we interviewed buys cards with an eye to the future. He gambles on a young player's success by stocking his cards before they get too expensive.
- Hockey, basketball and football cards, which have come out only recently, are usually far less expensive than baseball cards; therefore, they may be more fun for collectors with little money to spend.
- Many items such as bats and caps can be bought from the teams. One collector was even given a pair of sneakers belonging to basketball star Bill Russell by the club trainer. In any case, a call to your local ball club can't hurt.
- Baseball cards can be bought in sets at great savings from most dealers. However, be

*Dizzy Dean Watches. (Collection of Robert Lesser)*

prepared to sacrifice the thrill of opening a pack of cards to find your favorite ball player or the missing card of a series.
- Addresses of sports stars can be obtained from hobby publications and other collectors. When asking for an autograph, always be polite and send a SASE.
- The first year a player appears on a card is generally the most valuable, but other factors such as rarity and condition of the card are also important.

## Publications

*Sports Collectors Digest*, Stommen Publications, 409 North Street, Milan, MI 48160 (subscription $9 for 24 issues; FREE sample issue). Designed for the novice collector. Features articles on all facets of the field, addresses of sports stars (to send for autographs) and tons of ads.

*The Trader Speaks*, 3 Pleasant Drive, Dept. FH, Lake Ronkonkoma, NY 11779 (subscription $9, FREE sample issue with 75¢ handling). Geared to the more experienced collector. Forbids advertising of reprints and exposes dishonest dealers and collectors.

*The Baseball Advertiser*, T.C.M.A., Box 2, Amawalk, NY 10501 (FREE sample issue)

*Sports Collectors News*, Rt. 1, Somerset, WI 54025

*Baseball Bulletin*, 286 Penobscot Bldg., Detroit, MI 48215

*The Sport Hobbyist*, Box 3731, Detroit, MI 48215

## Collecting by Mail

*Autographed Baseball* ($4.99) from Martin Friedman Specialty Co., Box 5777, Baltimore, MD 21208 (FREE catalogue with 25¢ handling, of political, sports and musical memorabilia.

# Golfing

**THE JIM NEWSOME COLLECTION** in Sun City, Arizona is noted for its quality and, as can be seen, is displayed with taste and beauty. His library contains all of the masterpieces of golf literature, his ball collection includes an *"Alan"* and a *"Gourlay"* and among his clubs are *"Philps"* and *"McEwans."* The golf caps, lined up on the top of the bookcase at left, represent each of the Clubs that hosted The British Open and the British Amateur since the first tournament in 1860.

*Advertisement*, dated 1923.

FOR HIS CHRISTMAS

THE **FRISK AUTO CADDY**

A distinctive and practical gift for the Golfer - Motorist. Instantly clamps to the running board of any type of car. Carries any style of golf bag. Eliminates discomfort to passengers. Protects upholstery and finish and adds to the appearance of the most elegant car.

$25.00

from your dealer or direct from Thos. E. Wilson & Co.

*"Rides on the Running Board"*

THOS. E. WILSON & CO.

NEW YORK    2037 Powell Ave. CHICAGO    SAN FRANCISCO    *Indispensable to the Golfer-Motorist*

*There is Wilson Equipment for every sport*

# A Bout with Boxing

Marvin Sloves won't go to a fight to see boxers. But he doesn't have to, because his office is filled with them. In one corner there's Jack Dempsey—that is, a life-size cardboard version. And in all the other corners and on the walls and shelves, the memorabilia of other boxers and fights are displayed. The reason for Sloves' interest is understandable—his father was a featherweight fighter from 1917 to 1921. But the collection was almost accidental. When friends saw his father's relics around, they started giving Sloves other boxing items. Since he likes to shop, it wasn't long before he began adding to these himself. The collection is so large now that it is divided between his office and home (where he has bronze statues of boxers, 19th-century English commemorative plates, scrimshaw with pictures of boxers, and more).

*Corner of Marvin Sloves' office* showing antique boxing prints, autographed photographs, posters; on the table, boxing gloves from the Tony Canzonni–Al Singer lightweight fight in 1930; boxing buttons; a bottle in the shape of two boxers; and a punching bag, a gift from partner Ed McCabe with his picture on it (Sloves is supposed to punch the bag when he feels like punching the partner).

*A Portrait of the Collector as a Boxer.*

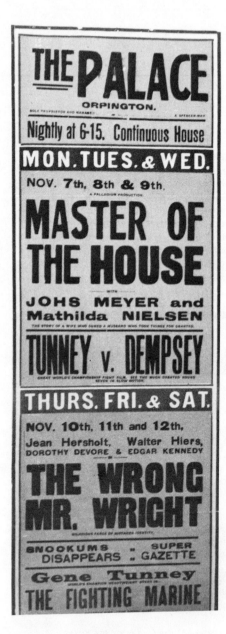

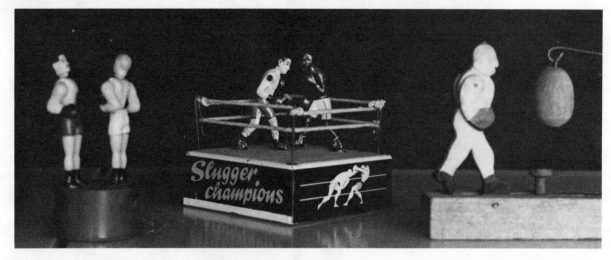

Closeups: Boxing Toys; Punch-out Games, Books and Autographed
Photographs; Trading Cards; Advertisements; Poster; Old English Buttons.
(Collection of Marvin Sloves)

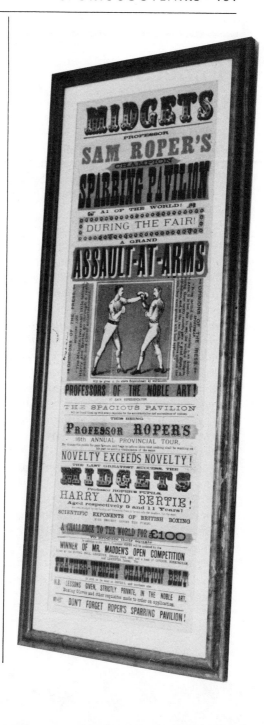

# Homecoming Badges

Anyone who has an interest in sports memorabilia might consider the merits in a localized collection, says Phillip M. Pollock, collector of Iowa State homecoming badges, or pinback buttons. He writes:

*"Most universities and colleges have used badges or ribbons as an integral part of their homecoming tradition. They form a rather personal collection because they remind the collector of his or her school or home town and are an exciting collectible because they can be located virtually anywhere (most of mine were acquired miles from the Iowa City campus) rather cheaply. I have seen the familiar coaching faces change on the buttons, along with the fate of the team, the Iowa Hawkeyes (whose greatest triumph was in the late fifties when they won two Big Ten championships and two consecutive Rose Bowls). The early designs—printing techniques, use of color and script—appeal to me, as does the archaic football gear of the twenties and thirties pictured. Completing the entire series of years could be incentive enough for me and other Iowa sports enthusiasts."*

A Large Celluloid Team Badge issued from 1909 to 1922, before the homecoming badge; *First Official University of Iowa Badge,* 1924.

*Hawkeye Player* graces the most desirable and rarest of all Iowa State Badges, 1928. Although 22,000 badges were issued, they are the hardest to find and many collectors in the Iowa area have paid handsomely for them, according to Mr. Pollock. *Typical Headgear* shown on a 1933 badge; *Coach Iri Tubbs,* 1937; *1939 Badge* popular and relatively common; *Coach Forest Evashevski,* 1953. *(Collection of Phillip M. Pollock)*

## Institutions

*National Baseball Hall of Fame,* Cooperstown, NY 13326

*Football Hall of Fame,* Canton, OH 44711

*Golf Collectors Society,* 638 Wagner Road, Lafayette Hill, PA 19444

*The International Tennis Hall of Fame,* Newport, RI 02840

*Boxing Hall of Fame,* 120 West 31st Street, New York, N.Y. 10001

*Sports Pennants behind a bunk bed. (Collection of Robert and Matthew Fogelson)*

*Sports Illustrated magazine covers. (Collection of Sidney Rabin)*

# SKIRTS AND SHIRTS, HATS AND SPATS

## Historical Hats, Hoods and Headdresses

With Tilly Mia Weitzner around, you'd better hang onto your hat—if she wants it, she may just walk up to you on the street and make you an offer! The result of her hankering for hats—which she often wears—is an extraordinary collection of over 400, including a headdress that belonged to Sitting Bull; a 19th-century Chinese executioner's hat with red silk cords (one for each victim); a Yemen hood of gold, silver and semi-precious stones that belonged to the Queen of Sheba 3,000 years ago; Anastasia's tiara; a Middle Eastern head "bank" made of real coins; and a 1,000-year-old Chimu ceremonial headdress from pre-Inca Peru, made from human hair. In addition to these museum-quality hats of historical and cultural note, Tilly collects "fashionable" hats, Victorian through the 1940s, from all over the world: France, Holland, Japan, China and South America. And to accompany her hats, Tilly Mia collects antique clothing and accessories, lace,

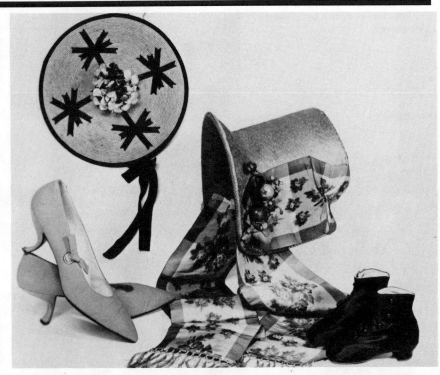

*Hat, Bonnet, Ribbon Ties, Pumps and Boots (Collection The Museum of the City of New York)*

*Antique Hat Molds*

gloves and "fun" jewelry. These appeal to her because of their "look," superior construction, workmanship, material and overall quality. As if she had nothing to wear, she also collects 18th- and 19th-century Chinese embroidered silks—dragon coats, robes, capes, skirts, emblems. The embroidery is so spectacular—with rich color and gold threads—that even if the article is in tatters, pieces or panels of it are often worth rescuing and framing. She advises dry-cleaning old clothing and embroideries; but if the piece is too far gone for the cleaner, Tilly Mia says the safest thing is to wash it with cold water detergent and then to lay it flat and perhaps iron it carefully on the wrong side.

**HE'S ALWAYS CHANGING HATS** Hat collector Robert Murch wears what he collects—hats acquired on trips, including unusual souvenirs such as a Portuguese sardine fisherman's cap and an English Bobby helmet. He also collects military and sporting hats, all arranged geographically or by occupation.

**CHINESE COOLIE HATS** Marguerite Johnstone specializes in inexpensive, contemporary Chinese hats (from local import shops) which she collects for their "golden color" and "lovely texture," and to use as decorations (along with Chinese baskets). She relates to the hats emotionally as well as visually, and feels that "the varied and intricate workmanship belongs to the last peasant handicraft in the world, and is an occupation of universal importance in China today."

*Coolie Hats* hung on dark red entrance hall walls. Also shown: *Chinese Fans, Tea Caddy* (under table) and *Wedding Basket* (in corner). Mail is "hidden" under the hat on table. *(Collection of Marguerite Rule Johnstone)*

# A Designer's Shoe Collection

Coty award-winning shoe designers Herbert and Beth Levine have a natural affinity for feet, and a large collection of miniature shoes and related objects that they have "accumulated" (not collected, they stress) over years of travel. Their prize possession is a snuff box from the French Revolution dated 1770, with a fleur de lis design and the inscription *Elle est une, indivisible. (Collection of Herbert and Beth Levine)*

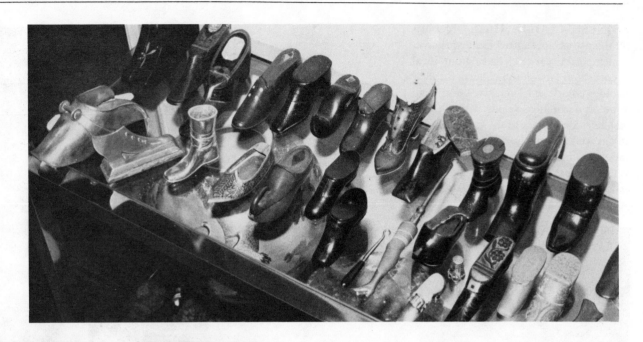

*Beth Levine's Personal Collection of Favorite Designs.* Collections of their shoes are in the Metropolitan, Smithsonian and Brooklyn Museums.

# Shoes of Celebrities

(Left to right) Satin shoe worn by Julie Andrews in *My Fair Lady*; leather sandal worn by Yul Brynner in *The King and I*, 1957; leather tap shoe worn by Eleanor Powell; velvet shoe worn by Richard Burton; leather boot worn by Mary Martin in *Peter Pan*, 1951; satin shoe worn by Irene Castle in *Watch Your Step*, 1951; ballet slipper worn by Marcel Marceau; leather shoe worn by Fred Astaire; leather shoe worn by Robert Preston in *The Music Man*, 1956; satin shoe worn by Marilyn Miller in *Sonny*, 1926; satin pump worn by Chita Rivera in *Bye Bye, Birdie*, 1961; satin shoe worn by Vera Zorina in *On Your Toes*, 1936; sandal worn by Martha Graham. *(Collection of Arthur Edelman and Capezio Shoes, from the exhibition "The Great American Foot" at the Museum of Contemporary Crafts of the American Crafts Council, 1978).*

*Assorted Small Shoes* that are also bottle openers, tape measures, pincushions, matchcases, ashtrays, salt and peppers, and beautiful intricate shoes that were shoemakers' models (detail above). *(Collection of Jane and Arnold Ginsberg)*

*Fine Snuff Boxes* on Art Deco stand.

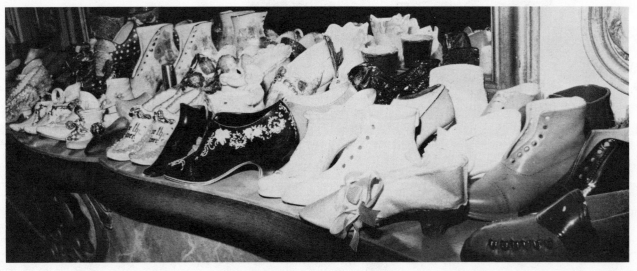

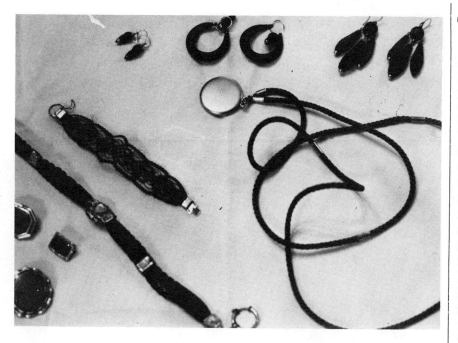

*Earrings, Bracelets* and *Necklace.*
*(Collection of Cecily Firestein)*

# Accessories

Hair work jewelry was popular first in Europe and then the rage around the middle of the 19th century in America. The last word in romanticism, the hair of a beloved one could be worked into elaborate mementos. It was not unusual for a man to carry a watch chain made from his sweetheart's hair, or for rings of the hair of someone recently deceased to be distributed among friends and relatives (sometimes referred to as "mourning jewelry"). Hair ornaments were made to order. But to assure authenticity, many Victorian ladies learned to do-it-themselves, and a popular drawing-room recreation evolved. As *Godey's Lady's Book* reported, "Of the various employments for the fingers lately introduced among our country women, none is perhaps more interesting than hair work, a recent importation from Germany, where it is very fashionable."

*Tortoise Shell Hair Combs*—Assembled around the middle of the 19th century by Joseph Fleischer, founder of the famous hairpiece company, these combs were handed down in the family (and some were given as gifts to royal clients, including the Queen of England).
*(Collection of Paul K. Fleischer)*

# Canes

Cane collecting has its roots in antiquity; in fact, Pharaoh Tutankhamon's tomb was filled with his collection. The most popular canes incorporated useful items into their design: watches, snuffboxes, stilettos, swords, daggers, umbrellas and long glass vials for a quick nip (called "nipsticks"). Cane-collecting specialties are: canes that belonged to famous men; canes from special places; and Presidential canes, such as the Carter cane with a peanut on top and the F.D.R. cane, extremely rare because it was quickly withdrawn from the market due to its obvious bad taste.

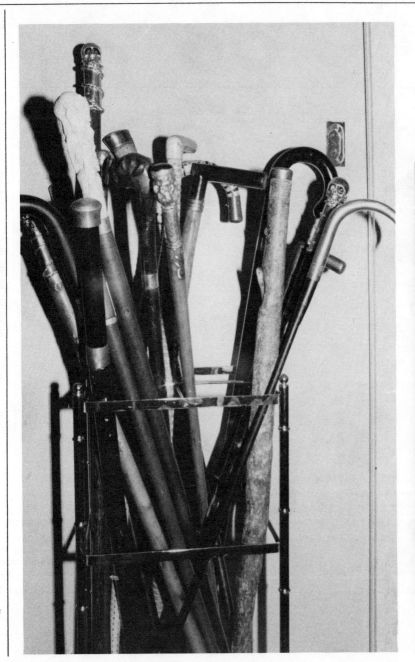

*Cane Collection*—a cane with a poacher's gun inside, two sword canes, a cane made on a whaling ship from shark vertebrae, the cane of a Japanese medicine man, several turn-of-the-century canes with skulls. *(Collection of Dr. Frank Miller)*

*William March "Boss" Tweed's Gold Tammany Tiger Cane* (the tiger was the symbol of the Tammany political organization). *(Museum of the City of New York)*

*Old Ties.*

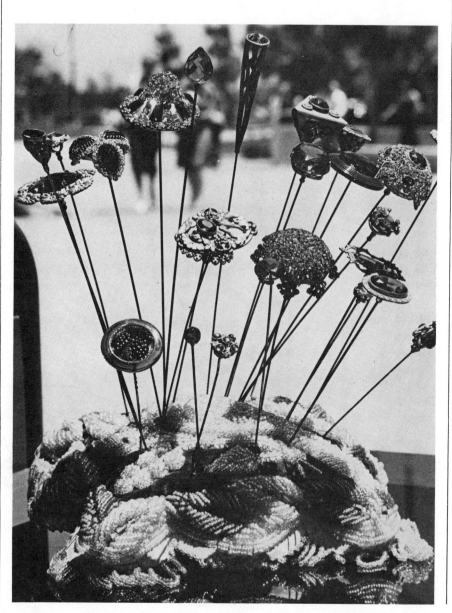

*Hatpins c. 1860–1920. (Collection Lillian Baker photograph by Ygnacio Nanetti)*

## What Other Collectors Collect

- *Gloves*–One collector has assembled over 400 gloves of historic interest dating from the 17th century to the present, and consisting of military, court and hunting gloves; 19th-century American cowboy gloves; and gloves that belonged to saloon or dance hall girls.
- *Ice Skates*
- *Hatpins and Hairpins* of famous actresses
- *Shoe and Belt Buckles:* gold, silver, silver plates, brass and other metals, decorated with precious stones or cut glass, or engraved, and in a variety of shapes—square, round, oval and rectangular

## Organizations

*Costume Society of America,* % Costume Institute, Metropolitan Museum of Art, New York, NY 10028

*International Club for Collectors of Hatpins and Hatpin Holders,* 15237 Chanera Avenue, Garden, CA 90249 Membership $15 FREE sample copy newsletter, 50¢ SASE

*Antique Eyeglasses* in a chrome and glass baker's cabinet *(Collection of Conrad Firestein)*

*Old Egyptian Beads* hung from "pushpins."

*Antique handbags*

# Buttons

Buttons originated as collectibles in antiquity and did not become fasteners until the Middle Ages. Worn as ornaments, they were collected for their beauty and value. Historians note that Louis XIV could barely stand upright under the weight of clothes decorated with gold buttons encrusted with diamonds, rubies and emeralds. In America, the colonists collected buttons to use over and over as an economy because buttons from Europe were expensive. In the 19th century, buttons were collected on strings like charms, and silver buttons were used by Navajo Indians as currency. Practically all art forms and events in history are repeated in miniature on buttons, in every shape, size and material. The National Button Society recognizes 400 classifications, any one of which would make a fascinating collection: dress and uniform buttons; shoe and coat buttons, theatre and opera buttons; buttons of cats, dogs, frogs, insects, food, buildings; buttons with pictures of movie stars, poets, playwrights and Peter Rabbit; buttons of the thirties plastic, shaped like butterflies and Mickey Mouse. Materials include: metal, wood, leather, glass, shell, precious stones, gold, silver, silk, plastic, pewter, coal, rubber, bone, enamel, jade, tusk, horn, pearl, shell, Wedgwood, Delft, Dresden, Meissen, china, crystal and shades of glass (milk, camphor, clam and black).

*Antique Buttons*—lithographed, mid-19th-century French court figures with metal decorative rim (top); *18th-century English paintings* on ivory (bottom). (*Collection of Diana Epstein*)

**JUST BUTTONS** Sally Luscomb began button collecting as the result of a radio program called *Hobby Lobby*. Aired during the Depression for people with time on their hands, the program was about low-cost, accessible hobbies. While many took up button collecting and the hobby boomed in that era, it is doubtful that anyone carried it as far as Sally Luscomb. She has thousands of buttons of every conceivable kind from all over the world. She has produced audio-visual programs and written *The Collectors Encyclopedia of Buttons;* she now operates the Just Buttons Museum and publishes *Just Buttons Magazine* (bimonthly subscription $5, sample copy $1). Address of museum and magazine: 45 Berlin Avenue, Southington, CT 06489.

## Collecting Clues

- From a collector's point of view, a button without a shank is not a button. Neither is a button that was not made to be sewn on a garment.
- To find buttons, look in your old aunt's button box, in her attic, on her old clothing; ask the dry cleaner if you can help him clear out his drawers.
- To display a button collection, use heavy thread to sew buttons onto stiff cardboard (the standard display size is 9″ × 12″ and can be covered with black velvet) or attach shank buttons by inserting them in a hole punched in the board and securing with a cotter pin, pipe cleaner or paper clip.

## Organizations

*National Button Society*, c/o Lois Pool, 2733 Juno Place, Akron, OH 44313 (membership $10; sample copy of *The National Button Bulletin* $1)

*Just Buttons Museum; 18th-Century Buttons* framed and displayed over antique desk in museum; *18th-Century Set*—painting on ivory under glass. *(Collection of Sally Luscomb)*

**TENDER BUTTONS** Many collectors start with a hobby and end with a business. Diana Epstein did the reverse—she bought a button shop before she became really interested in the field. Now she is a recognized authority, author of *Buttons* ($9 postpaid from her museum-like store, Tender Buttons, at 143 East 62nd Street, New York, NY 10021). Ms. Epstein says that many collectors concentrate on the pre-mass-production button of the 19th century or even rarer ones of the 18th century which can cost upwards of $100. But many 19th-century buttons can be had for $10 or less, and for the beginning collector there are worthwhile modern buttons (any button made after 1900) for a modest price. Rare Washington inauguration buttons, hand-engraved on copper, brass or silver plate, are the most coveted by collectors and also the most reproduced.

# WORKS OF NATURE

The best—and often most decorative —things to collect can be free. Natural objects like shells, minerals and butterflies are all around, waiting to be cared for and collected, to be appreciated for their beauty as well as for their scientific interest.

## In Search of Shells

The most beautiful and exotic shells are out in the open sea, many buried deep beneath the rocks; and you will have to take up scuba diving to find them. Those less adventuresome or more landlocked can look for shells during low tide and/or after a storm, under rocks and buried in the sand (they sometimes leave a ''trail,'' so follow it and dig where it ends). After you've found some special shells, carefully boil to kill any animals inside and remove them, if necessary; to whiten, deodorize and disinfect use houschold blcach; thcn polish thc shells with baby oil.

If you'd rather buy shells, be aware that their prices can, like non-natural collectibles, fluctuate wildly depending upon popularity and availability.

*Shinbone Tibia Shell, Turrid Shell; Regal Thorny Oyster.* (Dover Scientific Company)

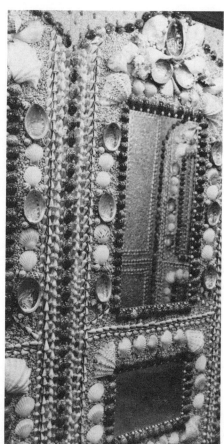

*Shells decorating mirrors in foyer.*

**ROYAL BEACH COMBER** Prince Albert I of Monaco (1848–1922) was an enthusiastic collector of both microscopic shells and giant clams weighing as much as 200 pounds.

# Lepidoptera

Some collections are limited by cost, by the availability of the objects, or by the time it takes to collect them; in a collection of lepidoptera no such limitations exist.

*"From March through September, on any sunny day, some butterflies will be flying; and on misty days eggs of caterpillars can be collected for rearing and to provide perfect specimens. In the U.S. and Canada, there are approximately 10,000 species of moths and 700 species of butterflies. The goal of many collectors is to have at least one male and one female of each species (either moths or butterflies or both), if not the numerous subspecies and forms of species. This hobby keeps the collector out of doors and healthfully exercising on sunny days, and in bad weather happily engaged in spreading and labeling and admiring his latest catch."* —Jo Brewer, lepidopterist.

It's all in the family—Dr. William David Winter, Jr., collects and is an expert on New England moths while Jo Brewer studies and photographs the life cycle of butterflies, lectures often, and edits the news of the Lepidopterists' Society. Jo has also written *Butterflies*, published by Harry Abrams, Inc. Together they have collected the butterflies of Sana Belle Island, Florida. They enjoy having

Rare butterfly. Ornithoptera Zalmoxis. *(The Butterfly Company)*

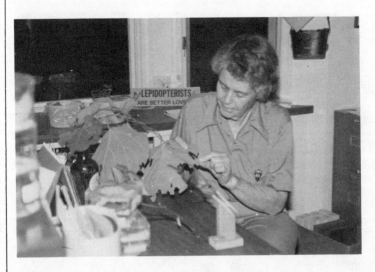

**Jo Brewer** with Butterflies, Caterpillars and Rearing Equipment.

others take pleasure in and learn from their work, and they look forward to the day when their collections may be available to the public and on view at museums.

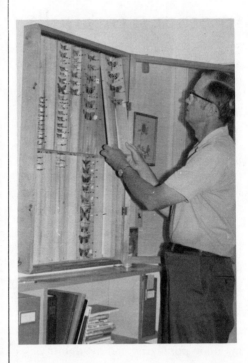

*Screened Wall Case for Drying Butterflies* on spreading boards.

**RIKER MOUNTS**—A low cost display mount made of heavy board, cotton filled with a glass cover to show off your specimens. The specimens are placed on the cotton bottom section and the glass upper section closes down over it to make a compact and safe haven for your collection. It has a ring for hanging on the wall. Riker mounts are also ideal for displaying rocks, minerals, fossils, gems, coins, medals, etc.

| Stock No. | Size | Price |
|-----------|------|-------|
| R-101 | 4 x 5 | 2.50 |
| R-102 | 5 x 6 | 3.00 |
| R-103 | 6½ x 8½ | 5.00 |
| R-104 | 8 x 12 | 6.00 |
| R-105 | 12 x 16 | 10.00 |

* Butterflies not included
NOTE: 20% discount on Riker mounts ordered in 1 doz. lots of each size.

*Display Cases or Riker Mounts* made of heavy cardboard and cotton, with glass cover, for coins, medals, buttons, jewelry, matchbooks and any other small collectible; also available from *The Butterfly Company*, 51-17 Rockaway Boulevard, Far Rockaway, NY 11691.

**THE BUTTERFLY COMPANY**   Whether you collect and mount your own or want to purchase a collection, The Butterfly Company, the world's largest dealer in moth, butterfly and insect specimens, can help. To give you an idea of what they do, I quote from their catalogue:

*Dear Customer,*

*Here is our new price list for your 18-page color catalog, showing well over 900 specimens of butterflies, moths and beetles. Please note we have added additional non-illustrated listings of sets, collections, and fine specimens. Since the insects are not manufactured, the supply and availability of any specimen constantly changes. However, specimens are arriving daily from all parts of the world. If you are interested in any particular species not listed in our catalog, or species marked "not available," please send us your want list and we will gladly quote you prices on those specimens we might have.*

*Our address is: 51-17 Rockaway Beach Blvd., Far Rockaway, N.Y. 11691. Telephone (212) 945-5400. We will have one of the nation's largest collections on exhibit. We would like you to come and pay us a visit. The only thing we ask is that you telephone first so we know when to expect you. We will gladly give you simple travel instructions. WE WANT TO SEE YOU–PHONE FIRST!*

*ALL SPECIMENS ARE SOLD WINGS CLOSED, UNMOUNTED. All specimens, unless otherwise noted, are first quality material. 1B quality where indicated means slight imperfections. Please give all information when ordering–catalog number, name, sex where necessary, price, etc. Please give alternate choices. As mentioned before, the stock of material is constantly changing. We may be out of your first choice in some cases. If no alternates are given, we will issue a credit voucher. No returns accepted without our prior written permission.*

*COLLECTORS AND BREEDERS–we are interested in buying or trading for first quality butterflies, moths, beetles, insects, spiders, live cocoons and chrysalids, etc. in QUANTITY ONLY. Please let us know what you have and we will make an offer.*

*If you have any questions concerning entomology and especially lepidoptera, please feel free to contact us. Your satisfaction is our goal.*
*(catalogue $1)*

### Collecting Clues

- According to Bernard D. Abrera and as reported by *The New York Times,* the butterfly has become the unlikely prey of a network of smugglers and black marketeers. With some endangered species now protected under an international covenant, an illegal and highly profitable trade in rare butterflies has sprung up. Even before it came under government protection, a giant birdwing butterfly whose wing span can exceed 12 inches brought $1,500 at auction and $1,800 on the black market. The major market for illicit butterflies is comprised of private collectors in the United States and Japan, many of whom specialize in a certain family of insect.
- Beetle and butterfly collectors often exchange specimens with collectors in other parts of the country and the world.
- Buy and use the Peterson "Guides"—*Field Guide to Butterflies,* etc.

**BIRD LISTING**   There are approximately 645 breeding species of North American birds, and Barrington Parker III has seen about 250 so far. He keeps track by listing the first sightings of each in a diary, along with the time, the place and relevant observations. With the help of a field guide, most birds can be recognized by their coloration and behavior, and birds in flight by their silhouette and the way they fly. The Audobon Society has a Rare Bird Alert telephone number (212-832-6523) in New York which recently reported that a prothonotary warbler was in the area of The Ramble in Central Park. Although Barrington spends a lot of time birdwatching in the park, he never did find this particular bird. And he is still searching the skies for the broadwing and sharpshin, to complete his list of hawks.

# Gems, Minerals and Fossils

There are many shows, clubs and organizations for those who like to collect minerals or fossils (the remains of plants and animals found in rocks) and many sites to be explored, as indicated by this clipping from a recent issue of *Gems and Minerals Magazine* (right).

*Shopping at a Gems and Mineral Show.*

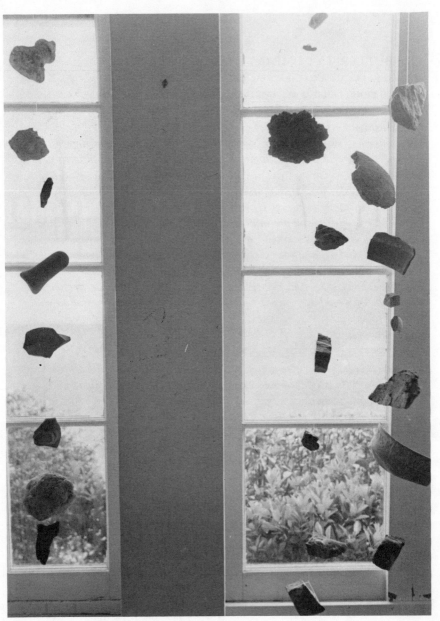

Rocks hung from fishing line, displayed in window.

# NEWS NOTES OF COLLECTING AREAS

**Important! Please Note.**

Notes in this column are obtained from a variety of sources believed to be reliable. They are published in good faith as a service to readers. Publication here does not constitute permission to collect at any area mentioned. Permission MUST be obtained before entering any private property. Corrections or additions to notes in this column are always welcome.

When collecting petrified wood on public land, remember to observe the limit in the amount set by law. In addition, remember H.E.L.P. Help Eliminate Litter Please!

Information for this column should be addressed to:

GEMS AND MINERALS
Editorial Department
P.O. Box 687
Mentone, California 92359

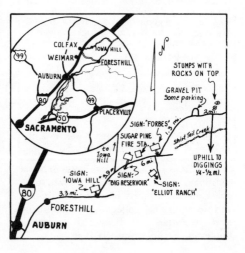

# Preserving Pine Cones, Leaves or Herbs

Early spring, before green leaves are injured, and early fall, as soon as the leaves have turned color, are the best times to collect. Cut leaves from a lower branch and get two specimens so that you can show both the front and the back. To remove moisture, press between two blotters (or sheets of newspaper) in a heavy book with additional weight on top. Mount in a scrapbook or frame with date and place noted. Pine cones should be thoroughly washed and dried on a radiator.

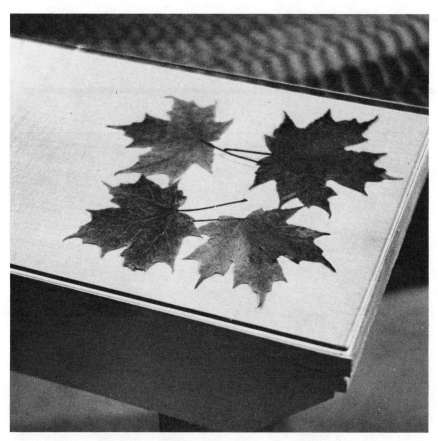

*Leaves* preserved under glass-topped table.

## Publications

*Collecting Rocks*, U.S. Geological Survey, 907 National Center, Reston, VA 22092 (35¢)

*Gems and Minerals*, 1797 Capri Avenue, Mentone, CA 92359 (monthly subscription $6.50; FREE sample issue with 50¢ handling)

*Rocks and Minerals*, 4000 Albemarie Street N.W., Washington, DC 20016 (monthly subscription $7; sample issue 75¢)

*Important Trees of Eastern Forests*, Forest Service USDA, Box 2417, Washington, DC 20013 FREE sample issue.

## What Other Collectors Collect

- *Roots* are popular ancient Chinese collectibles now enjoying a renaissance.
- *Spider Webs*—One serious collector keeps spiders in a simulated natural environment, then traps the web they weave between two pieces of glass and frames it.
- A French pharmacist has collected almost all the *Wild Medicinal Plants* in France.
- Someone actually collects the hairs from the tails of . . . elephants!

## Collecting by Mail

*Shells, Fossils, Minerals and Indian Artifacts*, Dover Scientific Corp., Box 6011, Long Island City, NY 11106 (catalogue 50¢)

*Malicks Fossils*, 5514 Plymouth Road, Baltimore, MD 21214 (catalogue $3.00). *Barter Offer:* "If you wish to exchange materials, kindly supply samples, collecting data, and a want list. If you prefer to sell materials, kindly supply samples, collecting data, and your best terms."

*Tropical Shell Institute.* This company will send you a catalogue for $1 and a whole "collection" of 150 shells for $12.95, with $3 postage and handling: Box 21490, Ft. Lauderdale, FL 33335.

## Organizations

*American Federation of Mineralogical Societies*, 6600 Cornelia Drive, Minneapolis, MN 55435

*Mineralogical Society of America*, U.S. National Museum, Washington, DC

*N.Y. Paleontological Society*, Box 287, Planetarium Station, New York, NY 10024

# MUSIC

## Antique Instruments: The Caplin Collection

*"Musical instruments are as basic to knowing a people's culture as the clothes they wore, the houses they lived in and the furniture they used."*

One has only to listen to Lillian Caplin play and re-create the sounds of the period on the instruments in her collection to realize the wisdom of her words. Because they were treasured and cared for, many antique instruments have survived in good condition. Those in the Caplin Collection are not only unique, but also beautiful, the result of a successful collaboration between designer and the musician whose demands he had to meet. Mrs. Caplin says that she collects casually here and abroad, buying from antique dealers who often do not know what they have. She is not afraid to make a mistake as long as it is not an expensive one, and seems to enjoy the thrill of discovering what others might overlook as junk in a box of old parts.

To complement the collection and to add to her wealth of technical informa-

*Instruments* on the living room wall of the Caplin home include (left to right): *Serpent Horn*, probably French 18th century; *Lyre Guitar*; *Base Horn*, 1820, French, with dragon head, ancestor of our modern-day tuba; *Early String Instruments*; *Arch Cittern*, late 18th century; *Wind Instruments* (on the lyre-shaped holder); and on the shelf below, an early 19th-century *Double Flageolet* (English), a *Bow*, a *Bugle* and a *Zither*.

tion, she collects reference books, some quite rare. She also admires, and collects, American folk instruments like the harmonica, dulcimer and pottery flute, which are uncomplicated and straightforward, with little skill required in designing them.

Edison Phonograph (Edison National Historic Site, West Orange, New Jersey).

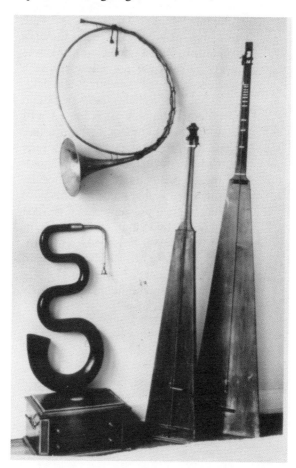

17th Century Hunting Horn, French Serpent Horn c. 1780 and Two Tromba Marina, monocord instruments used to accompany singers in the Middle Ages. (Photograph by Tony Mark, Collection of Lillian Caplin).

# Mechanical Music

Collector Allen Koenigsberg teaches college classics and, in his spare time, collects and writes about vintage phonographs—gramophones, victrolas and records. His speciality is pre-1913, and his prizes include a tinfoil Edison and a bisque-headed talking doll (German, with works by Edison). Mr. Koenigsberg says that collectors in this field are more interested in invention and mechanics than nostalgia,

Zonophone Grand Opera Phonograph with brass horn (plays 78-RPM records). (Collection of Allen Koenigsberg)

which is a good thing since a necessity of the hobby is being handy. Obviously, a working machine has far greater value than a non-working machine. But finding parts and someone to fix a machine may be harder than finding the machine, with the cost of labor higher than the cost of purchase. How did he get started? He saw one at an antique show, looked in vain for information, and became involved as much in the research as in the collecting (he also collects magic lanterns and kaleidoscopes). Mr. Koenigsberg has written a major reference work that documents 8,000 titles on wax cylinders: *Edison Cylinder Records 1889–1913*. He also writes *The Antique Phonograph Monthly*, 650 Ocean Avenue, Brooklyn, NY 11226 (subscription $8.00, free sample issue with SASE). Published 10 times a year, this journal is sent to approximately 1,300 subscribers.

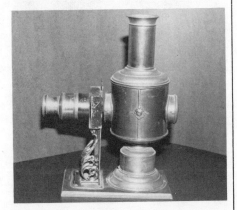

Magic Lantern c. 1890—kerosene burner, colors green and brass. (*Collection of Allen Koenigsberg*)

The famous Phono-Cinema-Theatre of 1900 utilized a L'Eclatant Lioretgraph.

## BEFORE *THE JAZZ SINGER*
### The Spoor Sound-Scriber and its Relation to the Sound Synchronization of Motion Pictures

Part One

T. C. Fabrizio

(Copyright Reserved)

# Golden Oldies: Records and Sheet Music

Like many things of a certain age, rare records—or golden oldies, as they are sometimes called—have come back in vogue. Collectors are interested in a wide variety of records—classical, jazz, opera, musical comedy, rock and roll, demonstrations—for a number of reasons. Some collect for the artist, some for the music itself, some for the performance, or for any combination of these. Rarity is also an important factor; records that are scarce because fewer were pressed can include Broadway shows that were not hits, or records by lesser artists like The Five Sharps, whose 78-RPM version of "Stormy Weather" on the Jubilee label is one of the hottest collector's items in the rock field.

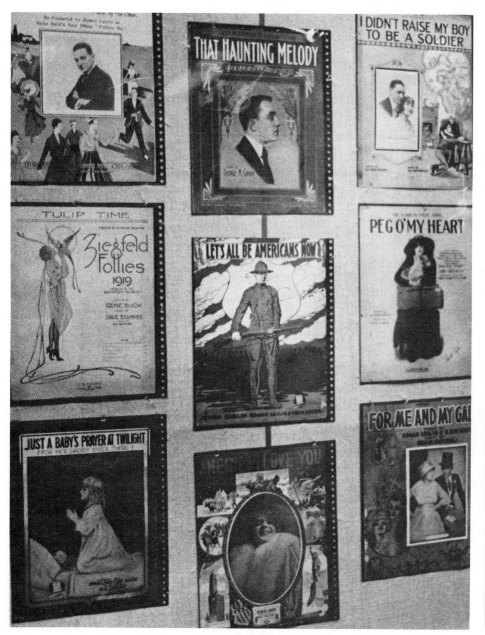

*Old Sheet Music* is collected for the song, style, composer or performer and for the visual appeal of its engraving and lithographs. Shown here: *19th-Century Sheet Music (Collection of Carl Haverlin, BMI Archives)*; *Early 20th-Century Sheet Music* by well-known American artists *(Collection of Abe Olman)*. (On exhibit at Songwriters Hall of Fame, 1 Times Square, New York, New York)

# Two Privately Owned Music Museums

*The Musical Museum*, Deansboro, NY 13328:

*"What began as a family collection of music boxes under the bed and a garage full of phonographs and nickelodeons in the kitchen for the Sanders family grew to a full-fledged museum in 1948 . . . to preserve and exhibit the instruments of our ancestors; visitors crank grind organs, play melodeons, operate early phonographs and enjoy hundreds of instruments."*

*Wiscasset Musical Wonder House* is a 19th-century sea captain's home partially turned into a museum (collector-owner Danilo Konvalinka lives in the back) of mechanical instruments ranging from snuff boxes with music to Victorian music boxes to grand pianos and organs, dating from 1795 to 1929. Konvalinka came to America from Yugoslavia where his father was a clockmaker who fixed music boxes as a sideline and his grandfather was a composer. Here he, too, worked at selling and repairing music boxes, and ultimately at collecting and establishing his museum. Filled to overflowing, the house and its extraordinary contents can be visited only in the summer. But the music from these instruments

*Wiscasset Musical Wonder House*

has been recorded and can be enjoyed all year long; Mr. Konvalinka sells by mail: ragtimes, cakewalks, waltzes, polkas, operas and religious music played by antique music boxes. The address: 18 High Street, Wiscasset, ME 04578.

## Organizations and Institutions

*The André Mertens Galleries*, Metropolitan Museum of Art, New York, New York—to hear as well as see antique instruments.

*Edison Museum at Glenmount*, West Orange, New Jersey

*American Musical Instrument Society*, 132 E. 71st Street, New York, NY 10021 (membership $12.50; FREE sample issue with SASE of AMIS Newsletter, Box 194, Vermillion, SD 57069)

*International Music Box Society*, c/o C.W. Fabel, Rt. 263, Box 202, Morgantown, IN 46160 (membership $10, initiation $5; FREE introductory brochure with SASE

*The National Sheet Music Society*, 1597 Fair Park Avenue, Los Angeles, CA 90041 (membership $8)

## Publications

*Sounds Fine*, The Rock Collectors Marketplace, Box 292, Riverdale, MD 20840 (FREE sample issue with 15¢ stamp)

*Goldmine* (world's largest record collector's publication), Arena Magazine, Box 61 F, Fraser, MI 48026 (sample copy $1)

*Collectors Guide to American Recordings 1895–1925* by Julian Morton Moss ($3.50 paperbound) and *Handbook of Early American Sheet Music 1768–1889* by Dichter and Shapiro ($6.95 paperbound). Both available from Dover Publications, 11 E. 2nd Street, Mineola, NY 11501 (add tax and 50¢ handling per book).

*Popular and Rock Records 1948–1978* by Jerry Osborne (O'Sullivan Woodside & Co., $7.95)

*Musical Instruments in the Metropolitan Museum* (Metropolitan Museum of Art bulletin, Winter 1977/78) includes a small 33⅓ record for $2.95 plus $2.85 postage and handling. Send to: Metropolitan Museum Mail Order Department, Box 255, Gracie Station, New York, NY 10028.

*Musical Instruments of the World* (Bantam, $9.95)

## Collecting by Mail

*House of Oldies*, 267 Bleecker Street, New York, NY 11014 (catalogue $1.50)

*Rare Records Unlimited*, 1723 Lake Street, San Mateo, CA 94403 (FREE sample issue). A collectors' mail-order record service that specializes in music of the fifties:
"We have one of the largest selections anywhere of 1950s Rock n' Roll, Rhythm & Blues, Rock-A-Billy, Blues, and White Doo-Wop on 45, 78, LP. We also list EP's and C&W (fifties) once in a while. Every two months we distribute a completely revised catalogue consisting of about 1,000 selections hand picked from our stock of over 200,000."

*The Vestal Press*, Box 97, Vestal, NY 13850 (catalogue $2). Books and manuals on musical machines, pianos, organs, etc.

*Automatic Musical Instruments*, American International Galleries, 1802 Kettering Street, Irving, CA 92714 (catalogue $3)

*Wiscasset Musical Wonder House*

## What Other Collectors Collect
● At the University of Michigan, Ann Arbor, there is a collection of *American Sheet Music* accumulated by Mr. and Mrs. Bly Corning that relates to historical events, including one of the only nine known original copies of "The Star Spangled Banner."
● Frank Warner, a folklorist, collected more than 1,000 *Songs of the Rural Eastern Seaboard*, including "Tom Dooley" (which he is credited with bringing to public attention).
● Radio collectors collect *Radio Magazines and Catalogues, Old Radios* and parts.

# PHOTOGRAPHICA

## Concealed and Antique Cameras

As a science teacher, collector Eaton Lothrop appreciates the technical achievement of cameras such as the box camera, which simplified and made available to the general public at modest cost a previously complex procedure; and the clever detective camera, about which he has co-authored the book *A History of Detective and Concealed Cameras*. (He is also the author of *A Century of Cameras,* and a columnist for *Popular Photography Magazine*.) His collection is diverse and includes some fine early cameras, more recent personality or novelty cameras, and ''go-withs'': film boxes, signs, advertisements and other literature. Lothrop's wife, Jean, has related collections: gold and silver charms in the shape of cameras, and small figurines holding cameras.

*Walkers Pocket Camera* c. 1881—a small boxlike camera.

*Quarter Plate Daguerreotype Camera* c. 1854, with some of the accessories necessary for making photographs. *(Photograph by Harvey Zucker)*

(Left to right) *Butchers Reflex Carbine* 1920s, the *Junior Reflex* 1912, and the *Brooks Reflex* 1932.

*Premo Reflecting Camera* 1905.

*Bullard Folding Magazine Camera* 1899.

*There is really nothing sacred, nothing that should be out of a collector's interest range. As the world delves more deeply into the history of photography, new areas in which photographers have concentrated will open up, to be of increased interest to collectors. Just as the camera is able to record infinite subjects, so will collectors be faced with infinite choices to make.*

*Specialization, therefore, will be the name of the game in future photography collecting, dealers and many collectors themselves forecast. With rising prices for historic prints, broad-based collections with first-quality images from 1839 up to the present will be harder to afford, or to put together even if funds are unlimited.*

*But what will be possible, and in many ways a great deal more fun for collectors, is to narrow in on one precise area of fascination, or on one school of photography.* –Landt and Lisl Dennis, in *Collecting Photographs: A Guide to the New Art Boom* (E.P. Dutton)

*(Items pages 208–209, Collection Eaton Lothrop)*

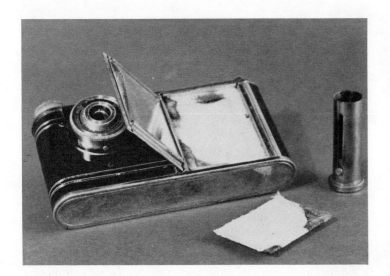

*Detective Cameras (clockwise):* Petite Vanity Camera; and Tisdell and Whittelsey Box Camera 1887; Book Camera 1893; Sovill and Adams Echo 8 Camera Lite.

*Personality Novelty Cameras*—cowboy star Roy Rogers and two different models of the Hopalong Cassidy.

*Charm Bracelet* with miniature cameras from all over the world, collected by Jean Lothrop.

*Two Mick-a-Matic Cameras*—the earlier model (left) has the ear acting as a shutter release.

*Other Camera Novelties:* Kodak toy truck, pins, film box.

# Vintage Photographs

**GIRLS DRESSED IN FLAGS** Keith de Lellis, like many others today, collects old photographs—daguerreotypes, tintypes, cartes de visite, stereoviews—but his specialty is singular and patriotic. As he puts it, ''In my search for 19th-century photographs (which has been going on since he was 15), I stumbled upon a daguerreotype of two girls dressed for a Fourth of July pageant in the 1850s. It has become one of my favorite photographs and spawned an interest in obtaining similar likenesses.'' He says that his flag ladies satisfy his combined interests in photography, history and antiques; and that he spends most of his spare time pursuing them at antique shops, shows and flea markets.

*An Early Daguerreotype* of two ladies decked out for a Fourth of July pageant. It is a highly tinted image by an anonymous photographer, c. 1853.

*A Tintype* of a girl in a patriotic outfit by an unidentified photographer, c. 1868.

## GLOSSARY OF VINTAGE PHOTO-GRAPHIC IMAGES

**Daguerreotype**—an early form of photography dating from 1837 to about 1860. The image was made on silver-coated copper plates, one at a time. Often delicately framed in leather and velvet cases trimmed with brass, the pictures of famous people and historic events are now in demand.

**Tintype** or **Ferrotype**—picture taken on lacquered iron (less expensive than daguerreotypes).

**Cartes de visite**—picturing famous people and places, made in large quantities in the 1860s and 1870s; meant to replace calling cards.

**Stereographs** or **Stereoviews**—double pictures of the life of the times which were put in viewers; popular at the turn of the century.

*Variation of the Goddess of Liberty* theme c. 1865 (*Photograph by Charles D. Fredricks*)

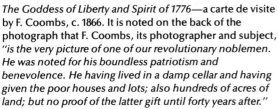

*The Goddess of Liberty and Spirit of 1776*—a carte de visite by F. Coombs, c. 1866. It is noted on the back of the photograph that F. Coombs, its photographer and subject, *"is the very picture of one of our revolutionary noblemen. He was noted for his boundless patriotism and benevolence. He having lived in a damp cellar and having given the poor houses and lots; also hundreds of acres of land; but no proof of the latter gift until forty years after."*

*Carte de visite* c. 1865

**THE SAMUEL WAGSTAFF PHOTO-COLLECTION** Samuel Wagstaff has, through his somewhat unorthodox approach, taken the mystique out of photograph collecting. In a recent exhibition of works selected from the several thousand photographs in his collection, nearly 80 percent were unfamiliar examples by major names. The point was made that all photographs should be appreciated, and that even the most mundane sources hitherto overlooked—such as trade and scientific books, commercial publications and publicity files—can produce giants (of which Wagstaff has many, including a Thomas Eakins for which he paid $9,000).

To quote from an interview with Wagstaff in *People Magazine*, ''Chances are that if you knew nothing you are going to pick out exactly the same favorite photo as the guy who knows the most.''

*Old Photographs* at a flea market cost under $1.

*Hippopotamus, Regents Park, 1852. (Photograph by Count De Montizon) (Courtesy Grey Art Gallery, New York University)*

**PORTRAITS OF MILITARY MEN**
Collector Dr. Mark Koenigsberg holding *The World's Largest Military Daguerreotype* alongside a half-plate daguerreotype of two frontiersmen with rifles and knives. The mammoth plate, measuring $9\frac{1}{4}'' \times 11\frac{3}{4}''$, shows a uniformed sergeant with sword and shako of the historic Seventh Regiment of the New York State National Guard. The image is contained in its original gold-leaf frame and was taken around 1854.

# Leica, the Cult Camera

For all the collectors who joyfully and freely share their ideas and information, there are others who jealously guard their privacy. This appears to be true of Leica collectors. For reasons of security, perhaps—Leica cameras and equipment are expensive—they are reluctant to talk, and shun publicity, which they certainly do not seem to need anyway. Leica was always a popular camera with photographers and a symbol of quality; now it is also highly sought after by collectors. Leica enjoys an unusual mystique shared by no other camera in the world, so much so that the "software"—brochures, ads, original catalogues and instruction books—are also heavily in demand. To service the growing number of enthusiasts, many books have been written and clubs organized, and The Leica Historical Society of America has branches all over the world.

## What Other Collectors Collect

• *Photographs of Photographers' Self-Portraits*
• Matthew Isenberg, who has a museum-quality collection of photographica, is now collecting *Stereo Cards* that depict the history of his home state of Connecticut.
• George Gilbert, well-known author of books about camera collecting, has a collection of *Sub-Miniature Cameras* dating back to 1893.
• *Photographs of New England Chimneys*

# PHOTOGRAPHICA

Volume X, No. 10      A publication of the Photographic Historical Society of New York      December 1978

*First passenger flight from New York to Washington, D.C., September 1919.*

## Focusing on Aviation's 75th Anniversary

## FREE Sample Publications

*Photographica*, Box 1839, Radio City Station, New York, NY 10019. Publication of Photographic Historical Society of New York, Inc. (Subscription included with membership, $17.50; FREE sample copy with SASE.)

*Shutterbug Ads*, P.O. Box 730, Titusville, FL 32780 (subscription $5, free sample copy with 50¢ handling). A monthly publication that carries classified ads of those who want to buy and sell photographic equipment and new or out-of-print photographic books. It is a useful price-guide, listing at least what is being asked, if not what is being paid.

*Photographic Memorabilia*, P.O. Box 351, Lexington, MA 02173 (subscription $3, FREE sample copy with SASE). *A Camera Collectors Newsletter* is a quarterly publication offering cameras and books for sale, published by Myron Walt. He is also the author of *Blue Book Illustrated Price Guide To Collectible Cameras, 1839–1979*. Hundreds of photographs and listings, in complete technical detail and with comments as to collectibility and historical value. Articles on each category of camera comment on the historical significance, rarity, investment value, counterfeit efforts and so on ($9.95, check only).

## Collecting By Mail

*Janet Lehr*, Box 617, Gracie Station, New York, NY 10028. Catalogues $6 each: 19th and 20th Century, American landscape (Eakins, Sieglitz, Weston . . . ); photographically illustrated and reference books, albums, manuscripts; American photographs 1918–1950 (Hine, Steichen, Lange, Rothman . . . ).

## Institutions

*George Eastman House*, Rochester NY 14607

*International Center of Photography*, New York, NY 10028

# CAMPAIGN COLLECTIBLES

## Political Memorabilia and Buttons

*"The history of our nation is politics. Political memorabilia provide a means by which young and old can relive and experience the lively art of politics."* —Richard A. Budie, Publisher, *Campaign Americana.*

Political history is reflected in the myriad objects that can be collected under the umbrella of political memorabilia, going back to the early 19th century and rising and falling in value with the political fortunes of those portrayed. Buttons are the most widely collected item, but others include: pins, badges, prints, cartoons, ballots, lists of candidates, plates, mugs, vases, posters, flags, photographs, sheet music, umbrellas, hats, jewelry, combs, handkerchiefs, banners, posters and bumper stickers. Some people collect by candidate, others by era or party. There are fewer Republican buttons than Democratic ones. Many button collectors have subspecialties such as tabs, coattails, jugates (buttons that pair the picture of a Presidential candidate with his running mate), local candidates and losing candidates.

*Recent Presidential Buttons* offered for sale by Douglas Hoehn.

*Rare Abraham Lincoln Ambrotype (Campaign Americana)*

# Left-Wing Causes

John A. O'Brien is the coordinator and founder of *The Cause Newsletter* and *Cause Chapter* of APIC (American Political Items Collector) and has over 7,000 left-wing cause buttons in his collection: 1830s anti-slavery tokens (predecessors of buttons); 1930s anti-Fascist buttons; buttons from the suffrage movement and from the Socialist Party of 1900; the Scottsboro Boys, Eugene Debs and Tom Mooney buttons; early Labor peace rally badges; and an Irish Home Rule ribbon. His collection includes thousands of duplicates used for trading. One day he hopes to establish a "people's museum." In the meantime, he keeps his buttons fully catalogued on cards, enclosed in Riker mounts (all inside a file cabinet).

O'Brien says, "Cause items reflect history and change better than the more common candidate pin," and he identifies with the struggles they represent. He would like to hear from other collectors: 1213 N. Highland Avenue, Hollywood, CA 90038.

## The Making of a Collection

Memorabilia that has great personal significance in the home of historian Theodore H. White, author of *The Making of the President* series, *In Search of History*. (Collection of Mr. and Mrs. Theodore H. White)

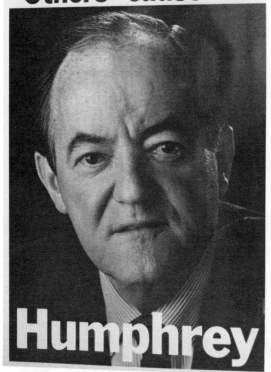

Some talk change.
Others cause it.

Humphrey

THE PRESIDENT

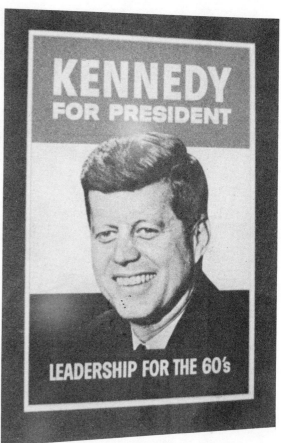

KENNEDY
FOR PRESIDENT

LEADERSHIP FOR THE 60's

*Presidential Plates*—early pieces show Lincoln, Jackson, Cleveland and General Scott, and new pieces have portraits of Gerald Ford, the Kennedys and Eisenhowers; the collection displayed in an antique corner cabinet.

*Official Inaugural Medals for U.S. Presidents*

## Collecting Clues

- Rarity can be more important in determining value than age (a Carter button may cost more than a McKinley button). If the candidate was a loser, fewer items may have been produced, making those that were scarce and expensive—for example, a James Cox for President (1920) can cost $1,200.
- Many pre-1896 items are overlooked, says APIC president Bob Fratkin, and can be bought very cheaply. He lists the George Washington inaugural buttons selling for $350 to $500, and 1840 Harrison tokens, which can go for $5, as particularly good bargains.
- Beware of fakes. Many items have been manufactured recently for the collector rather than for the campaign itself. While some are frankly advertised as new or reproductions, like the Carter peanut sack shown here, others, such as the set of Carter buttons with the names of six possible running mates, are designed to deceive the novice collector. In this case the company—one of the biggest in the business—had made plates with all the possible Vice-Presidential candidates so that it would be prepared to print the winning one as soon as Carter made his choice. With the plates available, the company capitalized on collector interest by printing up the losers and selling the set for $3. Newly made fake buttons are called Brummagem, and can sometimes be detected by checking for a manufacturer's name on the outside edge of a button.
- Political campaigns are the best source for free new buttons (but with rising costs, fewer are given away); mail order, antique shops and flea markets are good for older ones.
- Collect items outside your scope of interest and political persuasion for trading.
- One dealer gets boxes of discarded, mostly useless buttons from a manufacturer and rummages through to find a few salable items.

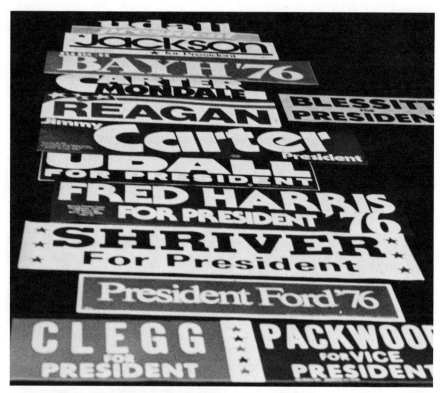

Bumper Stickers for 1976 Presidential Elections. (Collection of and photograph by Douglas Liman)

- Keep a record of each acquisition, including date, price and information (this can add to value) and photocopy it in *color*, if possible. It's easier to take sheets rather than actual buttons around, particularly if buttons are stored in, and must be removed from, a vault.

## Collecting by Mail (Auctions)

(NOTE: Even if you do not want to purchase from them, it makes sense to subscribe to one of the various mail-auction publications. They are a good guide to what is available and being offered, and then, as reported in subsequent issues, to what is realized or paid for particular items.) Some of the following may send a sample issue upon request:

*George H. LaBarre Galleries—American Collectibles*, 111 Perry St., Hudson, NH 03051 (subscription $13 for three issues—2,000 lots, profusely illustrated; sample copy $1)

*Hake's Americana and Collectibles*, Box 1444, York, PA 17405 (subscription $5 for six issues, sample copy $1)

*Ben Corning*, 10 Lilian Road Extension, Framingham, MA 01701

*Historicana*, 1632 Robert Road, Lancaster, PA 17601 (sample copy $1)

*Al Anderson*, Box 644, Troy, OH 45373

*Auction Americana*, Halottaway, 66 Norfolk Drive, Wichita, KS 67206

*Gary Smith*, 306 Peacock Trail, Hagerstown, MD 21740

*Leon Weisel*, 2180 Center Avenue, Ft. Lee, NJ 07024

Carter Peanut Sack, $3.75 from Martin Friedman, Inc. (see Collecting Clues)

Matchbook Covers for Local Candidates.

## Mail Order

*The Local*, Robert Platt, Box 159, Kennedale, TX 76060. Local buttons offered in catalogue.

*Campaign Americana*, Box 275, Merrick, NY 11566 (subscription $2 for six issues, sample copy 50¢)

*Tom Slater*, 622 W. Diversy Parkway, Chicago, IL 60614

*Pensland*, 4015 Kilmer Avenue, Allentown, PA 18104

*M. Friedman Specialty Co.*, Box 5777, Baltimore, MD 21208

## Mail-Order Posters

*World War I Poster* ($275). *Poster Americana Catalogue* ($1), 174 Ninth Ave., New York, NY 10011

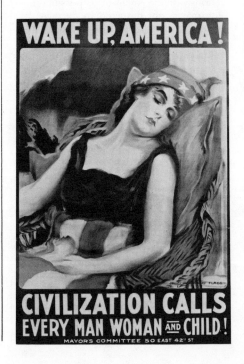

*APIC Adlai Stevenson Research Project*—Catalogued all collectibles issued in his campaign; includes telephone dialers, cigars and cigar boxes, baseballs, cups, shopping bags, etc.

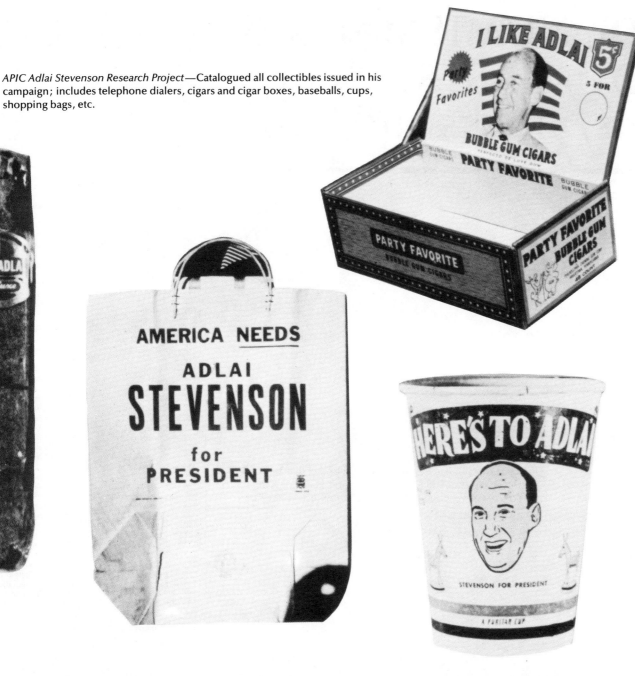

## Organizations

*American Political Items Collector* (APIC), Donald B. Coney, Secretary, 66 Golf Street, Newington, CT 06111 (membership $10). Publishes The Keynoter ($1 handling) and specialized research project, e.g., a book on all Adlai Stevenson collectibles, and a list of audio-visual material such as major Presidential speeches available on loan to members. Holds annual convention; has nearly 30 local chapters with over 2,000 members, and specialty subgroups including Locals APIC for those interested in items generated by local campaigns, e.g., governor, mayor, congressman. They alert members to the existence of fakes and will even arrange for insurance coverage. APIC may expand to include collectors of historical but non-political items in areas like Lindbergh, Vietnam protest buttons, NRA, Liberty Loan.

## Publications

*The Political Collector*, 503 Madison Avenue, York, PA 17404 (subscription $4.50)

*Political Merchant*, 201 Greenfield Road, Lancaster, PA 17601 (FREE sample issue)

*Political Buttons Book II 1920–1976* ($18 paperbound); *Political Buttons Book III 1789–1916* ($18 paperbound); *The Button Book* ($7.25). All by Theodore Hake, available from him: Box 1444, York, PA 17405.

*The Illustrated Political Button Book* by Richard Bristow ($5.95 plus 50¢ postage). Send to: P.O. Box 521, Santa Cruz, CA 95061.

# PHILATELISTS, NUMISMATISTS AND EXONOUMIASTS: Stamps, Coins, Tokens, Stocks and Bonds

## Philately

*"I commend stamp collecting to you because I started a collection when I was about 10 years old and have kept it up ever since. In addition to the fun of it, it has kept up my interest in history and geography, past and present. I really believe that collecting stamps makes a better citizen."* –Franklin D. Roosevelt

Not just the most educational, but by size the most portable and compact and by weight potentially the most valuable collectible, stamps have attracted over 22 million collectors. Rare stamps are as solid an investment today as always; but stamps can also be enjoyed for a minimal amount of money. A collection can be started by simply removing the stamps that come in the mail, or by buying first-day covers or plate blocks of new issues for face value (the cost of the stamps) at the post office. Most experts advise beginners to be wary of stamps that are manufactured just as collector's items, and to think about specializing in one of many categories.

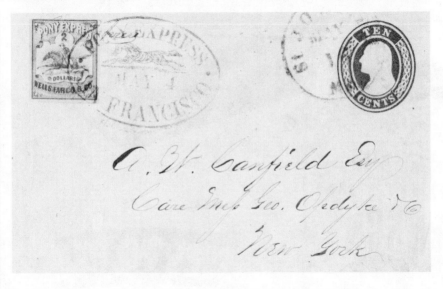

*Pony Express Cover*—Usually a first-day cover has no intrinsic value other than the value of the stamp; in this case, however, the value was in the envelope and postmark. *(From Jerome Hawley's collection of 200 Express Company covers auctioned by Sotheby Parke Bernet)*

### FIRST DAY COVERS AND STAMPS

When a new United States or foreign stamp is issued, it is canceled with a first-day-of-issue postmark from the officially designated post office, on a specially designed envelope. In 1971, Apollo astronaut Edgar Mitchell took 55 covers to the moon. Seven years later, one with his autograph sold for $4,200.

553 — Yugoslavia
554 — Zambia
555 — Zanzibar

**TOPICALS**

701 — General
702 — American Bicentennial
703 — Americana
704 — Animals
705 — Archeology
706 — Architecture
707 — Arctic/Antarctic
708 — Art
709 — Astrology
710 — Astronomy
711 — Atomic Energy
712 — Authors/Literature
713 — Automobiles
714 — Aviation
715 — Biology
716 — Birds
717 — Boats
718 — Bridges
719 — Butterflies
720 — Cats
721 — Centennials
794 — Chemistry
722 — Chess
723 — Children
724 — Christmas
725 — Churchill
726 — Coats of Arms
727 — Communications
728 — Composers
729 — Computers
730 — Copernicus
731 — Costumes
732 — Dogs
733 — Education
734 — Eisenhower
735 — Esperanto
736 — Europa
737 — Fairy Tales/Folklore
738 — Famous People

781 — Science/Scientists
782 — Scouts
797 — Shells
783 — Ships
798 — Skiing
784 — Space
785 — Sports
786 — Stamps on Stamps
787 — Transportation
788 — UN (Topic)
789 — Universal Postal Union
790 — Washington
791 — Waterfalls
792 — Women
793 — World Fairs

**GENERAL**

901 — Aerograms
902 — Air Mails (Foreign)
942 — Balloon Mail
903 — Booklets (Foreign)
904 — Cancels (Foreign)
905 — Censored Covers
906 — Christmas Seals
907 — Cinderellas
908 — Classics (Foreign)
909 — Coils (Foreign)
910 — Counterfeits
911 — Covers (Foreign)
799 — Dams
912 — Essays & Proofs (Foreign)
913 — EFO's (Foreign)
914 — FDC's (Foreign)
915 — Exhibition Covers
916 — First Flights (Foreign)
917 — Former Countries
918 — General (Global)
919 — Intl. Reply Coupons
920 — Jet Flights
800 — Lindbergh
921 — Locals (Foreign)
922 — Maritime Markings
923 — Military Mail

*Categories of Stamp Collecting. (Courtesy of American Philatelist)*

**TOPICALS: MOZART, CANADA** A philatelist of long standing, George T. Guzzio began by collecting stamps related to music, then narrowed his field to Mozart. This led him on a search for, and then philatelic documentation of, a town named for the composer.

## Philately honors Wolfgang Amadeus Mozart (1756-1791)

The first stamp to honor Mozart was an 1889 German local, and (right) the first Mozart stamp intended for general use was issued by Austria in 1922 (No. B51).

One of the portraits of famous people, a set from France issued in 1957 (No. 862).

In commemoration of the 150th anniversary of Mozart's death: A special cancel from Vienna (the stamp is German, No. B200), and No. B7 with attached label issued by Bohemia and Moravia.

The 200th anniversary of the composer's birth was honored by Belgium (No. B 588, above), and (right from top) Russia (No. 1879), Austria (No. 609), Germany (No. 750), and Czechoslovakia (No. 750).

Collection of Postmarks: Mozart, Saskatchewan, Canada, and a Collection of Mozart Stamps. (Courtesy of Scotts Monthly Journal)

Past Postmarks: The Haglof post office near Mozart existed from 1905 through 1918. Laxdal existed for about two years (1907-1909), then became the Mozart P.O. and relocated about 3½ miles from T. S. Laxdal's general store, site of its predecessor.

Above, first Mozart cancel, single broken circle, used 1909-22; and single circle steel handstamp. Left: Current handstamp — Steel die. (Note date, Jan. 27th, anniversary of W. A. Mozart's birth)

## Collecting Clues

● The condition dictates the price of stamps, and collectors look for perfection: clarity of color and picture, number and evenness of perforations, centering, the original gum back, and absence of canceling. Imperfections like tears, repairs, faded colors, tiny spots and streaks, thinning, and whether a stamp has been hinged affect value; but big imperfections enhance it. Here a 1918 24¢ airmail stamp, unused, has a "valid error"— the plane is upside down. It set a world record for a United States stamp when it brought $100,000 at auction in 1978. (Sotheby Parke Bernet)

## What Other Collectors Collect

● Postmarks (around 1900, in various shapes like triangles and hearts) and Cancellation Marks. Some people collect postmarks with odd names, the names of Presidents, or the same name as theirs.

● Early Post Office Equipment (vending machines, letter scales, and 19th-century hand-made postmark cancelers with slogans, designs of animals, geometric patterns, etc.)

## Organizations

*The Franklin D. Roosevelt Philatelic Society,* c/o Gustav Detjen, Jr., Clinton Corners, NY 12524 (membership $6, junior $3). An organization for those who collect stamps that honor F.D.R. or his wife (300-odd stamps exist issued by 54 countries), or that relate to the Roosevelt era. Includes stamps, covers, postmarks, postal slogan cancellations, related artwork such as post office posters, and programs of first-day ceremonies. Publishes newsletter *Fireside Chats.*

*American Revenue Association,* c/o Bruce Miller, 1010 Fifth Avenue, Arcadia, CA 91006 (membership $6).

*"Taxes have always been with us; when the first postage stamp made its appearance in 1840, revenue stamps had already been in use for almost 200 years! Every schoolboy knows that the American Revolution was provoked in part by the imposition of British stamp duties; less well known is the fact that there were revenue collectors who were contemporaries of George Washington! Among revenues may be found stamps rich in historical associations, stamps beautiful, quaint and novel in design, and stamps possessing an integrity of purpose sadly lacking in modern postage issues. And stamps far rarer than any 'airmail invert' at a tiny fraction of the price!"*

*United States Postal Service,* Philatelic Sales Branch, Washington, DC 20265 (FREE philatelic order list of all stamps and stamp products, *Stamps and Stories* $3.50, commemorative mint sets 1975–1978 $4.50 and $3.50, collecting kits $2—each kit has stamps with a theme like sports or space and includes an album and a guide on how to collect)

## FREE Sample Issues—Stamps

*The American Philatelist,* c/o Executive Secretary, American Philatelic Society, Box 800, State College, PA 16801 (50¢ handling)

*Olympic Stamps of Host Countries*—proofs, presentation sets and errors in lucite stands. (*Collection of Edwin H. Mosler, Jr., Chairman of the Olympic Fund*)

*Philatelic Observer,* Junior Philatelists of America, Box 1212, Pawtucket, RI 02862 (membership $6). To join: Box 09483, Bexley Branch, Columbus, OH 43209. Recommended: JPA's *Introduction to United States Philately* by R. Blum ($1.25 postpaid).

*Scotts Monthly Stamp Journal,* c/o Paula Pines, 3 E. 57th Street, New York, NY 10022 (50¢ handling)

*First Days* (50¢ handling), *American First Day Cover Society,* c/o Marge Finger, Executive Secretary, Box 23, Elberon, NJ 07740 (membership $7)

*Stamp Show News,* Box 284, Larchmont, NY 10538

*The Stamp Collector,* Box 10, Albany, OR 97321 (eight weeks free)

*Topical Time,* American Topical Association, 3308 N. 50th Street, Milwaukee, WI 53216 (50¢ handling)

*The Stamp Wholesaler,* Box 529, Burlington, VT 05402 (50¢ handling)

*Linns Stamp News* (world's largest weekly), Dept. G006, Box 29, Sidney, OH 45367. Recommended: *Linns World Stamp Almanac* ($10 postpaid).

# Numismatics

There are more than two sides to numismatics, or coin collecting, and more to it than just coins: paper money, bank notes, tokens, medals, old stock certificates and even canceled checks. It is a hobby that, like stamps, offers a wide range of subjects at every price level. A beginner can start by checking his pockets as Ferran Zerbe, an American newsboy, did in 1882. There he found a French 50-centime piece he had received as change. It became the first coin in what was to be the basis for one of the greatest collections of all time, the Chase Manhattan Collection (acquired from him). The coin ignited Zerbe's interest in foreign currency, and he went on to accumulate important coins, paper money and primitive currencies; Indian wampum, copper shield money, an Alaskan sealskin note, a clay "due-bill" from Babylonia c. 2500 B.C., and Egyptian gold ring money from 1500 B.C.

With more modest objectives in mind, perhaps, a collection may be formed from coins in circulation such as Lincoln pennies or Jefferson nickels, Mercury dimes or Washington quarters, and inserted into special boards according to place of minting (D means Denver, S is San Francisco, no make means Philadelphia) and date.

Experts agree that proof and commemorative sets minted for collectors, while of historic interest, appreciate slowly and are a very poor investment.

The Rise of Modern America 1873–1900 in money. (Smithsonian Institution)

# Exonoumiasts

Exonoumiasts, or token collectors, say coins lack challenge because they are almost all classified and nothing new can be discovered. Not so with tokens. They are privately minted, mostly by merchants, and their variety is endless. A token can be made of metal, wood and or plastic, and can be used as money everywhere—from a bakery to a billiard room to a bank (tokens worth 50¢ were given out to start a bank account). Civil War merchant tokens are collected (there is a Civil War Token Society) and so are present-day food stamp credit tokens (the law does not allow people using food stamps to receive change in coins, so tokens are used instead).

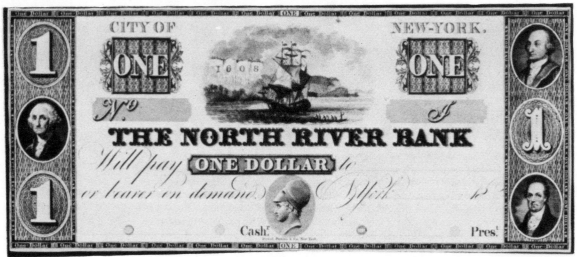

Banknotes of the 19th century were elaborately decorated (Metropolitan Museum of Art, Harris Brisbane Dick Fund)

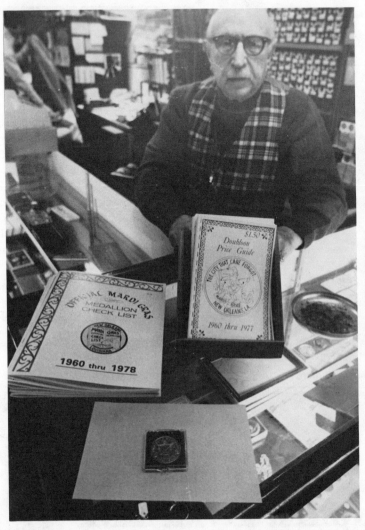

*Doubloons Dealer*—A few years ago a record number, (about 1,600) of different doubloons were made to raise money for the clubs (called krewes) that participate in Mardi Gras parades in New Orleans (coins are thrown from floats). That number of doubloons is too many to collect, and their value has become diluted. What was once an exciting local Louisiana tradition, which kept kids busy catching and then trading all year long, may be ending because of excessive production. The Lazard Coin and Stamp Company sells doubloons and also publishes an annual price guide, shown here with Mr. Calme L. Lazard.

## Organizations

Society of Paper Money Collectors c/o Harry Wigington, PO Box 4082, Harrisburg, PA 17111 membership $10

*Error Trends Coin Magazine,* Box 1588, Oceanside, NY 11572 (sample issue 60¢)

## What Other Collectors Collect

- *Enclosed Stamp "Tokens"*
- *Broken Bank Notes* issued in the 19th-century as currency by banks that later went broke
- *Early American Coppers*
- *Fifty-Cent Pieces*—A very successful but superstitious banker has at least 10,000 in a large chest, including the first 50 cents he ever earned.

## Free Sample Issues—Coins

*Coin World,* Box 150, Sidney, OH 45367. Also publishes *Basic Knowledge ($1.75)* and the important reference work *Coin World Almanac* ($10).

*The Numismatist ($1.25 handling),* The American Numismatic Association, Box 2366, Colorado Springs, CO 80901 (adult membership $12, plus $5 application fee; junior membership $9)

## FREE Coins

For five free coins from Brazil, Japan, the Philippines, Finland and Pakistan, or five free paper money bills from Formosa, China, Hong Kong, Yugoslavia and Indonesia; *Jolie,* Box 50FP, Brooklyn, NY 11224

## Publications

*Introductory Booklet on Coin or Stamp Collecting,* Boy Scouts of America, North Brunswick, NJ 08902 (55¢ each)

*U.S. Coin Collecting: The Red Book* by Richard S. Yeoman, edited by Kenneth Bressett (the author of Boy Scouts booklet on coins). Send $4.95 to publisher: Dept. M, Western Publishing Co., 1220 Mound Avenue, Racine, WI 53404. Required reading—a brief history of American coinage: early American coins and tokens; mint issues, private, state and territorial; gold and silver commemoratives and proofs; all illustrated and priced. (*The Blue Book* has wholesale price if selling.)

*Coins of the World ($1.95)* and *Paper Money of the World ($2.25)* by Dr. Richard Doty (Bantam).

# EXCERPT FROM 60 MINUTES, CBS NEWS, *November 12, 1978*

**MORLEY SAFER:** There's little doubt that with inflation people are looking for ways to invest their money, hoping that what they buy will increase in value as their dollars shrink in value. That, among other things, is what sparked the growth of companies that sell what they call "collectibles"— collections of commemorative stamps, plates, artwork, medallions and coins newly created and issued in what are referred to as "limited editions." A number of companies are tapping this market. Among them, Danbury Mint, Hamilton Mint, Columbia House (which is a division of CBS), Fleetwood, Lincoln Mint, and perhaps the best known, Franklin Mint.

Nearly all these companies are careful to avoid saying that their collectibles will increase in value, but many of their ads use words that might lead prospective buyers to believe just that: "rarity," "precious," "valuable," "scarcity," "heirloom." And if the object in question is something minted in precious metal like silver, the ads can be even more persuasive.

Which brings us to the Franklin Mint, the most advertised company in the field of collectibles, and the largest private mint in the world. You can hardly pick up a quality magazine without finding a very appealing ad for Franklin Mint products. Their best known are their numismatic products—medallions, coins and ingots.

Franklin Mint started out 15 years ago with a brilliant and profitable idea. They created the hobby of collecting Franklin Mint medals. Important Americans are paid to lend their names to some of the issues: "Gerald R. Ford chooses significant events in the Presidency"; Henry Kissinger chooses 50 portraits of greatness." The Mint stresses that these are "limited editions," but in most issues that means they are limited to the number of people who order them by a certain date; could be 2,000, could be 200,000.

Michael Kipperman is a New York businessman. His apartment has practically wall-to-wall Franklin Mint.

Did Franklin Mint encourage or discourage you from buying these as an investment?

**MICHAEL KIPPERMAN:** I read the articles to mean that it was an investment. Here is a typical example: Subscriptions must be postmarked by a specific date—a subscription deadline. And then there is an issue price guarantee, which is what really caught my eye. And their little paragraph: "In view of recent increases in the market prices of silver and the strong likelihood of further increases in the years to come, this is an extremely significant guarantee." And I think anyone would feel the same way I did. And there was a time that I needed the money. I went to turn in the sets, and I was horrified as to what they told me.

**SAFER:** Where did you go? Who did you take—

**KIPPERMAN:** Well, I first sent a letter with a copy of every issue that I owned, and I sent it to every coin dealer within a hundred miles of New York. Most of them were not interested whatsoever in the Franklin Mint, and only one person did make an offer and his offer was astronomically low.

**SAFER:** Did you complain to anyone?

**KIPPERMAN:** Who are you going to tell that you bought four or five thousand dollars' worth of ingots that aren't even worth half the price? P.T. Barnum's favorite statement, I think, was the fact that there was a sucker born every minute, and I am ashamed to say that I'm a living testament of it.

**MAN:** What they are doing is making artificial rarity. They are saying, "We will sell as many pieces as we get orders for, and then we will not sell any more." Well, that's true, but basically everybody that wanted that piece ordered it, and then that's the limited amount. The resale market is very limited, because they were offered on a national basis. Everybody that wanted that particular set would order it. There's just no place to go to sell them.

**SAFER:** So we went to Franklin Mint, to their chairman of the board, Charles Andes, to hear their side of the story. Would you say that investing in Franklin Mint collectibles is a bad investment?

**ANDES:** Do I think it would be a bad investment? No, I think it would be a good investment, but it depends upon what you . . . what you're looking for. If you're looking for the kind of things that most collectors are looking for—beauty, satisfaction, a thing . . . a product that endures and that you can have—then I think it's money very well spent.

**SAFER:** As a . . . as a financial investment?

**ANDES:** No, we don't ever recommend it as a financial investment.

*Marconi Wireless Telegraph Company*, dated 1920.

*Missouri, Kansas and Texas Railway Company*, dated 1914

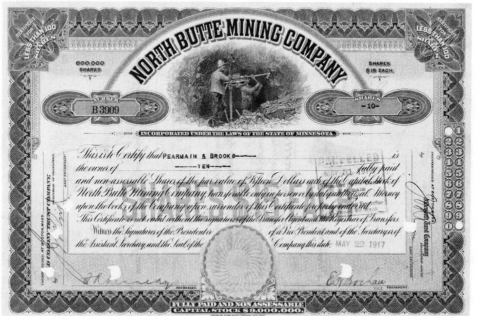

*North Butte Mining Company,* dated 1917.

*Boston Elevated Railway Company,* dated 1913.

# The Significance of Stocks and Bonds

Old, canceled stock and bond certificates are guaranteed to be worth far less today than when they first appeared. Although they may no longer have intrinsic value, they do have value as collectibles. Not only is it fun to own for pennies a piece of paper once worth hundreds, perhaps thousands of dollars (and sometimes signed by such famous magnates as Vanderbilt, Morgan or Rockefeller), but these beautifully engraved certificates (the intricate detail helps to avoid counterfeiting) are a fascinating document of business history. Dealer-collector Ken Prag prizes his certificates with signatures of Thomas Edison and Robert Morris (a signer of the Declaration of Independence), and a certificate dated 1792. Shown here are examples from his collection and catalogue, including railroad, mining and communications company certificates. For a free issue (25¢ handling) of his bimonthly catalogue, write: Box 531, Burlingame, CA 94010.

# BOTTLES

No wonder bottle collecting is one of the fastest-growing hobbies. It offers something—from ancient glass to Avon bottles—for everyone, from the amateur archeologist to the auction addict.

## Avon Calling

*"You eat, sleep and dream Avon,"* says Herbert Tomaschefsky, who once, in desperation, sold his whole collection, only to buy it all back. His first bottle, in the shape of a gavel, was a funny gift, sort of a souvenir from friends upon the successful completion of his divorce proceeding—they said justice had been done! Now he has all kinds of Avon collectibles—bottles, awards, plates—filling three rooms of his home; but he has one room just for his specialty, test bottles. He has over 250 of these rare bottles, the largest collection ever assembled, he says. Test bottles are samples made by several glass companies for Avon products and sent to them for approval. The sample that is accepted becomes the test bottle that Herb Tomaschefsky collects. Besides using the standard sources, Herb adds to his collection by buying from Avon representatives and buying and trading ("one for one")

Bud Hastin's Book—410 pages, with over 9,000 Avon items priced and pictured (previous edition sold out at 365,000 copies). Available from Bud Hastin Enterprises, Box 9868, Kansas City, MO 64134 ($14.95 postpaid).

*Avon Automobile Series.*

with members of Avon clubs from all over the country whom he visits or corresponds with. "You find the bottles in the monthly Avon papers printed by the Avon clubs. You write to people or call them up and eventually find what you are looking for, plus an Avon friend." Herb is president and founder of the Avon club of Cudahy, a member of eight other Avon Collecting Clubs, and author of *Herb's Guide to Avon Test Bottle Collecting,* "*The most comprehensive display of test and production bottles of Avon collectibles ever published and photographed side by side.*" The book is dedicated to a young friend, Jimmy Sayler, who has Reye's Syndrome, and $1 of the purchase price is donated to help defray his medical costs.

For the hobby or the club write to Herb at: 1237 Wakefield Rd., Grafton, WI 53024.

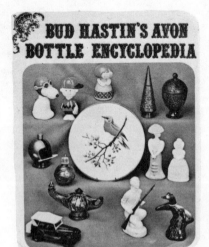

# Alice Creswick's Canning Jars

Ms. Creswick writes about the antique canning jars she collects and has had several books on old fruit jars published. The current book is the *Red Book of Fruit Jars No. 3*, an illustrated price guide.

*Turn-of-the-Century Barber Bottles.* (Collection of Robert Blake Powell)

*Canning Jars of the 19th Century:* Cohansey 1877, Eagle 1858, Automatic Sealer 1885, The Dandy 1885, Eureka 1864, Clark 1885, All Right 1868.

*American Bottles of the Late 19th and Early 20th Centuries*—medicine, bitter, ink, food and beverage bottles selected for their size, shape, color and for the historical interest in the impressed brand name or ad. The collection is displayed on glass shelves in a kitchen window that looks like stained glass when the sun shines through. (*Collection of C. Leonard Gordon*)

# THE UTTER FACTS ABOUT MOO (Milk Bottles Only Organization)

When he was president of his local archeological association and looking for colonial artifacts, Fred Rawlinson found another hobby—bottle collecting. His specialty is old milk bottles, and he has over 600 (mostly acquired through trade), including: two Thatchers from 1884 (to be the first milk bottle on the market); early Whitemans; Smalleys with metal handles from Boston, 1898; and many others with tin tops, from around 1890. There are 200 MOOers, members of MOO, an organization he runs (Box 5456, Newport News, VA 23605—membership $5; ads free).

Rawlinson writes the monthly newsletter *The Milking Parlor,* and has also authored *Old Bottles of the Virginia Peninsula,* about wine, beer, medicine and milk bottles; *Make Mine Milk,* on milk bottles; and *Brad's Drink,* a primer for Pepsi-Cola collectors.

## THE MILKING PARLOR

MARCH, 1978    VOL. 9, NO. 9

DAIRY INDUSTRY IN AMERICA BOOKS - About 30 MOOers have sent in the money for the book. I have been waiting until all money was in and now you should be receiving your books in a couple of weeks. Thanks for waiting.

FOR SALE - WANTED - TRADES - For Sale, round & square, : embossed & painted, quarts, pints, 1/3 quarts from Wisconsin and surrounding area. Send SASE with a list of your wants and I will send you a list with prices. Dick Kempinger, 247 W. 16th Ave., Oshkosh, Wis. 54901.............For Sale - Milk Bottle Jewelry, pins, tie tacs, tie bars, hand carved in wood with slogan "Grade A Milk". $2.00 each postpaid. Wanted to buy milk bottles from college or universities. Tom Morton, 103 W. Park Place, Newark, Del. 19711.............Wanted - Two milk bottles from Fred F. Field Holstein Company, Dutchland Farms, Brockton, Mass. This was my grandfather's milk company and I'd like to give these to my sons. Fred F. Field, 84 State St., Suite 726, Boston, Mass. 02109.............Mr. Moo quarts or ½ gallons, square amber, $5.00 each includes shipping. Other good milks for sale. R. Henry Schneider, 525 Forum Ave., Louisville, Ky. 40214.............Wanted - A bottle from Zack Dairy, located in or around Fairmont, N.J. Mrs. Carolyn Eroh, Rt. 1, Box 384, Belvedere, N.J. 07823.............For Sale - Square Cop-The-Creams $20 postpaid also some baby face and double baby faces, quarts at $20 each postpaid. A few ½ pint baby faces at $15 each. Also want embossed bottle from my old home town, Jordan, N.Y. Also wanted a top for Cop-The-Cream shaped like a policeman's hat. Dave Vrooman, 2383 Flamingo Dr. #7, Miami Beach, Florida, 33139.............For Sale - Square bottom, long neck, blue paint, Stroups Dairy, Palmerton, Pa. With cow on back, 12 per wooden case. Approx 15 cases. $5 per case. Clarence Getz, 19 Maple Rd., Weissport, Pa. 18235.............Wanted - Bottle from Kleppinger's Dairy (or creamery) Havertown, Pa. Nancy Brey, 1988 Miller Ave., Emmaus, Pa. 18049........Wanted - War Slogan milks. Also have many new bottles, some amber, SASE. Bob Ciesinski, 5704 Delores Dr., Castalia, Ohio, 44824.............Frank Shellhamer, 279 S. Geyer's Church Rd., Middletown, Pa. 17057 will buy your milk bottle collection, any amount (quarts) round, embossed or round painted. Would like mint or near mint condition, city & state must show on bottles.............For Sale - Kleen Dairy, sq. amber quarts and some Reed's Guernsey Milk, sq. amber quarts with long necks. $4 Kleen, $5 Reed's, post and ins. paid. Some case wear. R.S. Riovo, 686 Franklin St., Alburtis, Pa. 18011......Wanted- Elsie The Cow items. Will trade. Also want license plates especially Bicentenial plates. Artie Klatt, 128 Suburbia Ter., Jersey City, N.J. 07305......Wanted-collectors of restaurant creamers contact Kay Cooley, Box 7, Osborne, Kan. 67473.

## The Utter Facts From MOO
## Milkbottles Only Organization
## box 5456. newport news. va. 23605

Page from *The Milking Parlor.*

*Milk Bottles.*

*Thatcher Milk Bottle,* dated 1884.

# Figural (Miniature) Liquor Bottles

*"Miniature liquor bottles have for the most part been produced in the 20th century, usually for use on airplanes as individual 'one-shot' drinks. Bottles are generally grouped into straights (replicas of standard-size bottles) figurals, jugs, pitchers, etc. They are produced in many countries and in such diverse materials as earthenware and porcelain. We specialize in figurals, most produced outside the U.S. Interesting items include a pretzel bottle, complete with salt spots, made in Germany at the beginning of the century; a six-piece majolica Italian chess set (rare—fewer than 300 were manufactured—and probably worth close to $500); and a set of Dutch townhouses (27 were made by Delft and given to first-class passengers on KLM airlines starting in 1959). Other collectors specialize in Scotch, of which there are literally hundreds of different brands and bottles from pre-Prohibition days." (Anonymous Collector)*

*Wall-Mounted Figural Bottle Openers*—(clockwise) Amish man, Mr. Peanut, top hat man, wall-mounted drunk. A "new collectible" and becoming scarce due to the introduction of the twist-off bottle cap. (*Collection of Michael Jordan,* president of the newly formed *Figural Bottle Opener Collectors*)

*One hundred fifty Miniature Soda Bottles. (Collection of Ellen Sue Levy)*

## What Other Collectors Collect

- *Character Bottles (a bottle in the shape of a person, object or animal used for cologne, syrups, liquors and medicines)*
- *Coca-Cola Bottles* from foreign countries
- *Infant Nursing Bottles* from the latter part of the 19th century
- *Historical Flasks and Bottles* of the early 19th century with embossed pictures of famous figures such as George Washington, Andrew Jackson, Benjamin Franklin

## Collecting Clues

- To guard against copies, recognize these marks of age: imperfections and unevenness in the glass; pontil marks (round, rough scars on the bottom) that indicate the bottle was hand blown, thus made before 1860; the location of the mold line on the side (the nearer the mouth it is, the newer the bottle).
- Bottles are valued according to rarity (with embossed names more desirable); color (clear bottles with the patina of the earth or sun, or colors no longer made, like blue); condition (scratched, stained, presence of the original stopper); and local appeal (many collectors specialize in one area).
- Many valuable bottles can be unearthed with just a little hard work at dumping areas (often found behind old houses and barns). Digging advice: While it is easy to locate newer dumps and demolition sites (a metal detector may help, but be sure to get permission before digging on private property), it is good to research in town documents and libraries for the site of older dumps, homesteads, deserted mining and military camps, etc. Use a shovel, a probe and a potato hoe for digging; wear gloves for protection, and take along a box to transport your treasures home.

*Free Sample Miniature Bottles of Perfume. (Collection of Emily Liman, photograph by Douglas Liman)*

## FREE Sample Issues

*Antique Bottle World Magazine*, 5003 Berwyn, Chicago, IL 60630

*Bottle News*, Box B48, Kermit, TX 79745 ($.25 handling)

*World Wide Avon News*, c/o Jeanne Monnette, 18740 Welby Way, Box 1184, Reseda, CA 91335

*The Old Bottle Magazine*, Box 1000, Kermit, TX 79745

*The Collector*, Kermit, TX 79745

*The International Chinese Snuff Bottle Society Journal*, 2601 N. Charles Street, Baltimore, MD 21218 ($1 handling)

## Organizations

*Federation of Historical Bottle Clubs*, Barbara Robertus, 50001 Queen Avenue N., Minneapolis, MN 55430

*Figural Bottle Opener Collectors* (17 members but growing), 95 Apple Valley Rd., Stamford, CT 06903 (membership $10)

*Chinese Snuff Bottle*

# MECHANICAL MARVELS

## Vending Machines

Although coin-operated vending "machines" were used in ancient times (the Romans had a device that dispensed holy water for three drachmas), it was really not until the latter part of the 19th century that they became big business. Made from materials like cast iron and oak, the finest machines were works of art created at the turn of the century by skilled and very imaginative craftsmen. These mechanical marvels dispensed diverse necessities of the day: eggs, wine, collar buttons, tobacco, cigars, chocolate, gum, pencils, perfume, divorce papers, music, medical treatment and information.

The machines in this collection not only look good, they also work perfectly. (Because so few people can, or will, do repairs, an important part of collecting any working apparatus is to be able to restore it yourself—to find parts and, in this instance, the authentic items, like gums cards, etc., that were dispensed.) Luckily, this collector was mechanically inclined and actually started his hobby by volunteering to help the owner of an antique shop with repairs in exchange for a vending machine. Being handy is only half the battle, though. Research is

also important. The Patent Library is a good source of information for any patented machine, while other, similar machines—ones beyond repair, perhaps—may be good sources of missing parts.

*A Group of Turn-of-the-Century Machines*—(left to right) *"Niagara" Figure* tips hat, and gum comes out of friend's mouth, 1904; *Match Dispenser* 1905; *Spanish Peanut Orbit, Jr.*

*Perfume Dispenser*—Squirts come out of the flower the lady is holding.

*Toilet Paper Dispenser* 1902, in collector's bathroom.

*Electric Treatment for Headache, Neuralgia and Other Ailments.*

*Penny Service Shoe Brusher* with local ads, 1915.

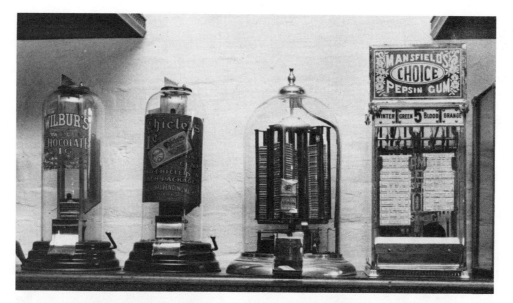
Match, Chocolate and Gum Machines.

*Blinking Eye Soda Mint Gum Machine, 1907.*

*Teddy Bear Gum Machine*

*Decorative Bubble Gum Machine.*

*Very Rare Coin-Operated Dictionary 1902—Insert coin and it will open to page desired.*

*Smiling-Sam Peanut Dispenser* 1931.

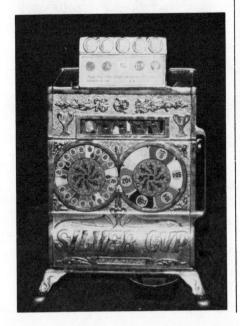

*Peanut Machines* in the kitchen.

## Publications

*Drop Coin Here* by Fran and Ken Rubin ($12.95, Crown; or $13.95 postpaid from K & F Publishing, Box 240, Brooklyn, NY 11202 (with price guide supplement, $17.50)

*Loose Change,* 21176 S. Alameda Street, Long Beach, CA 90810 (monthly subscription $22, FREE sample issue with $1 handling)

## Organizations

*The Society for the Preservation of Historical Coin Operated Machines,* 100 N. Central Avenue, Hartsdale, NY 10530. For information, send SASE. As its name indicates, this organization is dedicated to preserving coin-operated machines, and one of its current activities is to lobby for change in laws that prohibit possession of gambling machines. According to one of the founders, it is illegal under most state statutes to own a gambling device, whether or not it works or is used for gambling (ironically, it is not illegal to own an antique gun that *does* work, and a permit for one is not necessary). The law has now been changed in California due to the efforts of an irate collector whose entire collection was confiscated when the police answered his "For Sale" in a local paper. Since them, 12 other states have followed suit.

# Locks and Keys

The variety of locks and keys to be collected is a direct result of the battle between locksmith and thief—as civilization advanced, the design of the lever end of the key and the lock became more complex. And ever since the days when the master of a Pompeian household kept a two-foot-long key to his wine cellar and front door chained to a slave (who could also use it as a lethal weapon to knock out an intruder), ingenuity has prevailed.

**WATCH KEY COLLECTION** From the 16th century, when they were first used, up until the middle of the 19th century, timepieces were wound with a watch key. One of the most complete collections of these keys—1,200 representing practically all general types ever made—was assembled by Dr. and Mrs. Eugene Randolph Smith. (*Permanent collection, The Cornell Fine Arts Center, Rollins College, Winter Park, Florida*)

**STEWART'S BIT-STYLE KEYS** Mr. Stewart has about 4,000 keys in his catalogued collection—some framed, all "hanging around the house and store." A former lumber and construction company owner, he began collecting old bit-style keys about 30 years ago, when he found himself on a job replacing old locks and new equipment. He has a natural affinity for junk, Mr. Stewart explains, so he saved these until things got out of hand. Then he sold everything but his real treasures. He collects keys for enjoyment only, and not for their value or for any technical reasons. He was never a locksmith, so he did not develop the desire to collect locks.

**LAWYER CHARLES CHANDLER** head of the 400-member Lock Collectors Association, has one of the nation's best collections of old and unusual padlocks, handcuffs, leg irons, prisoner collars, ball chains and other restraining devices.

(Collection Lock Museum of America)

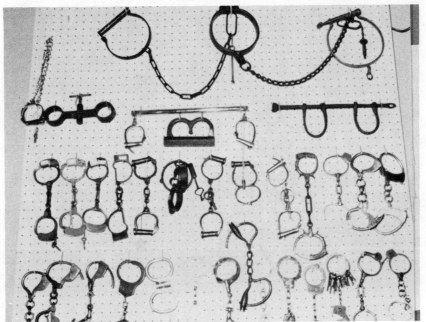

(Collection of Charles Chandler)

## Organizations and Institutions

*American Lock Collectors Association,* 14010 Cardwell, Livonia, MI 48154 (membership $5; FREE sample of bimonthly newsletter with SASE)

*Lock Museum of America,* 114 Main Street, Box 104, Terryville, CT 06786. America's first lock museum, it has the largest, most varied collection of American locks.

## Publications

*The Key Collectors Newsletter* ($8 per year) and *Standard Guide to Key Collecting 1850–1975* ($7.95 postpaid)—both from Don Stewart, Box 9397, Phoenix, AZ 85068. Inquiries answered —just send SASE.

## What Other Collectors Collect

• *Jail Keys, Hotel Keys, Car Keys, Night Latchkeys, Push Keys, Bell Keys, Safe-Deposit Keys, Railroad Switch Keys, House Keys, Common Bit or Stamped Keys, New Keys from One Manufacturer, Keys with an Unusual Design, Trunk Keys*

## Collecting Clues

• A locksmith can make a key for an old lock, and may be a good source for old keys.
• Wash keys with soap and water, rubbing carefully with a little steel wool; then sort according to size and style.

# HAND TOOLS AND WROUGHT IRON

## A Houseful of Hammers

Just as the history of tools, so intertwined with our social and economic development, is a study in ingenuity, so is the adaptation of one common form of hammer for so many trades and in so many variations. The honesty of the hammer—its economy and simplicity of design—is what attracted collector Daniel J. Comerford III at first. He started off buying a few hand-wrought pieces in college, but became fully involved about 10 years ago. He now has around 1,500 hammers in the collection, including practially every type ever made: a Roman claw hammer, c. 1 B.C., found in a Roman ruin; several 14th-century hammers; an American Indian war hammer, stone with a buckskin handle; bronze, copper and brass hammers (used where there is volatile material); hammers for tenderizing meat, leatherworking, log marking, crate opening, woodworking, metal working, stone dressing; mallets, beetles, tack and sledge hammers; and combination hammers such as one with a wrench, pliers, glass cutter and screwdriver at-

tached. Comerford, a teacher, is fascinated with facts about the function of a hammer, particularly those no longer in existence, such as the snowknocker and wagon pin hammer.

*"A snowknocker is a hammer used to knock the snow and ice out of the hollow part of a horse's hoof. The pick end of the hammer is used to pick out more stubborn pieces of ice. Many have clips on them for easy fastening to the horse's harness. Wagon pin hammers were used originally on Cones-*

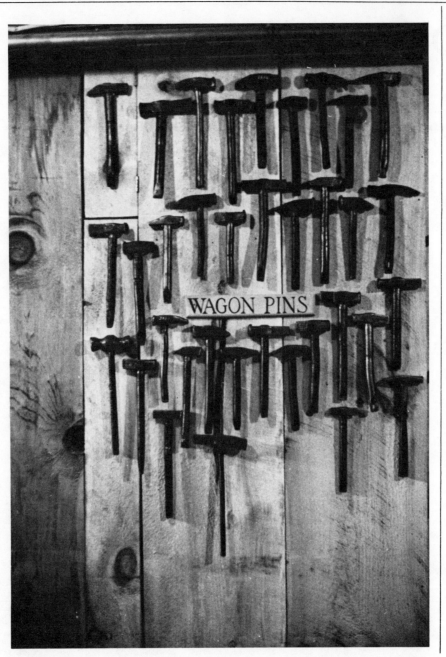

WAGON PINS

*toga or covered wagons and later on work wagons of all types. In order to save weight—so important on the long journey west—these hammers were multi-functional: they were used to pry out axle linchpins, as a general all-purpose utility hammer, and to hold the double tree (a piece of wood between the team of horses) to the rear end of the wagon tongue."*

Mr. Comerford says you can still find hammers for $1. Most, however, are in the $25 to $35 range, with a price tag of $100 to $200 on the more expensive ones. Besides the reasonable cost of this collectible, there are, of course, many other attractions: "The joy of acquiring a new piece, the excitement of unexpectedly finding a rare item; or the hunt itself and the warm friendships developed with fellow tool collectors across the country through my active participation in Early Americans Industries Association (EAIA)." The EAIA has 100 members with limited membership subject to approval, publishes a magazine and holds three-day weekend meetings at historical restorations. For information write John S. Watson, Box 2128 Empire Station, Albany, NY 12220. *(Photographs by Marty Rownin)*

P.S. *In self-defense, no doubt, Mrs. Comerford collects tool prints, kitchen utensils, toys, banks and statues of Scottish terriers.*

# The Wonder of Wrought Iron

One of the largest collections of old wrought iron belongs to James Sorber, a lover of antique furniture, a carpenter, cabinetmaker and sometime forger-by-hand. Grandson of a blacksmith, he was attracted as a child to the technical achievement and strong graphic design of Early American metalware. What began as an avocation has become a business for Mr. Sorber, who sells originals, as well as labeled reproductions that he makes, at his home in West Chester, Pennsylvania. The collection is divided into several categories: hardware, utilitarian cooking and other tools, and items relating to the Conestoga wagon.

*Pennsylvania Pincushion* c 1827—Cushion was sewn through the holes in the top of the clamp.

*Eighteenth-Century Pennsylvania Foot Scraper.*

*Eighteeth-Century English Pipe Tongs,* used to remove hot coals from the fireplace and put in pipe.

*Late 18th-Century Pennsylvania Suffolk Thump Latches.*

*Hinges* showing Pennsylvania German influence and a *New English Suffolk Thumb Latch* dated 1814–15 (the top of the latch is a snake head with eyes, and the bottom of the latch ends in the snake's tail). *(Collection James Sorber)*

# Early American Planes

Dan Semel's collection of Early American planes started with an interest in woodworking. He hunted in flea markets for the tools he needed, and soon realized that these old tools not only had utilitarian worth, but investment and historical value as well. Now, besides using and collecting planes and other tools, he is interested in researching their past and writing about it. Like all woodworkers, he keeps his tools in a tool chest—and his large tool chests are collector's items, too. To go along with all this, he has old catalogues, lists, a library of books—and, above all, a tolerant wife and careful children. His advice on cleaning:

*"Cleaning is an 'art.' Each tool requires a different approach, and experimentation with solvents is the name of the game. Proceed slowly and try to preserve the patina. Overcleaned tools are worthless to me. I 'restore' rather than 'refinish,' and I end off with butcher's wax as a final finish."*

*Wildung Tool Collection. (The Shelburne Museum)*

## What Other Collectors Collect

- *Tools of Carpenters, Shipwrights, Coopers, Blacksmiths, Cobblers, Tinsmiths, Cabinetmakers, Coachmakers, Craftsmen*
- *Primitive Tools*
- *Clockmaker's, Watchmaker's, Farmer's Tools*
- *Tools for Jobs That No Longer Exist,* such as soapmaking
- *Tools in One Specialty*—A Connecticut collector even has his own fully equipped forge!

## Collecting Clues

- It is said that in the 1930s the great art collector and Argerol king Edward Barnes would go knocking on farmhouse doors in pursuit of old tools for his collection. Even today it is possible to acquire some from the craftsman himself or his descendants.

## Collecting by Mail

*Catalogue of Tools and Books About Tools,* Iron Horse Antiques, Rt. 2, Poultney, VT 05764 ($2)

## Publications

*Knife World,* Box 3395, Knoxville, TN 3791 (Monthly Subscription $7. FREE Sample copy SASE by special arrangement with The Collecting Book)

## Institutions

Sloane/Stanley Museum, Kent, CT 06757

*Group of Knives, and a Farrier's Knife* used to operate on horses. The latter has a bone saw and a key to open the barn door. (*Collection of Dr. Frank Miller*)

# GROOMING AND HEALTH

## Robert Blake Powell's Barberiana

Retired from his job in air traffic control, Robert Blake Powell has a new occupation. He has turned his hobby of collecting barberiana into a business; as his search for barber shop items became a search for information, what started as a modest interest mushroomed. Powell is an authority in the field now, and his two self-published books are scholarly works, considered the Bibles of barberiana: *Antique Shavings Mugs of the United States* ($17.95, 272 pages) and *Occupational and Fraternal Shaving Mugs of the United States* ($17.50, 256 pages). Both are available from him: Box 833, Hurst, TX 76053. He writes the following about his collection:

*"I have over 300 shaving mugs (all categories or types), barber bottles, early century barber/surgeon shaving/bleeding basins, and all related memorabilia of the past. Among my prized pieces are P.T. Barnum's personal shaving mug; a pewter shaving/bleeding basin once owned by one of the Pope Leo's and later in the William*

### Antique Shaving Mugs of the United States

#### CONTENTS

Partial Contents Page of *Antique Shaving Mugs of the United States.*

Randolph Hearst collection; and a 3,000-year-old Greek razor. My collection was started because of my fascination for both history and unusual antiques, especially those with great eye appeal and those which few person knew anything about.

*"I have been collecting for over 20 years. Some items were acquired from descendants of the orginial owners. I have bought from antique publications*

Barber/Surgeon Shaving/Bleeding Bowls or Basins—very rare 17th-century Delft (above); French Faience c. 1830–40 (below).

ads and selectively from antique shops.

"The collection is displayed in original barber shop wall racks and cabinets in my home (visitors are welcome, but the visit must be pre-arranged). Selections from it have been publicly exhibited at the State Fair of Texas, at public libraries, at The Institute of Texan Cultures Museum in San Antonio, Texas, and several branches of The Lincoln Savings Bank in New York.

"I buy, sell and trade mugs and other related items, and keep a current 'want list' for collectors all over the country. My advice to new collectors is to learn all they can about their hobby before investing too heavily. I welcome questions from anyone who sends a stamped envelope with their letter."

Robert Blake Powell with *Bleeding Bowl* in front of portion of *Shaving Mug* collection.

*Shaving Mugs:* rare early pewter shaving utensil, English, c. 1790–1820, Brittania-handled brush, carved bone-handled razor (original owner, Mr. Powell's grandfather)

White opalware glass (milk glass) mug patented Dec. 26, 1876

Rare Belleck China mug, 1894.

*Porcelain Container* for bear grease, a male hair preparation.

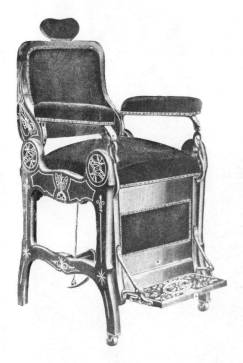

Early Advertisement for Koken's Patent Reclining Barber's Chair.

*Occupational Shaving Mugs*—a few of the thousands of different styles, each originally personalized with the owner's name and a picture representing his business, trade, profession or avocation; hand-painted by painters who worked for the barber supply companies, a practice that ended in 1920.

*Barber Shop Rack* with mugs, restored in 1895; *Koken Barber Chair; Spittoon;* and *Barber Pole.* All in Robert Blake Powell's home.

**THE BARBER BOWLS OF GOV-
ERNOR FAIRCHILD** General Lucius
Fairchild was a Civil War hero, three-time
Governor of Wisconsin and an avid collector of barber (or shaving) bowls. Said to be
possibly the largest collection in the
United States (but not the best, as it consists mainly of Spanish tin glaze with only
a few French, Japanese and Chinese
pieces), it was hung all over the walls of
his home, as shown here. (*Iconographic
Collection, State Historical Society of
Wisconsin*)

# Toothpicks, Toothbrushes and Tongue Cleaners

A collection of antique oral hygiene implements was started 40 years ago by Dr. Isadore Hirshfeld, author of *The Toothbrush's Use and Abuse*.

*Toothpick Holders of the 19th Century—Ivory, porcelain, glass.*

Wood Toothpicks, probably carved and owned by Thomas Jefferson.

*Eighteenth- and 19th-Century Gold and Silver Toothpicks—Some are telescopic, decorated with semi-precious stones.*

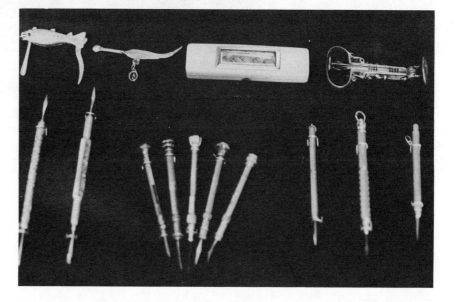

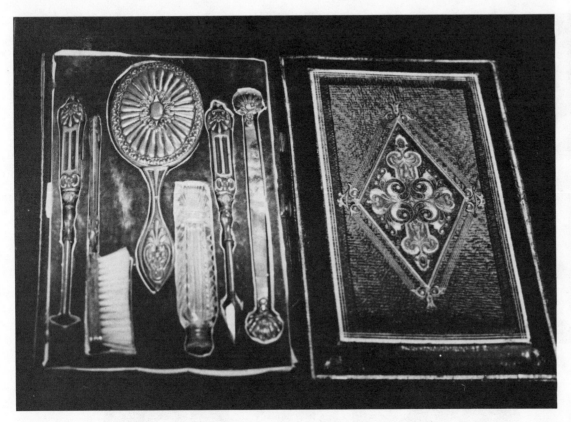

*Talcum Powder Tins.*

*Home Care Cases: Man's Necessaire* contains two hollow
master handles, knife razor, scissors, architect's rule,
pencil, toothpick and earspoon. (*Collection Dr. Isadore Hirshfeld.*)

*French 18th-Century Etuis*—boxes or cases for glasses, cigars,
and, as shown, for grooming tools. (*Collection of jewelry
designer Lucy Feller and M. Richard Feller*)

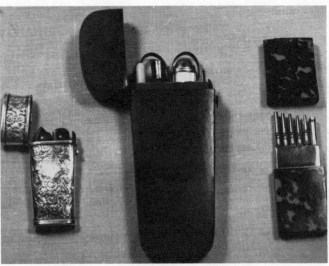

*Pharmacy Museum*, New Orleans, Louisiana, is filled with interesting pharmaceutical antiques—apothecary jars, mortars and pestles, pill cutters, cosmetics, drug jars, figural thermometers.

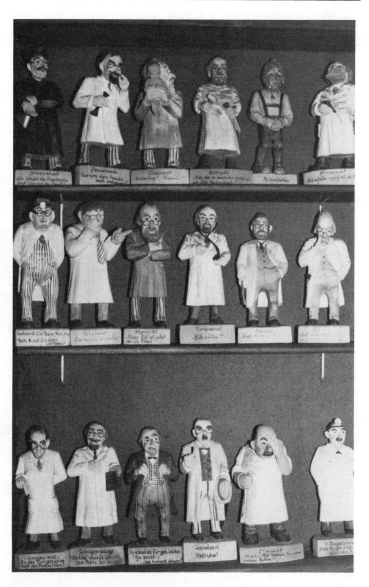

*Hand-Carved Doctors* depict different specialties. (*Collection of Doctor Richard Gibbs*)

# BESTIAL BRIC-A-BRAC

*Ch'ien Lung Dogs*, Chinese 1700–80. One of the more than 100 works of art reproduced from The Nelson Rockefeller Collection, for sale to the public (the dogs cost $350).

*Pugs*—The first one he bought was real and his name was Listo. To keep him company, a collection of fine old china pugs. ("Good antique pugs have clipped ears; after the mid-19th century they were made with full ears.") The pugs come from fine factories—Meissen, Worcester, Sevres. One pug is a perfume bottle. Pugs are displayed on a table, covered with a simple plexiglass cube. (*Collection of Ruben De Saavedra*)

Cane with dog-head handle,
Massachusetts. c. 1830 (*Collection of Mr.
and Mrs. Lawrence Kalstone*)

Pins for a Nine Pin Game, Maine. Early 20th Century. (*Collection of Molly Epstein*)

*It's a Dog's World at Recent Show,* with over 170 representations of dogs in all forms of art: furniture, needlework, textiles, painting, pottery and sculpture. The show was an excellent example of the variety possible in one area of collecting. (*"The American Dog," Museum of American Folk Art*)

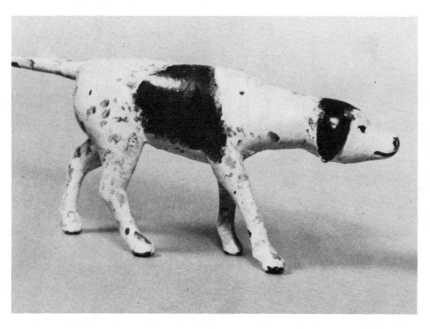

Hooked Rug, California. Early 20th century. (*Collection of Suzanne Paterson*)

Iron dog, Ohio. Late 19th century. (*Collection of Mr. and Mrs. William Gilmore*)

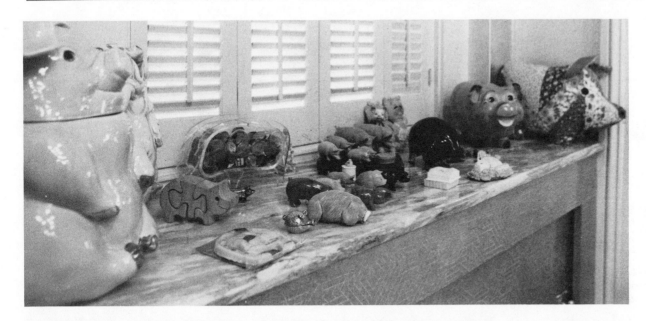

*Pigs in the Powder Room*—a pig pillbox, puzzle, piggy bank, pocketbook, hot water bag, matchbox; pigs in pottery, brass, silver, glass and cloth, given as gifts to collector Lynn Revson.

*Hippos. (Collection of James Warren)*

*Parading Elephants. (Collection of Eleanor Brenner)*

*All Manner of Mice* in gold, silver, bronze, glass, ivory, plastic, pewter, porcelain, fabric (and a mouse stamp collection to go with them) are replacements for the first—a live laboratory mouse—that the collector, Ellen Youngelson, brought home from college. (Photographs by Ira B. Newman)

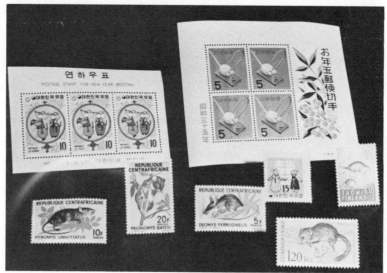

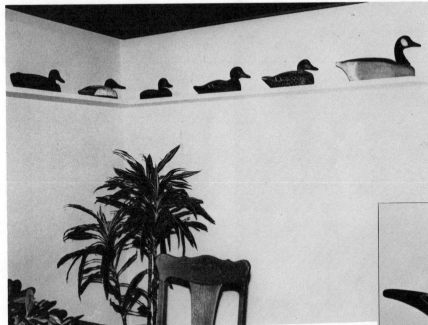

*Decoy Ducks*—Used in hunting, many are masterpieces of carving and painting, made to scale to look like real ducks, geese, grouse, woodcocks, etc. These ducks were carved and used by the collector, who gave them to his children to proudly show off in their dining room. (*Collection of Marguerite Rule Johnstone*)

*Bruce Matteson's Duck Decoys*, from the collection of the well-known illustrator of wild life and fowl. Pictured above are two *Drake Pintails* and left are two *Drake Mallards* of different quality—the ones above sold for more money. (*Christie, Matson and Woods International, Inc.*)

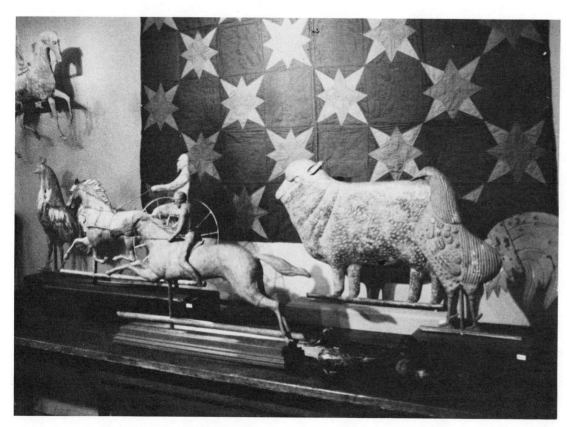

Weathervanes. (Collection of George E. Schoellkopf)

Foxhound Weathervane, Massachusetts. c. 1883 (Collection of Ben Mildwoff)

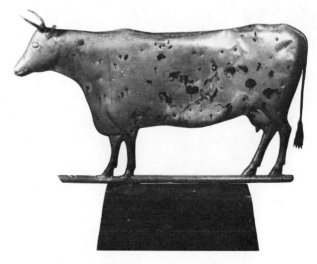

Cow Weathervane c. 1875, Pennsylvania. (Collection of Mrs. Jacob M. Kaplan, gift to Museum of American Folk Art)

Carousel Carvings—Horse. (Collection of Henry Kibel)

Animal Cause Buttons. (Collection of John O'Brien)

# TRANSPARENT TREASURES

## Carnival Glass Collector

Originally called "taffeta" for its iridescence, and referred to as the "Poor Man's Tiffany," carnival glass dates from the first quarter of the 20th century. It was manufactured in many colors and patterns and was very inexpensive. For a dollar you could buy a dozen pieces. How times have changed!

*"We do not advertise our collection or the pieces we own because of the danger of theft, and only people we know are invited to our home to view the glass," writes Lee Markley. And as with many other popular collectibles, copies are common. "I gradually began studying the Hartung books (e.g.,* Carnival Glass *by Marion T. Hartung) to learn more about the patterns and to aid in avoiding reproductions. These can be a problem, but study and observation helped me to minimize expensive mistakes."*

Ms. Markley's collection of 400 pieces is displayed on glass shelves that are installed between the frames of blocked-up windows.

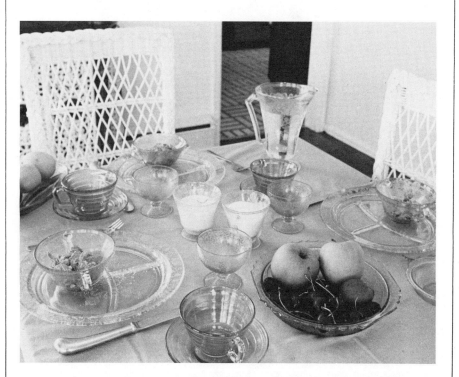

*Dining with Depression Glass*—So cheap, this colorful machine-made glass, primarily of the Depression era (1929–40), was often given away as premiums or at fairs. Now, with prices rising to meet collector demand, it will soon be getting too good to eat . . . on. *(Collection of Sara Lee Singer)*

*Art Glass Objects,* French and American, early 20th century: Tiffany, Lalique, and Thomas Webb cameo glass, in a lit cabinet that is both the focal point of and a divider between living and dining rooms.

# Paperweights

Although the manufacture of paperweights dates back to ancient times, those sought by collectors are relatively new and the finest, from the factories of Baccarat, Clichy and St. Louis, are not more than 100 years old. First made in Europe in the mid-19th century and later in America, they were the great technical and artistic achievements of glass making. Everything from fruit to famous people to flowers and minutely detailed millefiore ("a thousand flowers" made by arranging canes or rods of colored glass) was encased under a magnifying dome of crystal. Limited-edition paperweights are manufactured and collected today, but the real action is in the once modestly priced older and finer weights. A piece that sold in the thirties for $100 was resold in the seventies for $20,000.

*Jennie H. Sinclair Collection*—One of the world's biggest (over 500) and best collections was bequeathed to the New York Historical Society by Jennie H. Sinclair, wife of the co-founder of Sinclair and Valentine, makers of printing inks.

(left to right) Dahlia, c. 1870–90, Millville Rose, New York, c. 1900–12, Floral Bouquet, New York, c. 1852–80

Ship Paperweight c. 1900

King Louis Phillppe, Baccarat, France c. 1845–50

*Art Deco Crystal* on open glass shelves which serve as bar and show off collection.

*French Enamel and Glass Vases* by Faure, c. 1920.

## TWO MAJOR GLASS MUSEUMS

*Sandwich Glass Museum*, Sandwich, MA 02563

*Corning Museum of Glass*, Corning, NY 14830

*Overlay Lamps. (Collection Sandwich Glass Museum)*

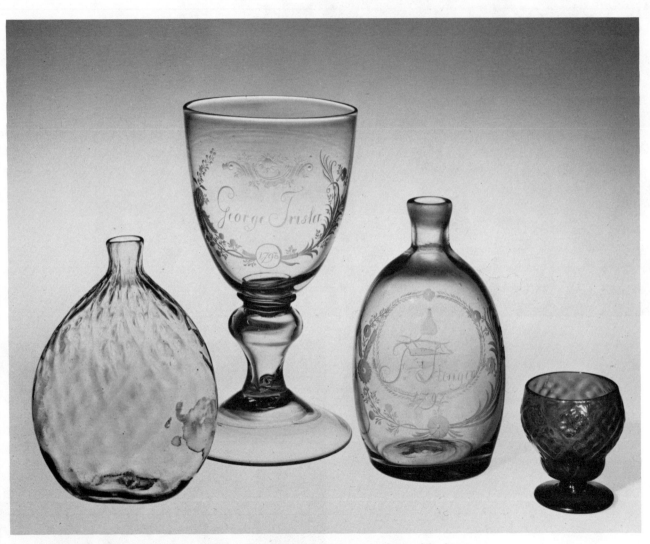

Glasses made at the Maryland glass manufactory of John Frederick Amelung, producer of the finest American glassware of the late 18th century. Note presentation goblet dated 1793, flask 1792. (Corning Museum of Glass)

*Lacy Pressed Glass* c. 1827–40, United States (Midwest and New England). (Corning Museum of Glass)

## Organizations and Publications

*National Depression Glass Association,* c/o Ada E. Wilson, 230 N.W. 126th Street, North Miami, FL 33168 (membership $4; FREE sample issue of journal with SASE)

*International Carnival Glass Association* (around 1,200 members), Lee Markley, RR1, Mentone, IN 46539 (membership $4)

*Paperweight Collectors' Association,* Box 128, Scarsdale, NY 10583 (no membership fee)

*Depression Glass DAZE,* Box 57RR, Ofisville, MI 48463 (monthly $6.50)

*Glass,* Box 2315, Costa Mesa, CA 92626 (monthly $6)

The Early American Glass Club, Mrs. James A. Collins, Corresponding Secretary, 195 Fullen Road, Lexington, MA 02173

*Compote, Vase and Bar Bottle* in pressed loop pattern. *(Collection in Sandwich Glass Museum)*

*Nineteenth-Century American Pharmacist Glass* in window of Pharmacy Museum.

# ANCIENT GLASS: Confessions of a Collector

"I started collecting ancient glass about 20 years ago as a result of a trip to Turkey. I bought an ancient glass vase at the underground bazaar simply because it looked beautiful. It was carefully wrapped; but when I opened the package in London (where I was living at the time), I found the vase had shattered. I felt terribly guilty about this, as the antique dealer from whom I had purchased the piece had explained that it had been made about 2,000 years before and had miraculously survived the ravages of fire, flood, earthquake, etc.

"All of this made me decide to learn more about the object that was shattered. I started reading on the subject, visiting museums, haunting antique shops, and, of course, collecting.

"In the 20 years, I've collected several hundred pieces; the bulk of the collection dates from 100 B.C. to about A.D. 300. However, several pieces date to 700 B.C. or earlier and my youngest piece was made around A.D. 1000. I chose to focus on the period of 100 B.C. to A.D. 300 because it was the period when glass making flowered. This was due to the discovery of glass blowing. This technique allowed glass to be made into shapes and forms as diverse as the maker's imagination. Prior to the discovery of glass blowing, many beautiful pieces were made but within strict technical limitations. The technical breakthrough of glass blowing stirred the imagination and vitality of the craftsmen and resulted in a massive outpouring of beautiful, elegant and varied glass objects.

"Since the discovery of glass in about 1500 B.C. , many people have attributed mystical qualities to it. After all, glass is made principally of sand. It is made by heating sand along with minor amounts of other ingredients and this causes a magical fusing to take place. Out of the sand comes a substance which is clear—you can see through it. Also, it casts almost no shadow, which was a matter of great importance to people 3,000 years ago. The other characteristics of glass were unmatched by any other substance known to early man. It could be made in almost any color; it was rock hard but still easily broken; it could be cut, painted, carved, drawn, fused, engraved, pressed in a mold, blown, etc., etc. It will take almost any shape and, once made, will hold that shape indefinitely, or that shape could be reheated and made into another shape.

"It is easy to understand why glass captured man's imagination . . . and the years between 100 B.C. and A.D. 300 brought together this imagination and the technique of glass blowing.

"Since I broke the first piece of glass that I bought, I've gone to great pains to avoid a recurrence. I have a tin can specially made for each piece so that I can cover the piece with cotton matting and slip it into the can. This results in a tight fit and the piece is well protected. The cover of the can is also tight fitting and labeled.

"Many of my pieces are displayed in my apartment. I have a cabinet in the vestibule of my apartment and about 30 pieces are displayed there. Another 80 or 90 pieces are displayed on four large glass shelves in my dining room. From time to time I rotate the pieces on display with those in storage.

"The pieces range in size from an inch and a half in height to about a foot in height. Many of the pieces were actually in everyday use as perfume jars, water pitchers, cosmetic containers, oil vessels, as well as decorative items. Several pieces that I highly prize are known as Janus vases and are in the shape of two heads protruding from either side of the vase. Other pieces are traceable to a specific town and factory where they were made because of the characteristic moldings on the piece. Still other pieces have religious significance and bear the distinctive symbols of the Jewish or Christian faiths.

"There are relatively few collectors of ancient glass in the United States and, as far as I know, there are no clubs, conventions, etc. However, the Corning Museum of Glass publishes a book annually containing various learned articles on the subject. Some other museums have catalogues describing their glass collection such as the Toledo (Ohio) Glass Museum. On occasion, magazines such as *Scientific American* will publish an article on the scientific and technical aspects of ancient glass making. In addition, there are a number of books on the subject which for the most part are themselves collector's items. These books are hard to find as they have been out of print for a good many years. Here in New York there are several excellent places to view glass—mainly the Metropolitan Museum of Art, the Brooklyn Museum and the Jewish Museum. Further afield, the Yale Museum of Art in New

Haven has an outstanding collection, but 95 percent of it can be viewed only in the Catacombs (by special request). In Washington, D.C., the Freer Art Gallery has an outstanding collection of cane glass, but this too can be viewed only by request. Of course the Toledo Museum, and most of all, the Corning Museum have incredible collections, and probably the Corning Museum has the best collection in the world.

"Outside of the United States, ancient glass is well represented in the collections of the British Museum, the Louvre, etc. The Germans were very active in glass collecting and some of the very best ancient glass is on view there. By and large, I thought the Cairo Museum was disappointing and God knows what remains of the wonderful collections that used to be on display in Lebanon.

"In the past 10 years, the price of glass has gone up very substantially. Perhaps the increase has been four or five times, and maybe more. Of course the number of fakes has also increased along with the price. From time to time in the past, I've been fooled by fakes and will probably be fooled in the future. By and large, experience is a good teacher. When you see enough pieces and handle enough pieces, you begin to sense when something's wrong. Many fakes are composites of broken pieces disguised to look like the complete and whole piece. The fakers are ingenious and one must be philosophical about collecting.

"There are no special sources for collecting glass; you just have to take the time and visit dealers in archeological artifacts, and of course it is important to follow the auction houses." –Harvey L. Karp

*Bedouin and Old Yemenite Glass*—first- and second-century Palestinian.

# FABRICS AND NEEDLEWORK

## Crib Quilt Collector

These child-size American quilts crafted in the 19th century for cribs or trundle beds appealed to collectors Irwin and Linda Berman because of their colorful, very "modern" graphic design and their rarity. Dr. Berman writes:

*"There are well under 1,500 fine crib quilts of early vintage left in America. This (rarity) has been accentuated by the increasing interest in small quilts through exhibitions in major galleries. A truly fine crib quilt is not a scaled-down knock-off of a full-size quilt. Indeed, the great quilt is a product of the inspired admixture of one or more of the ingredients or the fabrics, their age, the final image and the uniqueness of the whole. How fortunate were the sleeping babies of those lost generations to have been the objects of such effort and inspiration for 'only a crib.' "*

*Rose Cross*, pieced and appliquéd crib quilt, Pennsylvania c. 1880.

*Delectable Mountain,* cotton crib quilt, New Jersey c. 1870–80.

*Lady in the Lake,* Amish pieced crib quilt c. 1910–20.

*Pomegranate,* appliquéd summer spread, third quarter 19th century. (Collection of Irwin and Linda Berman)

*Winged Square,* Pennsylvania, early 20th century. (Collection of Irwin and Linda Berman)

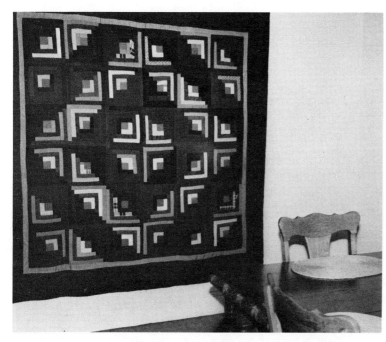

*Full-Size Quilt* of woolen and homespun is an eye-catching wall hanging. Ohio, 1870s. (*Collection of Marguerite Rule Johnstone*).

*George Washington Flag Quilt* c. 1875. This commemorative hand quilt was created for the first centennial of the United States. It is made with pieces of flags of different nations put together and quilted around George Washington's head. (*Collection of Bette Klegon*)

*Sampler* c. 1859: "Selura Aldrich wrought this AD 1819 while God dothspare for death prepare."
(*Collection of Electra Havemeyer Webb, Shelburne Museum*)

# Samplers

*American Sampler 1797.* One of the samplers that provided the designs for packaging of Whitman's Chocolates, from their collection of over 500 at the Philadelphia Museum of Art. (*Photograph by A.J. Wyatt, staff photographer.*)

*Fantasy Fabrics and Clothing*—Dell Pitt Feldman is an artist-craftsman and author (*Crochet, Discovery & Design,* Doubleday) who collects assorted antique remnants (old tapestry, lace, knitted pieces) and trifles (fur tails, stones, jewelry) for the purpose of incorporating them into the crocheted body adornments she creates. Shown are petit point and needlepoint remnants worked into a *Crochet Skirt; Crocheted Neckpiece* with antique cameo, metallic threads and beads.

# Printed Textiles

Susan Meller collects printed and woven fabrics—predominantly 19th- and early 20th-century—for her own library of textile designs. A background as a textile designer and a lifelong love of fabrics coupled with a strong collecting urge started Susan and her husband acquiring patchwork quilts, which led in turn to ferreting out the individual pieces themselves. Now they are primarily concerned with design, rather than with fabric construction or merely age, and are collecting printed textiles. They mount each of their examples on white paper, date them whenever possible, and file them in metal file cabinets according to design categories, e.g., paisley, leaves, animals, birds, small floral stripes, diaper prints and so forth.

# Stevengraphs

In 1854 Thomas Stevens of Coventry, England, programmed the Jacquard loom to make silk-woven bookmarks and pictures depicting such subjects as royalty, politics, sports, religion and mythology. There are 187 Stevengraphs of different subjects, and Lewis Smith has collected all about 20 of them. Mr. Smith started collecting in the early 1930s when he was given a horse-racing scene as a gift. Today his comprehensive collection is quite valuable (some Stevengraphs sell for $1,000 or more), and he is the president of The Stevengraph Collectors Association, formed in 1965 when he invited the six known collectors to a meeting in his home.

*Stevengraph Collection on Library Walls* includes some pictures manufactured by other companies such as the Grant Company and the American Silk Label Company. The subjects shown include portraits: the Marquis of Salisbury, Her Majesty Queen Victoria, Abraham Lincoln and Betsy Ross; sporting pictures: racing, bicycling, tennis and footballs; scenes of London: the Crystal Palace; and souvenir bookmarks from the town of Abbington.

## Collecting Clues

• *"Keep pieces out of the light and store in other textiles like a cotton pillowcase or sheet–not in a plastic bag that does not breathe. Refold fabric from time to time to cut down on permanent creasing and wear on fibers. When washing, never put in a washing machine or dryer, but hand-wash gently with a mild neutral soap or detergent such as Ivory liquid or Woolite. Block a small piece on an ironing board (but do not iron) by smoothing with your hand and pinning to board with straight pins; and when drying larger pieces observe the rule: Dry it on the lawn, never on the line."* –Patsy Orlofsky, Director, Textile Conservation Workshop, Main Street, South Salem, New York (914-763-5919)

## Organizations

*Stevengraph Collectors Association* (over 200 members worldwide), Irvington on Hudson, NY 10533 (membership $5, initiation $5; FREE booklet with SASE, *Thomas Stevens and His Silk Ribbon Pictures* by Alice Lynes, F.L.A.)

*Center for the History of American Needlework*, Box 8162, Pittsburgh, PA 15217 (membership $10; FREE bibliographies with SASE)

*Signing of the Declaration of Independence (Collection of Lewis Smith)*

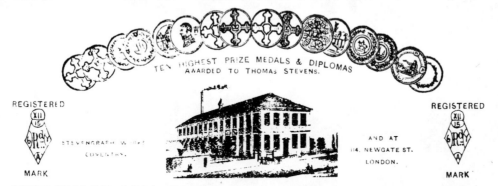

## What Other Collectors Collect

- *Antique and Oriental Batik* —Inger McCabe Elliot, the creater and president of the design company China Seas, collects antique Oriental batiks; she stores them, folded, beneath plastic cubes on shelves.

- *Fabrics for the Home*—antique fabric and wallpaper pieces, dresser scarves, doilies, antimacassars (used to protect the upholstery back from a man's head of macassar hair oil), napkins, runners, tablecloths

*William Shakespeare.*

# POTTERY AND PORCELAIN

## Staffordshire Pot Lids

(NOTE: Because of the fine quality of clay available for pottery making, many 18th- and 19th-century manufacturers produced a variety of wares in the Staffordshire district of England.)

While most collectors are satisfied to have containers without tops, the pot lid collector is happy to have only the top, or lid, of these mid-19th-century Staffordshire pottery jars, which are decorated with underglaze color and finely detailed picture transfer prints.

At the same time that she bought one as a house gift, Nancy Brown purchased another one for herself, the first in her collection. Now she has a fairly representative selection of lids with scenes that whimsically show: nursery rhymes (Little Red Riding Hood); historical events and famous people and places (Garibaldi, Victoria and Albert Memorial, Shakespeare's home in Stratford-on-Avon); allegories and myths; and scenes of daily life.

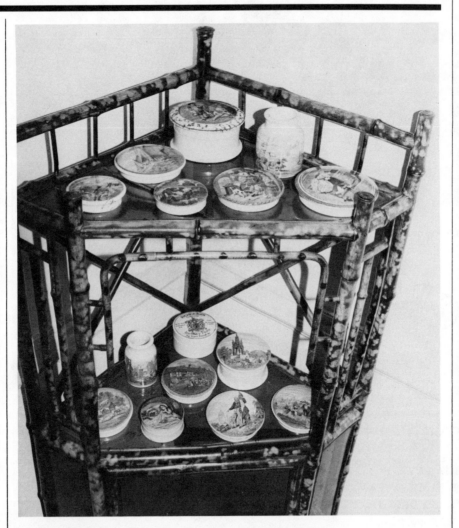

The contents once held in these jars are almost as intriguing as the decoration on them: bear's grease pomade for the hair, fish paste, potted meats, and other pastes and salves of the time. (Collection of Mr. and Mrs. Robert B. Brown)

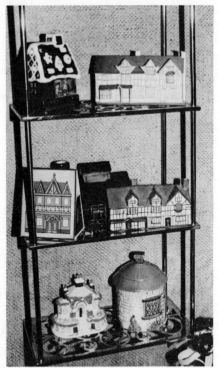

*Collection of Buildings,* including Staffordshire houses, designed as incense burners.

*Historic Staffordshire* (or *"Old Blue"*)—early 19th century. Using the transfer process, often in blue, these dinnerware pieces depicted every aspect of American life: scenes of Bunker Hill and the landing of Columbus; portraits of Washington, Franklin and Lafayette; pictures of steamships, railroads, your college or home town.

*Blue and White China Collection* of different (Early American, Chinese) but compatible patterns.

# American Redware Pottery

The stratospheric price of Redware, possibly the oldest fired-type pottery made (from the same common red clay as bricks), belies its earthy origin and appearance. Only recently, a mid-19th-century Redware lion sold at auction for $18,000, a record for a piece of American ceramics.

Notwithstanding cost, the objects in this collection—*Redware: Pie Plate, Cereal Bowl and Pickle Jar (but not the "Pig" Liquor Flask)*—are actually used. *(Collection of Mr. and Mrs. Robert B. Brown)*

*Poodle,* Bennington, Vermont, mid-19th Century. *(Collection of Mr. and Mrs. Martin Leifer)*

*Early American Stoneware*—jars and crocks in a Victorian pantry of the period.

*Stoneware Jug,* J & E Norton, Bennington, Vermont, 1850–59. *(Collection of Mr. and Mrs. Charles B. Hagler)*

*St. Clement French 18th-Century Faience.*

*Japanese Imari Porcelain* on Japanese cabinet. (*Collection of Diane Love*)

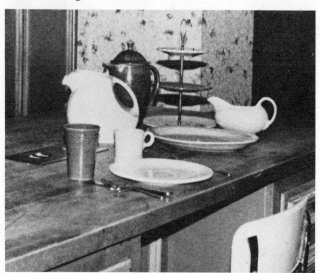

Fiestaware—Each piece in place setting is a different bright color. (*Collection of Mr. and Mrs. Arnold Ginsburg*)

Ceramic Cookie Jars. (Collection of Mr. and Mrs. Arnold Ginsburg)

Antique European Cups and Saucers, Hotel Due Torri, Verona, Italy.

# The Plate Lady

While most collectors think in terms of complete sets or matching pieces, Bernice Levy buys only the *odd* piece (or plate). And this is the charm of her collection, eye-catching in its variety and composed without any restriction except cost (odd pieces can be bargain pieces), made up of whatever she finds aesthetically pleasing. It is displayed on built-in shelves that line the walls of her living room. The plates come from almost every important manufacturer: Meissen, Coalport, Minton, Royal Crown Derby, Limoge, Wedgwood, to name a few. Mrs. Levy buys only at antique shows and flea markets, and cautions: *"If you really love it, buy it then and there. You may never see it again. But don't buy 12 plates just to get that special one."*

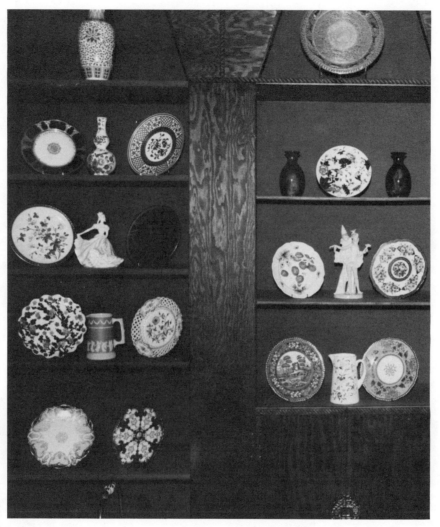

*Tiffany Design Plate* with lifelike molded walnuts was a gift from Mrs. Levy's husband and the beginning of the collection.

**LIMITED-EDITION COMMERORATIVE PLATES** are generally issued as a series by well-known companies in a "limited" quantity and/or for a "limited" period of time. Often decorated by famous illustrators like Norman Rockwell and Kate Greenaway, they are usually highly promoted, creating a wide and sometimes unstable price range. Dealers like to tell about how the first such plate issued at Christmas 1895 for $50 by Bing and Grondahl has appreciated to well over $2,000; but like other new limited editions that flood the market and are created especially for collectors, they can be a risky investment.

# Pitchers and Teapots

Pitchers come in a variety of shapes and colors, and each piece has its own intrinsic beauty.

*"I have been collecting them—especially large pitchers with white backgrounds—for about 10 years. I use them as decorations thoughout the house—for flowers, for kitchen utensils and for serving juice, cider and wine."* (Collection of Raquel R. Levin)

*Chinese,* handmade of native clay in the shape of (left to right) dog, monkey, rat and frog.
*(Susan Mills Teapot Collection)*

*The Susan Mills Teapot Collection at Mills College—Minton; Spode* with inscription: "We'll take a cup o' kindness yet for days O'Auld Lang Syne".

## What Other Collectors Collect

- 19-century American Ceramic *Spatterware* and *Ironstone*
- Early 20th-century *American Art Pottery* (Newcomb, Roseville, Rookwood, Weller and Dedham are only a few)
- ABC (Alphabet) *Plates;* giant-size *Farmer's Cups* (some could hold a quart of coffee); *Egg Cups;* and *Wine Labels* of Delft, Battersea and Staffordshire
- *Assorted Antique Dinnerware* (also glassware) for mixing and matching: a different plate for a different course and/or the motif or design coordinated with the dish—a fish design for a fish course, a fruit design for a dessert course, an herb or foliage design for salad

## FREE Publications

*The Glaze,* Box 4929, Springfield, MO 65804

*The Plate Collector,* Box 1041, Kermit, TX 79745 (25¢ handling)

*American Wedgwoodian,* 55 Vandam Street, New York, NY 10013

*The Bradford Exchange,* Current Quotations, 933 Milwaukee Avenue, Niles, IL 60648. Pamphlet of over 900 plates; also includes price guidelines.

## 525 Porcelain Veilleuse Theires

There are almost more Veilleuse Theires, or night-light teapots, in the tiny town of Trenton, Tennessee, than people. As the name indicates, they are part lamp (the bottom) and part teapot (the top). Used to warm soup or tea at the bedside of sick aristocrats while simultaneously supplying a soothing light, they were manufactured by every important ceramics factory in Europe from 1750 to 1860. Not surprisingly, this was the collection of a doctor, Frederick C. Freed. He apparently did not have to sit at the bedside of too many patients and had time to travel all over the world buying teapots. The collection is almost unique in the world (Frances Parkinson Keyes had one of the others). It is on permanent exhibition in the Municipal Building in Trenton.

*(photograph by The Commercial Appeal)*

# BASKETS, BOXES AND TINS

## Handmade Japanese Baskets

40 to 100 years old, some signed with the name of the maker, and one with a poem and signature.

*"I love the baskets because they are superb examples of a functional folk art, showing in their variety the vivid imagination of the craftsman. The Japanese have the greatest respect for nature, and the ingenious way they have of incorporating natural roots and branches and vines into the basket is, in my mind, the most perfect blend of art with nature. The baskets are sculptures in themselves and also wonderful containers to use for flowers. The unending variety is what makes collecting these baskets a perpetual pleasure."* (Collection of *Diane Love*, designer)

Contemporary Chinese Baskets. (Collection Marguerite Rule Johnstone)

Baskets on the wall. (Collection of Sara Lee Singer)

Baskets Beneath the Dining Room
Sideboard—On her travels, designer Eleanor
Brenner buys baskets for their shape and
texture.

# Miniature Enamel Boxes

For pills, coins, snuff and secret love potions, with delicate transfer-printed scenes of court ladies and cavaliers, landscapes and portraits, these were made at Battersea, England, in the middle of the 18th century. The factory flourished for only a few years, but boxes in this style continued to be made, and the term "battersea" became generic, referring to all similar enamels. (*Collection of Catherine Westin*)

*Assorted Papier Mâché, Lacquered and Other Boxes.*

*Painted Box* c. 1830, New England, stenciled wood and metal. (*Collection of Mr. and Mrs. Howard Lipman*, gift to the Museum of American Folk Art)

# Old Tins

Particularly popular and ''in'' tins include those used for smoking—flat tobacco pocket, cigar and cigarette tins. Also very collectible are coffee, tea, spice and cocoa tins. Value is determined by scarcity, graphics and condition. (A flat tobacco pocket tin called TAXI depicting a nostalgic 1920 New York scene and taxi sold for $695.00 at a recent auction). Peanut butter tins (one series has pictures on it of Jackie Coogan) and Talcum and Face Powder tins (valued for their Art Deco designs or lovely illustrations of girls in 20's costumes), story tins (Peter Rabbit), pictures of Americana, the Old West, sports, birds, Indians are very popular collectibles. So are tins of unusual shape: Log Cabin Syrup tins in the shape of a cabin, lunch box tobacco tins (when empty they were used for carrying lunchs), British biscuit tins like those manufactured by Huntley and Palmer in unusual shapes of telephones, windmills, and sets of books. The choicest tins of all, the Roly Poly's (early 20th century) were made for Mayo's Tobacco in a series of six funnyfaced people (the challenge for collectors is to complete the set, which no doubt contributes to their rise in price from $50 a piece a few years ago to over $500 now)

*Tobacco Pocket (Collection Tony Gianti, Photograph by Ken Tannenbaum Studio)*

*Roly Poly Tobacco (Collection Tom Ryan)*

*Tobacco Pocket (Collection Tom Ryan)*

*Cigar Tobacco (Collection Jim and Timmy Challenger)*

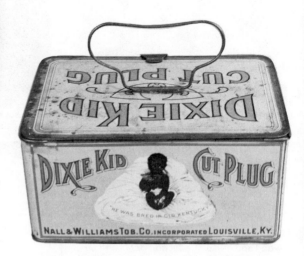

*Tobacco Lunch Box (Collection Tom Ryan)*

*Marshmallow Tins from Canada (Collection Pam and Jack Coghlan)*

*Peanut Butter (Collection Lila and Warren Green)*

*Coffee Tins (Collection Lila and Warren Green)*

## Collecting Clues

- Best sources for obtaining tins are by word-of-mouth, flea markets, tag sales, antique shows and dealers. Be on the lookout for tins from Canada as good American tins are becoming increasingly hard to find.
- Tins should be in good condition, free from rust, discoloration, dents (and with lids intact). Beware of tins that have been retouched or repainted (their value is greatly decreased). Tins can be cleaned, brightened and protected by using a mild liquid wax (Sani wax); test first in an inconspicuous spot to be sure colors do not run. Dents can be removed by gently "kneading" them out with the back of a wooden kitchen spoon.

*Huntley & Palmers Biscuit Tin (Collection Lester Barnett)*

*Mop head Tin (Collection Jim and Timmy Challenger)*

*Animal Fly Spray (Collection Jim and Timmy Challenger)*

*Women's Talcum Powder*

*Cosmetic Tins*

*Men's After Shave Talcum (Collection Jim and Timmy Challenger)*

## Organizations

*The Tin Container Collectors Association*, Box 4555, Denver, CO 80204 (membership $15; FREE sample issue with SASE of newsletter *Tintype*).

## What Other Collectors Collect

- *Early American Round Woodenware Boxes* (sometimes called pantry boxes) for spices, cheese, meal, butter, herbs and even pills
- *Hat Boxes* covered with old papers
- *Collar, Cuff, Glove, Button and Jewelry Boxes*
- *Indian Wedding Baskets* from the twenties, worth as much as $16,000

# WRITING UTENSILS

## Typewriters, Tools and Ribbon Tins

*"The typewriter is a machine intended to take the place of the pen. That such a machine is a necessity of the age has long been an acknowledged fact. Genius as well as labor have been freely bestowed upon efforts to supply this want and until recently without satisfactory results."* –from a brochure for the first typewriter, Densmore Yost & Co., Agents, 1874

So many inventors or "tinkerers" tried their hand at making a writing machine that it is little wonder so many of the early machines varied greatly in design and mechanics. Some used ink pads, others ribbons; type might be on a wheel or cylinder, or in a radial arrangement. One of collector Julian Marwell's prized pieces is a Sholes and Glidden c. 1873. It was the first mass-produced machine, complete with a table, decorated with flowers and activated by a foot pedal. Other early typewriters in his collection are the "new" Crandall c. 1885 (inlaid with mother of pearl), Hall and Norris c. 1885, Oliver c. 1894, Sun c. 1885, Odell c. 1886, Blickensderfer c. 1893 and Hammond c. 1880.

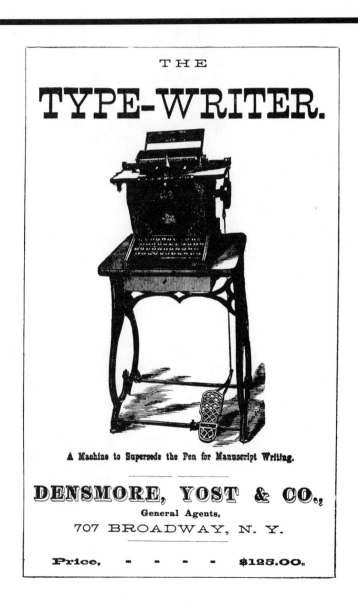

THE

## TYPE-WRITER.

A Machine to Supersede the Pen for Manuscript Writing.

**DENSMORE, YOST & CO.,**

General Agents,

707 BROADWAY, N. Y.

Price, - - - - $125.00.

*Odd and Very Early Typewriters* on view in the Marwell home. The unusual stand allows him to rotate the display.

For someone who only recently started collecting (he fell upon his first old machine in 1974 at a yard sale and paid $5 for it), Marwell has an impressive array of over 150 machines, 200 typewriter ribbon tins and other ''go-withs'' such as medals for good typing, brushes, repair tools, and postcards with pictures of typewriters.

Finding one source of 25 machines—a retired typewriter dealer—helped to accelerate Marwell's rate of collection. The man was discovered in Colorado by Marwell's nephew, who was traveling across the United States handing out Marwell's ''Want Antique Typewriters'' card. The typewriter dealer's collection was too large, so Marwell held a mail auction to sell off duplicates and those machines he did not want.

The Blickensderger Featherweight Typewriter, the first successful portable, 1893. On exhibit *Ten Thousand Years of Recorded Information*, Xerox Corporation Headquarters, Stamford, Connecticut *(Typewriter courtesy of The Stamford Historical Society)*

*Typewriter ''Go-Withs'':* postcards, rulers, brushes, tools and tins. (Collection Julian Marwell)

## FIVE HUNDRED TYPEWRITERS IN FOUR ROOMS

Judd Caplovich advertises actively and, as a result, now has over 500 typewriters, most dating from 1873 to 1910. He, too, started by literally stumbling upon an old machine, an 1892 Blickensderfer, at an auction he attended with his parents. He was fascinated by the mechanical gadget and bought it for $3.50. He was only 13 at the time and did not appreciate the value of the purchase. Now he does. Judd likes to buy machines made before 1920 that are in good working condition. He seems to specialize in firsts: he has the first Sholes and Glidden, Blickensderfer, Williams, Hammond and Hall; the first Portable, Practical, Indicator Usable, Even Typing, Braille; even the first toy typewriter, a Simplex. Judd keeps the collection in four rooms, about half on view on racks in the center of the room and the rest on tables under the window. With such a space-consuming collection it is hard to believe that Judd has room to breathe, let alone house other collections. But he does manage to squeeze in the following:

- Old office equipment: adding machines, staplers, pencil sharpeners, check cancelers
- Eight thousand 78-RPM records
- Porcelain license plates from Connecticut (1905–16)
- Old radios (1914–25)
- Old cameras (1886–1919) and stereoptic viewing cards (1858–1901)
- Connecticut maps and town history books (1825–1918)
- World's Fair maps and books (1876–1904)
- Several hundred mechanical kitchen gadgets (1850–1904), including apple peelers, grinders, raisin and cherry seeders, irons, ice cream makers, a carpet sweeper and a washing machine
- Finally, eight roller organs (1878–1900), five pianos, one theatre organ and one pipe organ (1832–1950) . . . and a 1911 Evinrude outboard motor. And he's not even an antique dealer—he's a computer analyst.

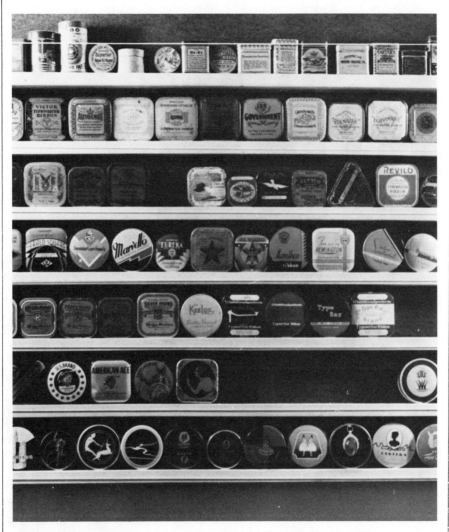

*Typewriter Ribbon Tins* are kept on a shallow shelf. (Collection Julian Marwell)

# THE POINT OF THE PEN FANCIERS

Cliff Lawrence has 1,000 quality pens in mint working condition made by four old-line pioneers: Wahl-Eversharp, Parker, Shaeffer and Waterman. The most valuable are a Waterman number 20, worth over $1,000, and a Parker Lucky Curve Black Giant, worth $500. He not only enjoys collecting these pens—for their beauty, style and quality—but he also likes to use them and promote them as ideal collectibles too, and as president of The Pen Fanciers Club he tells how it was started and how it is sustained:

*"When I started pen collecting seriously in 1975, I found that most pen collectors felt that they had an odd and very unusual hobby and as a result kept their interest pretty much to themselves. In September of 1976 I had an article on pen collecting published in Joel Sater's* Antique and Auction News. *In this article, I expressed a desire to start a club for pen collectors. I envisioned this club as organizing collectors, putting them in touch with each other, acting as a clearinghouse for pen information, and bringing respectability and recognition to our wonderful hobby. This first article obtained our first nine members for us. In*

*Waterman Pens* (1920–27)—The largest one, called "Giant Ripple" (1923), is red and black and valued at $105 in Lawrence's book.

*Waterman Pens* (1884–1920)—The large pen in the center is the famous number 20. According to Lawrence, Waterman is the most sought-after make; pens from the twenties, the most popular.

*the less than two years that have ensued, our membership has grown to nearly 300. At first we obtained new members through articles, classified and display advertisements. As our club has grown, however, referrals have become our main source of new members. As the club grew, we realized that most of our members wanted us to make top-quality pens and pencils available to them at reasonable prices and on a money-back-if-not-satisfied basis. We started the Pen Trading Post. The proceeds of this successful service are used to finance the club promotion and overhead. We buy quality old pens and pencils for resale and operate on about a 20 percent profit margin. Thus we are a clearinghouse for quality pens as well as information. Since the first of this year (1978), we have been organizing local chapters throughout the world."*

*The Pen Fancier's Club*, Box 413, Clearwater, FL 33517 (membership $10; free sample issue of monthly newsletter with SASE). *Fountain Pens—History, Repair and Current Values* by Cliff Lawrence can be ordered from the club ($7.95 postpaid).

*Wahl-Eversharp Art Deco Pens* of the twenties—beautiful colors, fancy trim and top quality make these pens very popular with collectors.

*Parker Duo-fold Pens* (1923–29).

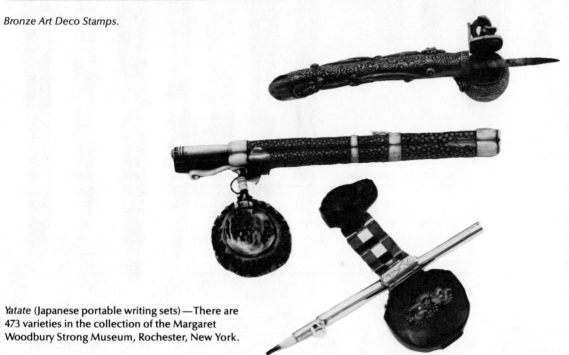

*Bronze Art Deco Stamps.*

*Yatate* (Japanese portable writing sets) — There are 473 varieties in the collection of the Margaret Woodbury Strong Museum, Rochester, New York.

## What Other Collectors Collect

- *Inkwells* in every kind of material: pottery, majolica, Delft, faience, stoneware, iron, pewter, brass, copper, tin, tole, bronze, silver, gold, enamel, glass and papier mâché
- *Desk Sets, Letter Openers, String Holders, Magnifying Glasses, Blotters*

## Organization

*The Society for the Collection of Brand-Name Pencils* ℅ Arthur Kroeber, 226 St. John's Pl., Brooklyn, NY 11217

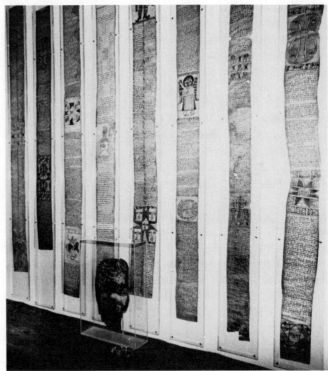

*Ancient Coptic Scrolls* from Ethiopia hang over long hall table.

# THE MILITARY AND SCOUTING

## Military Miniatures: Toy Soldiers

No longer a hobby for children (lead soldiers are expensive and cannot be legally sold as toys), military miniatures are bought for their historic interest and for the quality of their decoration, as well as to join whole armies in the war games of their owners, the war history buffs. At a sale in 1977 of film star Douglas Fairbanks, Jr.'s, collection, one bidder paid $1,392 for 21 figures representing a Royal Marines band, and the total of 3,000 pieces realized $16,120. (This collection had been displayed on shelves lining the walls of a room in Fairbanks' house; behind the shelves, diorama backgrounds illustrated the various historic periods in the collection, ranging from Roman to modern times.)

For fun and maybe to save a little money, some collectors, including television producer Av Westin, buy unpainted lead models. After careful study and research, they hand-decorate these soldiers with suitable uniforms.

*Av Westin's Collection of Military Miniatures* —(foreground) Napoleon's troops retreating from Moscow; (background) British cavalry and American Revolutionary figures. These stand on wood bases, carefully labeled. Other groups in the collection include Prussian, Bavarian, German and Austro-Hungarian soldiers; French military of the 18th and 19th centuries; and miniatures depicting the wedding and portrait-taking of Charles, Prince of Wales.

## Organizations

*American Military Historical Society & American Model Soldier Society*, 1524 El Camino, San Carlos, CA. A dual society founded in 1960, it has 400 members worldwide. It publishes a quarterly bulletin and, to quote director Frank Frisella: *"The club encompasses members from war gamers to military modelers to historians, tacticians, artists—most every facet involved in military collecting. We have members with extensive Civil War Americana collections, German regalia, British militaria and so forth."*

*Military Posters of World War I,* a perfect complement to this collection, line the wall of the Westins' den.

## Collecting Clues

• Comments of a dealer: "The market is in a state of flux, the soldiers are hard to get and there is no price guide. I do not collect in order to avoid a conflict of interest with my customers, who would then suspect me of keeping the best pieces for myself. And I hate kids. They take up time and they don't have the money to spend!"

# Military Medals

Joseph Copley of New Castle, New Hampshire, collects military medals, badges, insignia and buckles, specializing in medals of the Mexican and Civil War. He has a group of medals worn by General George H. Thomas in the Civil War, and the earliest known belt buckle of the regular United States Army, worn in 1789 by a First Regiment infantryman. He says that a small collection inherited from an uncle, a veteran of 30 years' service in the United States Army, formed the basis for the collection, and the hobby offers him the opportunity to relive history by researching how the medal came into existence and why the recipient earned it. Copley advises beginners:

*"Try to collect in one category, e.g., lifesaving, a war, one branch of the Armed Forces. Don't try and rush, as a good collection is built in time and research; a good reference library is a must; try to obtain all the data possible on items you acquire, as it is the bits of history 'collected' that makes the hobby and the collection more interesting."*

*Militaria*

*Imperial German Militaria*—rare transitional model, Garde du Corps officer's helmet c. 1897, of bodyguard to Kaiser Wilhelm II. *(Collection of Richard Mundschenk)*

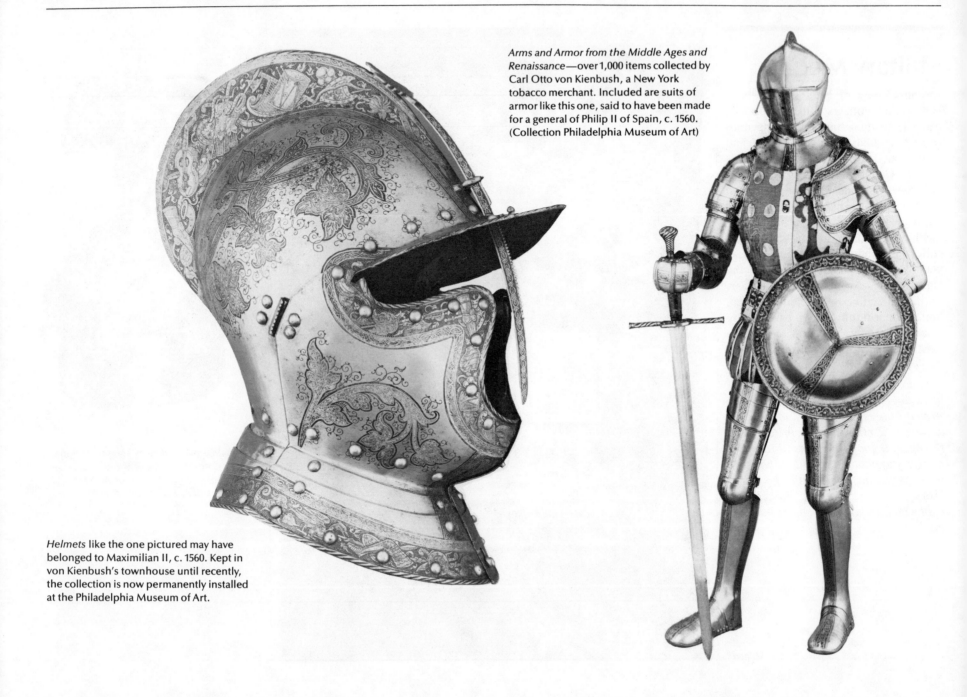

*Arms and Armor from the Middle Ages and Renaissance*—over 1,000 items collected by Carl Otto von Kienbush, a New York tobacco merchant. Included are suits of armor like this one, said to have been made for a general of Philip II of Spain, c. 1560. (Collection Philadelphia Museum of Art)

*Helmets* like the one pictured may have belonged to Maximilian II, c. 1560. Kept in von Kienbush's townhouse until recently, the collection is now permanently installed at the Philadelphia Museum of Art.

# BOY SCOUTS

Judge Sheldon Levy's collection of Boy Scout memorabilia is an offshoot of 10 years of collecting Scout stamps. He specializes in Scout figures and Lord Baden-Powell (founder of the Scout movement) china, which are displayed on the shelves and walls of his den.

## Collecting by Mail

*The Soldier Shop, Inc.*, 1013 Madison Avenue, New York, NY 10021 (catalogue of antique and model soldiers, rare militaria, books—$4)

*Military Medals and Decoration Catalogue*, Sydney Vernon, Box 387, Baldwin, NY 11510 (subscription $2.50 for eight issues; sample copy 50¢)

*Militaria Collectors*, Quincy Sales, Box 7792, Tulsa, OK 74105

*Peter Hlinka Historical Americana* (militaria and war relics catalogue), Box 310, New York, NY 10028 (sample copy 50¢)

*Campaign Americana*, Box 275, Merrick, NY 11566 (sample copy 50¢, subscription $2 for six copies)

*EPCO Publishing Company* (books and reprints), 75-24 64th Street, Glendale, NY 11227

*N. Flayderman & Co.*, New Milford, CT 06776

*Harry Thorsen, Jr., with a Model for a Scout Fair.* He has been collecting for 53 years—since boyhood—and operates a private museum (open to visitors by invitation) of Boy Scout memorabilia which includes uniforms, stamps, seals, books and badges. Thorsen is also the publisher of *Scout Memorabilia*—7305 Bounty Drive, Gulf Gate Woods, Sarasota, FL 33581 (FREE sample copy with SASE).

## Organizations

*Orders and Medals Society of America,* John Lelle, 3828 Ronald Drive, Philadelphia, PA 19154 (membership $12). "For those interested in the study and/or collecting of the insignia of the orders of knighthood and merit, the decorations of valor and honor, the medals of distinction and service, and allied material and historical data." Maintains an official library (books may be borrowed by mail) and a ribbon "bank" supplying suspension ribbons. Holds conventions and publishes an official journal, *The Medal Collector.*

*American Society of Military Insignia Collectors,* George Duell, Jr., 526 Lafayette Avenue, Palmerton, PA 18071 (membership $10). Publishes a quarterly magazine, *The Trading Post,* a bimonthly bulletin, and catalogues that list all known insignia.

*Scouts on Stamps Society International,* Carl Hallman, 253 Sheldon Avenue, Downers Grove, IL 60515 (membership $5)

*Zitelman Scout Museum,* 708 Seminary Street, Rockford, IL 61108

*Civil War Round Table of New York,* 289 Hyde Park Road, Garden City, NY 11530

# LIVING WITH YOUR COLLECTION

**IN HOMES**

*"Everything that you collect should be displayed or used constantly and enjoyed with your family and close friends—for they are the royalty of all guests."*

–Eleanor Brenner, fashion designer

Her mother's *Toby Jugs*, her children's *Bronzed Shoes and Artwork*, *Photographs* and *Pretty Things*. *(Collection of Eleanor Brenner)*

*Art Deco Posters* on walls in foyer.

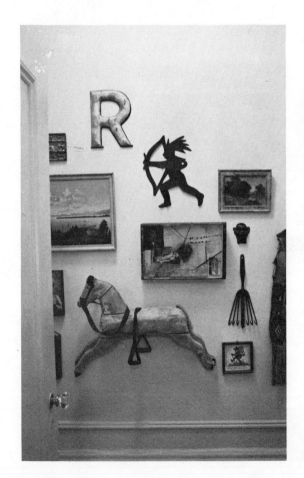

*Tools, Toys, Pictures and American Folk Art displayed in hallway.*
*(Collection of Eve Propp)*

*Ancient Palestinian Glass* and *Ancient Persian Bronzes.*

*Jade* in recessed and lit cabinet. *(Collection of Mr and Mrs. Arnold Ginsburg)*

*Art Nouveau and Art Deco Statues and Vases*

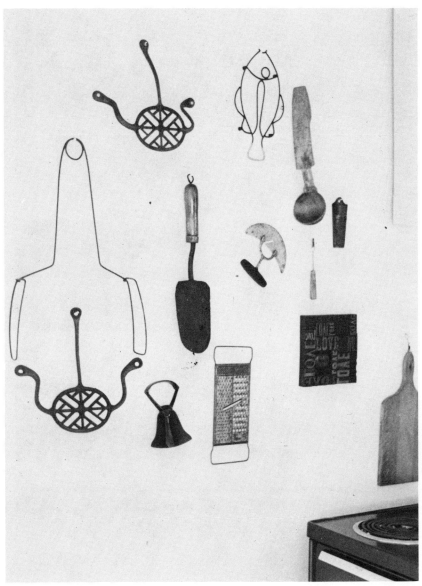

Assorted Kitchen Accoutrements. (Collection of
Sara Lee Singer)

Glove collection in dinette area (Collection of and photograph by Bernard Askienazy)

Art Deco Silver

*Antique Tins* in kitchen cabinets.

*Toys and Circus Posters* in child's room.

*Bronze Stamps* on glass shelves in bathroom.

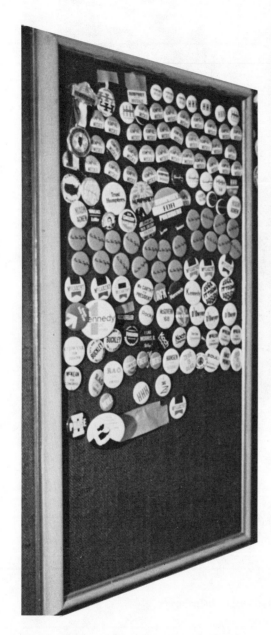

*Wall-to-Wall Campaign Memorabilia (Collection of Lewis Liman)*

*Framed Political Buttons (Collection Edward Costikyan)*

## IN HOME MUSEUMS

*Basement Gun Room*—Dr. Frank Miller's extensive collection of antique weapons: American pre-Revolutionary to modern, an English musket and officers' pistols from the Revolution of 1762; turn-of-the-century goose guns; Kentucky guns; guns that belonged to Albert Speer, Rommel and Theodore Roosevelt; peace pipe tomahawks c. 1620; a furrier's knife; powder flasks; military badges; and antique gun books and catalogues (including the military goods catalogues of Francis Bannerman & Sons, 1897–1963).

# Gilbert Stanley's Firehouse

All this full-time museum and part-time den/bar/guest room needs now is a dispatch center and a fire engine. Gilbert Stanley is building the former, and as for the latter—well, he did own one once and still has a lot of the parts and equipment in other locations along with two-thirds of his firefighting collection, which can't fit into this room.

*"My first item was a fire helmet, then a playpipe (large brass nozzle approximately three feet long); finally the whole thing took off and I started to collect virtually anything old connected to the fire service. (At the same time I joined the local volunteer fire department which I served for 12 years and I am now in my fifth year as a fire commissioner.) My grandfather had been a fire chief. As evidenced by the wide variety of items in my collection, I would say that this would have to be one of the most all-embracing areas of collecting possible—indeed, there are collections within the collection (toys, equipment, postcards, prints, buttons, books, etc.). There are some people who even specialize in monitoring fire calls on special radios, tape them and exchange the tapes with other people throughout the country. I have five such radios (car and home) but consider them part of the collection and*

*Back Bar* Showing, play pipe, speaking trumpet, lantern from horse-drawn fire engine and brass model of hand pumper.

*not a specialty. Further, there are still others who collect full-size fire engines; I myself had a full-size 1942 American La France Pumper for about five years. And believe it or not, there are some people who go to major fires and record pump pressure (water) readings from the dials on the fire engines (fortunately I'm not that far gone).*

*"My particular specialty is toy and model fire apparatus. I have over 400, many of which I have built myself. Outside the toy/model area, my favorite item is an antique, early 1900s fire-alarm dispatching system, i.e., a visitor to my mini-museum can actually pull a fire alarm box (just like the one on the street corner) and see and hear what happens as the alarm is received at the firehouse or dispatcher's office."*

*Display Cases Holding over 200 Toy and Model Fire Engines.* On top of cases is a selection of antique fire helmets. At left of cases is operating fire alarm box. Over alarm box is wire frame in shape of fireman's helmet—used by florists to intertwine flowers forming casket piece for fireman's funeral. At right is a fire axe reportedly used at infamous Triangle Shirtwaist fire (many woman workers perished and this led to radical revisions of labor laws). Also shown are *Cast-Iron Toys, Fire Parade Trophies,* a pressed steel 1920s *Toy Steamer Fire Engine,* inside workings of a typical *Fire Alarm Box* and *Lanterns* from early horse-drawn and motorized fire engines.

# The Mansion of Margaret Woodbury Strong A Museum of Collections

*Starting a Museum Is Easy; Just Acquire 300,000 or So Curios*

Heir to Buggy-Whip Money, Mrs. Strong Leaves Dolls, Circus Items in Her Estate, Dec. 23, 1977

by Raymond A. Joseph, *Staff Reporter of* The Wall Street Journal

ROCHESTER, N.Y.—Wealth was a strong suit for Margaret Woodbury Strong. At her death in 1969, aged 72, she was the largest single shareholder in this city's most famous institution, Eastman Kodak Co., with Kodak shares worth $60 million at 1969 prices.

But more interesting to posterity are the odds and ends that she had accumulated during a lifetime of collecting: 473 yatate, or Japanese writing implements; 27,000 dolls; 600 doll-houses; about 2,000 paintings; Winslow Homer's personal library; thousands of antique advertising cards; hundreds of circus artifacts; and, among other things, collections of napkin rings, ship models, Victorian furniture, canes, ceramic tiles, door-

*Toy Ferris Wheel* c. 1915, German—one of hundreds of circus artifacts.

stops, sleds, fossils, bone carvings, bells, bicycles, apothecary jars, thimbles and candlesticks.

"She was a compulsive buyer," says Anne Hotra, who served as Mrs. Strong's secretary for many years. "She bought everything herself because she distrusted experts. In my traveling with her from 1955 on, she kept repeating, 'How fascinating!' And whatever fascinated her, she bought—in great numbers at times."

It seems that Margaret Woodbury Strong was a collector from early childhood. She was born in 1897, the only child in a family that made some money in the buggy-whip business and in milling. Her parents invested early in the venture of George Eastman, and their wealth grew as Eastman Kodak prospered.

## Empty Bag to Fill

The Woodburys traveled widely, and young Margaret was encouraged to turn her hand to collecting. Each day when she went shopping with her parents in a foreign city, she was given a bag and told she could buy objects until it was filled.

Margaret Woodbury continued collecting after her marriage to Homer Strong, a Rochester lawyer, in 1920, and after the birth of the couple's only child, Barbara, in 1921. Barbara Strong died in 1946, and Mr. Strong in 1958. The widow then "turned to collecting almost on a full-time basis," says Mrs. Hotra, the secretary. Living with only her staff for company, she added wings to her mansion as the jumble of her collections grew.

Her interests were wide. Once she bought 40 bathtubs at an auction. She was interested in any kind of doll, and that collection grew from 600 in 1960 to the 27,000 she owned at her death.

## Dolls in Demand

The resulting hodgepodge, more than 300,000 objects in all, ranges from the commonplace to the rare. Mrs. Strong's doll collection, for instance, is considered to be among the world's best, and its French dolls have been borrowed by the Louvre for display.

Mrs. Strong's legacy could have formed the basis for several specialized museums. Instead, she chose to leave her collections to her own museum, founded shortly before she died and christened the Museum of Fascination, to be sustained by the income from her Kodak stock. Mrs. Strong couldn't have guessed how she thus, at a stroke, created work for scores of people for years to come.

Sorting, appraising, cataloging, cross-referencing and displaying the donor's objects have proven such formidable tasks that, nine years after her death, the museum remains closed to the public and will continue to be closed for some years to come. One problem: The 300,000 objects don't fit in the 75,000 square feet of floor space

*Decorative Doorknobs*—(left to right) porcelain, glass gearshift knob for a car, brass, Bennington flint enamel.

of the mansion Mrs. Strong left to house the collections. *Reprinted by permission of The Wall Street Journal, Dow Jones & Company, Inc. All Rights Reserved 1977.*

## A Restaurant Full of Remingtons

Behind the famous Iron Gate of New York's "21" Club hangs one of the most impressive collections of paintings by Frederic Remington to be found anywhere in the world. A lover of Western art and of horses, the late Jack Kriendler, owner of the club, bought his first Remington painting in 1929; his brother and partner Peter Kriendler carried on the tradition after Jack's death in 1947. Peter has many entertaining stories about how particular works were acquired, such as the one about the customer who had run up a large debt and offered in lieu of payment the Remington he kept under his bed. To enable others to enjoy this collection, "21" and publisher Harry Abrams have joined together in a business venture that will make limited-edition copies of six of the paintings (reproduced in a slightly smaller size to avoid confusion) available to the public.

*Rare Pewter Oil Lamps* c. 1700–1850 on display in office of Arthur Carter

## IN OFFICES

*Nineteenth-Century Ivory Toothpicks* and assorted *Toothpick Holders* on display in waiting room of dentist Isadore Hirshfeld.

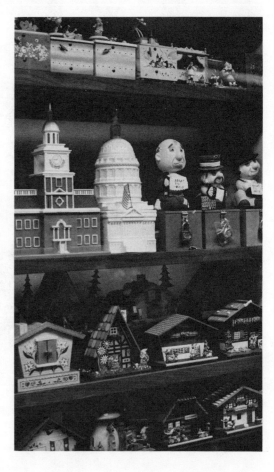

The vast toy bank collection of Edwin H. Mosler is housed in wall-to-wall, floor-to-ceiling glass-fronted cabinets.

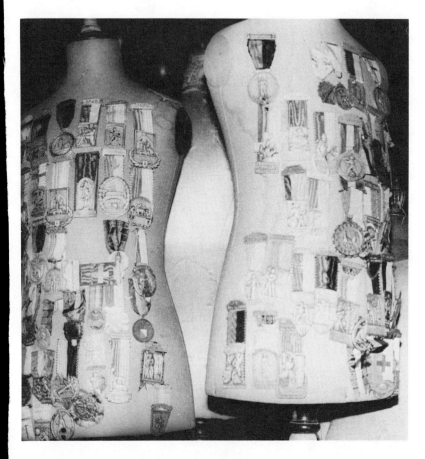

Medals hung on dressmaker's models; for fun.

Labels and Patches on car.